GREAT MYTHS OF
EDUCATION AND
LEARNING

Great Myths of Psychology

Series Editors
Scott O. Lilienfeld
Steven Jay Lynn

This superb series of books tackles a host of fascinating myths and misconceptions regarding specific domains of psychology, including child development, aging, marriage, brain science, and mental illness, among many others. Each book not only dispels multiple erroneous but widespread psychological beliefs, but provides readers with accurate and up-to-date scientific information to counter them. Written in engaging, upbeat, and user-friendly language, the books in the myths series are replete with scores of intriguing examples drawn from everyday psychology. As a result, readers will emerge from each book entertained and enlightened. These unique volumes will be invaluable additions to the bookshelves of educated laypersons interested in human nature, as well as of students, instructors, researchers, journalists, and mental health professionals of all stripes.

www.wiley.com/go/psychmyths

Published

50 Great Myths of Popular Psychology
Scott O. Lilienfeld, Steven Jay Lynn, John Ruscio, and Barry L. Beyerstein

Great Myths of Aging
Joan T. Erber and Lenore T. Szuchman

Great Myths of the Brain
Christian Jarrett

Great Myths of Child Development
Stephen Hupp and Jeremy Jewell

Great Myths of Intimate Relationships
Matthew D. Johnson

Great Myths of Education and Learning
Jeffrey D. Holmes

Forthcoming

Great Myths of Personality
M. Brent Donnellan and Richard E. Lucas

Great Myths of Autism
James D. Herbert

50 Great Myths of Popular Psychology, Second Edition
Scott O. Lilienfeld, Steven Jay Lynn, John Ruscio, and Barry L. Beyerstein

GREAT MYTHS OF EDUCATION AND LEARNING

Jeffrey D. Holmes

WILEY Blackwell

This edition first published 2016
© 2016 John Wiley & Sons, Inc.

Registered Office
John Wiley & Sons, Ltd, The Atrium, Southern Gate, Chichester,
West Sussex, PO19 8SQ, UK

Editorial Offices
350 Main Street, Malden, MA 02148-5020, USA
9600 Garsington Road, Oxford, OX4 2DQ, UK
The Atrium, Southern Gate, Chichester, West Sussex, PO19 8SQ, UK

For details of our global editorial offices, for customer services, and for information about
how to apply for permission to reuse the copyright material in this book please see our
website at www.wiley.com/wiley-blackwell.

Library of Congress Cataloging-in-Publication Data
Names: Holmes, Jeffrey D., author.
Title: Great myths of education and learning / Jeffrey Holmes.
Description: 1 | Hoboken : Wiley-Blackwell, 2016. | Series: Great myths of psychology |
    Includes bibliographical references and index.
Identifiers: LCCN 2015043943 (print) | LCCN 2016001622 (ebook) |
    ISBN 9781118709382 (hardback) | ISBN 9781118709399 (paperback) |
    ISBN 9781118760482 (ePub) | ISBN 9781118760505 (Adobe PDF)
Subjects: LCSH: Learning, Psychology of. | Educational tests and measurements. |
    BISAC: PSYCHOLOGY / Education & Training.
Classification: LCC LB1060 .H636 2016 (print) | LCC LB1060 (ebook) |
    DDC 370.15/23–dc23
LC record available at http://lccn.loc.gov/2015043943

A catalogue record for this book is available from the British Library.

Set in 10/12.5pt Sabon by SPi Global, Pondicherry, India
Printed and bound in Malaysia by Vivar Printing Sdn Bhd

1   2016

For Sheila, Lila, Mom, and Dad

CONTENTS

INTRODUCTION

Human behavior seldom lends itself to black and white assertions. Learning and education in particular involve countless intersecting influences that are often difficult to study in isolation, and that can seldom be portrayed accurately with brief, simplistic claims. Some of the beliefs presented in this book are completely at odds with scientific evidence, while others contain kernels of truth that provide some validity under limited conditions or in certain contexts. The beliefs as stated in the chapter titles are demonstrably at odds with the bulk of scientific evidence. None of the chapters represent (or could represent) a comprehensive review of every existing study on a particular topic, but I have striven to accurately represent the scientific evidence as it currently stands. Some chapters are longer than others – reflecting differences in the amount and complexity of the research on various topics.

Scientifically weak ideas often persist rather than fading over time. One reason for this is confirmation bias, in that once we come to believe something, we tend to notice and remember confirming evidence even against a backdrop of broad contrary evidence. Social influences also play a role in maintaining beliefs. Since many of the beliefs examined in this book are widely shared, they are constantly reinforced and strengthened by those around us. Finally, sheer repetition of the ideas over time makes them seem ever more credible. In preparing this book, I have endeavored to allow the existing published scientific evidence on each topic to speak for itself. All beliefs in this book have wide endorsement, and each is represented by invested proponents who would assert that it is a myth to claim that these claims are myths. Many of the beliefs are repeated over and over without supporting evidence. It is not uncommon to read statements asserting that research supports some claim, with no reference to actual research. Claims of the existence of supporting research are then repeated – sometimes giving the impression that there is strong evidence and scientific consensus when in fact there is little actual evidence.

One of the most meaningful insights I acquired while researching and writing this book is that the line of belief between adherents and skeptics is often the same line that separates those who conduct the research in a particular area from those who do not. For example, it is difficult to identify neuroscientists – experts who study brain function – who agree that people are left- or right-brained, or that education can be tailored to activate one brain hemisphere or the other. It is similarly challenging to identify psychometricians – those who study the measurement of psychological characteristics – who assert that standardized tests do not predict important outcomes including academic performance, or cognitive scientists who assert that teaching should be matched to student learning styles.

The nature of scientific inquiry is such that research findings are not necessarily final. However, this book includes topics about which there is a divide between what many people believe and what the scientific evidence currently supports. As is always the case when a widely-held belief is portrayed as a myth, reactions to the research presented in this book are likely to include claims that I have missed or ignored evidence. I would encourage anyone – teachers, administrators, journalists, students, parents, etc. – to demand that claimants favoring any belief about education provide references to specific, obtainable, and peer-reviewed scientific studies. Too often, research findings are misunderstood or misrepresented, or claims that "researchers have found …" are created seemingly out of thin air. I would further encourage readers to remember Gottfredson's (2007) admonition that "scientifically successful explanations rest not on single studies (all of which have limitations) but on a dense nomological network of empirical evidence." Isolated contradictory studies – when they exist – do not justify abandoning established scientific trends. This assertion is not meant to communicate cynicism; rather, it is merely an endorsement of an evidence-based perspective.

References

Gottfredson, L. S. (2007). Applying double standards to "divisive" ideas: Commentary on Hunt and Carlson (2007). *Perspectives on Psychological Science, 2*, 216–220.

ACKNOWLEDGMENTS

I want to thank Scott Lilienfeld and Steven Lynn, whose editorial expertise greatly strengthened this book. I am also grateful to Barney Beins for his tireless mentoring. Likewise, I thank my many colleagues at Ithaca College and at the Society for the Teaching of Psychology, whose collaboration and friendship have greatly enriched my personal and professional life. Most of all I thank my wife, my daughter, and my parents for their unceasing love and support.

"Uncertainty is an uncomfortable position. But certainty is an absurd one."

Voltaire

1 MYTH: STUDENTS ARE ACCURATE JUDGES OF HOW MUCH THEY KNOW

Most teachers have probably had the experience of asking students whether they have any questions on a particular topic and receiving confirmation from the students that they understand the material, only to learn from later exam results that this was not the case. Sometimes students may be too shy or anxious to speak up, but often they genuinely believe that they know more than they do. Students often express a great deal of confidence in the degree to which they have learned something (e.g., Shaughnessy, 1979; Sinkavich, 1995). However, students' evaluations of their own learning can be extraordinarily inaccurate. Bjork, Dunlosky, and Kornell (2013) assert that students' overconfidence arises because they misinterpret information about their learning and have inaccurate views about what learning strategies are most effective. It is therefore possible for students to be confident that they know something without actually knowing it. One team of researchers even found that students' predictions regarding how well they would remember information they had studied were negatively correlated with their actual memory (Benjamin, Bjork, & Schwartz, 1998). That is, students had poorer memory for information they were more confident they would remember than for information about which they were less confident. Students' ability to accurately assess their own knowledge has enormous implications for their capacity to select appropriate study strategies, effectively allocate their study time, and know when they have reached an appropriate level of mastery (Nelson & Dunlosky, 1991; Bjork et al., 2013).

Researchers have used two types of studies to test the accuracy of students' estimates of their own knowledge pertaining to academic

Great Myths of Education and Learning, First Edition. Jeffrey D. Holmes.
© 2016 John Wiley & Sons, Inc. Published 2016 by John Wiley & Sons, Inc.

information. In some studies, students judge their own performance relative to a given standard by estimating how well they did on an exam or how many items they answered correctly. In other studies, students judge their knowledge or performance relative to other students. As demonstrated by the research results reported below based on both types of studies, students' judgments of their own learning are often quite inconsistent with objective measures of that learning. However, the accuracy of self-judgments of learning is not consistent across students. Specifically, high-performing students are much more accurate than low-performing students in judging their own knowledge. Moreover, high-performers tend to underestimate their own performance, whereas low-performing students tend to exhibit overconfidence in their performance.

In one illustrative study (Langendyk, 2006), advanced medical students in Australia completed an assignment requiring them to make a complex diagnostic assessment. The assignments were then evaluated according to specific criteria by the students themselves, by student peers, and by faculty. Low-achieving students tended to give themselves and their peers higher ratings than those provided by faculty, but high-achieving students gave themselves lower ratings than those provided by faculty. According to Langendyk, students who were low achievers with respect to the assignment were simply "unable to assess accurately the quality of their own work" (p. 173). Because the students in this study were advanced medical students, most of them performed adequately in an absolute sense; however, the study shows that even academically advanced graduate students do not always have insight into their own performance and are sometimes unable to distinguish high-quality from low-quality work. The low-achieving students were unable to accurately judge the quality of their own performance or the performance of higher-achieving peers.

The tendency for lower academic performers to have difficulty judging the quality of their own performance has more frequently been the subject of research involving undergraduate students. Shaughnessy (1979) studied introductory psychology students as they completed four multiple-choice exams over the course of a semester. As students responded to each exam item, they also rated their degree of confidence that their answer was correct. For the first three exams, students later studied their answers and their confidence judgments; therefore, they received feedback both on their test performance and the accuracy of their judgments. Shaughnessy reported that students' self-judgment accuracy was positively correlated with test performance. That is, students who knew more information were much more capable of evaluating how much they knew.

Similarly, Sinkavich (1995) assessed students' confidence in their responses on multiple choice exams. Students rated their confidence in their responses and later received individualized feedback, compared their feedback with that of other students, and received encouragement to try to improve their ability to identify what they did and did not know. Consistent with earlier findings, and despite repeated individualized feedback, students who did well on the exams (those in the top third of the class in terms of exam score) judged their level of performance much more accurately than did poor performers (those in the bottom third of the class). In a more recent study (Ehrlinger, Johnson, Banner, Dunning, & Kruger, 2008), college students completed a difficult exam in class and then rated their performance immediately afterward. Students in the bottom quartile in terms of exam performance rated their performance at the 61st percentile, and their estimates of their own raw scores were inflated by an average of 20%. In contrast, those in the top quartile were more accurate, but tended to underestimate their performance both in terms of test score and standing relative to other students.

In a more complex classroom study (Hacker, Bol, Horgan, & Rakow, 2000), researchers again had undergraduates estimate their exam performance – this time both before and after taking exams. Immediately prior to taking an exam, students estimated the proportion of items they expected to get correct. Immediately following the exam, students reported the proportion of items they believed they had answered correctly. This procedure was repeated twice as the semester progressed. Throughout the course, the instructor emphasized the importance of accurate self-assessment and provided instruction on how to accomplish it. The week before each exam, students also completed practice tests on which they received feedback. The researchers replicated the results of other studies and provided even greater detail: students earning As and Bs were most accurate in their judgments; students earning Cs and Ds were highly overconfident in their predictions before the exam, but were much more accurate in their self-judgments after they had completed exams; and students whose exam scores were below 50% were grossly overconfident in their self-judgments both before and after taking the exams. Students in this lowest-performing category overestimated their actual exam performance by as much as 31 percentage points, and the lower their exam scores, the greater their overconfidence.

Laboratory studies of student self-knowledge provide additional insight into the findings from classroom research cited above. Kruger and Dunning's (1999) research allowed them to evaluate student self-knowledge in a more controlled environment than that of a conventional classroom. In one of their studies, college students completed a logical reasoning test. The students then estimated the number of items they had answered correctly and reported how they believed they had performed relative to other students. Similar to classroom studies, students in the bottom quartile of test performance greatly overestimated their performance on the test itself as well as their performance relative to others. Not only did these low-performing students overestimate their performance, they also estimated their performance as above average: on average rating their performance at the 62nd percentile when it was actually at the 11th. Again mirroring classroom studies, students in the top quartile were more accurate and tended to underestimate their performance. Kruger and Dunning reported similar findings with respect to grammatical skills. Students in the bottom quartile of performance on a grammar test grossly overestimated their performance – rating themselves at the 61st percentile when their performance fell at the 10th percentile. Students in the second and third quartiles also overestimated their performance, but were more accurate than the lowest-performing students. Only students in the top quartile were accurate in their estimates of their absolute test performance, but, again, they tended to underestimate their performance relative to other students.

It is interesting to note that judgments of students' own knowledge and performance – particularly among the majority of students whose performance is at or below the level that would earn them a B according to conventional grading standards – tend to be quite inaccurate whether the students predict their performance before or after taking an exam. Kruger and Dunning (1999) explained the inaccuracy of self-judgments, in particular those made by low performers, by asserting that "incompetence ... not only causes poor performance but also the inability to recognize that one's performance is poor" (p. 1130). To illustrate, they cited the ability to write grammatically correct sentences which, they observed, requires the same skills necessary to recognize grammatical errors. In other words, someone who is incapable of good writing will be unable to recognize and correct bad writing. Dunning and his colleagues referred to this as a "double curse" because "in many intellectual and social domains, the skills needed to produce correct responses are virtually identical to those needed to evaluate the accuracy of one's responses" (Dunning, Johnson, Ehrlinger, & Kruger, 2003: 84–85). Skill or knowledge deficits prevent students from knowing whether their answers are correct, and also from recognizing that other students' performance is superior.

High-performing students sometimes misjudge their own performance, but to a lesser degree. Moreover, high performers tend to underestimate their performance – at least relative to that of other students. Dunning (2005) explained that strong students underestimate the uniqueness of their performance. Because they are more knowledgeable, they are better able to accurately evaluate the quality of their work. Therefore their self-evaluations tend to be more accurate than those of low-performing students with respect to the proportion of test items answered correctly. Because they are more knowledgeable, they are likewise better at recognizing when they do not know something. However, strong students often make the false assumption that because they know something, most other students must know it as well. This leads them to overestimate the performance of other students (Ehrlinger et al., 2008).

Yet another factor contributing to students' difficulty in making accurate judgments of their own knowledge is hindsight bias: the tendency to assume once something happens that one knew all along that it was going to happen (Fischhoff, 1975; see also Hawkins & Hastie, 1990, for a review). When students receive feedback suggesting that their knowledge is incomplete, such as getting an exam item incorrect, they may respond by telling themselves that they actually did know the information. Although they do not have a strong grasp of the material, they feel as if they do because they recognize something about the item content. Looking back, once they know the answer, the solution seems obvious. This feeling of familiarity can lead students to have an exaggerated sense of what they know. Hindsight bias therefore reinforces the feeling that their failure was due to the nature of the assessment rather than the nature of their knowledge – which makes it more difficult for them to learn from feedback.

Koriat and Bjork (2005) postulated a contrasting phenomenon that they termed foresight bias, which leads people to overestimate how well they will recall information when they predict their future performance at a time when the information to be learned is available to them. That is, people fail to account for the fact that the memory cues available to them while studying will not be available when they are asked to recall the information. The relevance to academic performance is clear, in that students often judge their own learning and make decisions about additional studying at times when they have the relevant academic material available to them. Bjork and colleagues (2013) similarly explained that learners often mistake their sense of fluency regarding information to be learned as evidence of actual learning. When information seems easy to learn, or seems to come to mind easily in the presence of specific memory cues, students believe that they genuinely understand the information even when they do not.

Ehrlinger (2008) pointed out that one's motivation also plays a pivotal role in the accuracy of one's self-judgments. She noted that people will be motivated to recognize the limits of their knowledge only if their primary objective is to increase that knowledge. If, instead, one's primary goal is to see oneself in a positive light, the person will tend to avoid or distort feedback that suggests a lack of knowledge. Ehrlinger suggests that people motivated primarily by a desire to maintain a positive self-image will have difficulty acknowledging and learning from feedback indicating that they are not doing well. This observation is consistent with the finding that despite repeated testing and ongoing feedback and reflection on their performance, students tend to base their self-assessments on their beliefs and expectations about themselves, rather than on their past performance (Hacker et al., 2000).

There is mixed evidence concerning the extent to which students can improve the accuracy of their self-evaluations. As cited earlier in this chapter, Kruger and Dunning (1999) gave students a test of grammar and had the students rate their own performance. Several weeks later, the researchers invited participants who had scored in the top and bottom quartiles on the grammar test to return to the lab to grade tests completed by five other participants, and then to rate their own performance once again. Students in the top quartile became more accurate in their self-judgments after seeing the work of other students. Those in the bottom quartile failed to gain insight into their poor performance even after seeing the work of stronger students. Hacker and colleagues (2000) likewise found that although high- and low-performing students were inaccurate in their self-judgments at the start of a course, the high-performing students became much more accurate over time while the low performers showed no improvement in accuracy. Kruger and Dunning found that it might be possible to train students to judge their work more accurately. The catch is that the way to do this is simply to help them improve their skills on the relevant task. That is, students rated their skills more accurately as their skills increased. Nonetheless, they still overestimated their performance relative to other students.

A slightly different pattern of results emerged in another classroom study. Miller and Geraci (2011) noted that improving student metacognition (i.e., knowing what they know) is more challenging in the classroom than in the laboratory. These researchers had students predict their own exam performance immediately prior to completing each of four exams. High scorers were again more accurate than low scorers, and accuracy did not improve over time despite the incentive of extra credit for making accurate predictions. In a second study, Miller and Geraci provided students with more explicit feedback on the accuracy of their self-judgments. This time, low-performing students demonstrated some increase in accuracy over time, but appeared to reach an accuracy ceiling. The researchers speculated that there may be a limit to how much low-performing students can improve their self-evaluations. More importantly, however, the increase in accuracy did not lead to an improvement in exam performance. Low-scoring students improved their accuracy by lowering their predicted scores, rather than by improving their test scores.

Other researchers have similarly investigated whether students can improve the accuracy of their self-judgments if provided with adequate incentives. As noted above, Miller and Geraci (2011) found that offering extra credit for accurate predictions did not lead to increased accuracy. In a more complex test of the effects of incentives (Hacker, Bol, & Bahbahani, 2008), researchers again found that offering points for accuracy had no overall effect on judgment accuracy. However, the researchers qualified this conclusion because high-performing students were accurate throughout the course so a ceiling effect would have prevented significant improvement. In contrast, low performers were less accurate, but improved slightly in their ability to judge their performance after taking an exam. Unfortunately, there was no such improvement in their ability to predict their performance before the exam, which is arguably more important because it is this factor that would help them to determine whether they were sufficiently prepared.

The findings from laboratory studies on the effectiveness of incentives for increasing the accuracy of student self-judgments parallel the findings from classroom research. Ehrlinger and colleagues (2008) tested the impact of a particularly strong incentive. The researchers had students complete a 20-item multiple-choice test of logical reasoning ability and then predict the number of items they answered correctly. Students were offered $100 if their predicted score exactly matched their actual score, and $25 if their predicted scores were within 5% of their actual scores. Consistent with other studies, low scorers overestimated and high scorers underestimated their own performance. The large monetary incentive had no effect on the accuracy of self-judgments. The researchers reported similar results with respect to social incentives. Students taking a test of logical reasoning ability who were told that they would be interviewed by a professor regarding their rationale for their responses on the test were no more accurate in judging their performance than students with no such incentive.

Aside from finding ways to help students learn more, which is always a priority in education, the best hope for helping students to become better judges of their own knowledge and performance is to have them engage in frequent and repeated self-assessment. Lopez and Kossack (2007) conducted a study in which students in one class did not engage in self-assessment of their knowledge, students in a second class self-assessed on the first and last days of class, and students in a third class self-assessed on the first day of class and also following each of four exams. Only students who self-assessed after each exam became more accurate in their judgments by the end of the course. The researchers concluded that students can improve their ability to gauge their own knowledge if they do so repeatedly and systematically. Unfortunately, the findings do not permit a comparison of students at various performance levels, which is an important consideration given research (e.g., Kruger & Dunning, 1999; Miller & Geraci, 2011) suggesting that interventions to improve students' self-assessment accuracy have only modest effects on low-performing students whose self-ratings tend to be the least accurate.

Accurate self-evaluation can play an important role in student learning. As Shaughnessy (1979) points out, students who cannot judge their knowledge accurately are likely to study less efficiently and effectively: spending too much time reviewing familiar content and failing to recognize and review content they do not know well. Existing research suggests that students often misjudge their level of understanding and performance with respect to academic material, and that low-performing students are at particular risk because they tend to grossly overestimate their performance. This pattern creates a paradox, in that low-performing students might improve their self-evaluation skills if they more effectively mastered course content, but their deficient self-evaluation skills make learning more difficult. Current research suggests that, although the overall effects may be small, the most promising strategy for improving the accuracy of students' self-judgments is to have them in engage in ongoing, systematic self-evaluation and to provide them with feedback on the accuracy of their evaluations. Moreover, students should not assess their knowledge immediately after studying because self-evaluations become more accurate after a short delay (Dunlosky & Nelson, 1992). With continued practice and feedback, students may learn to be better judges of what they know.

References

Benjamin, A. S., Bjork, R. A., & Schwartz, B. L. (1998). The mismeasure of memory: When retrieval fluency is misleading as a metamnemonic index. *Journal of Experimental Psychology: General, 127,* 55–68.

Bjork, R. A., Dunlosky, J., & Kornell, N. (2013). Self-regulated learning: Beliefs, techniques, and illusions. *Annual review of Psychology, 64*, 417–444.

Dunlosky, J. & Nelson, T. O. (1992). Importance of the kind of cue for judgments of learning (JOL) and the delayed-JOL effect. *Memory & Cognition, 20*, 374–380.

Dunning, D. (2005). *Self-insight: Roadblocks and detours on the path to knowing thyself.* New York: Psychology Press. doi: 10.4324/9780203337998.

Dunning, D., Johnson, K., Ehrlinger, J., & Kruger, J. (2003). Why people fail to recognize their own incompetence. *Current Directions in Psychological Science, 12*(3), 83–87. doi: 10.1111/1467-8721.01235.

Ehrlinger, J. (2008). Skill level, self-views, and self-theories as sources of error in self-assessment. *Social And Personality Psychology Compass, 2*(1), 382–398. doi: 10.1111/j.1751-9004.2007.00047.x.

Ehrlinger, J., Johnson, K., Banner, M., Dunning, D., & Kruger, J. (2008). Why the unskilled are unaware: Further explorations of (absent) self-insight among the incompetent. *Organizational Behavior and Human Decision Processes, 105*(1), 98–121. doi:10.1016/j.obhdp.2007.05.002.

Fischhoff, B. (1975). Hindsight ≠ foresight: The effect of outcome knowledge on judgment under uncertainty. *Journal of Experimental Psychology: Human Perception and Performance, 1*, 288–299.

Hacker, D. J., Bol, L., & Bahbahani, K. (2008). Explaining calibration accuracy in classroom contexts: The effects of incentives, reflection, and explanatory style. *Metacognition and Learning, 3*(2), 101–121. doi: 10.1007/s11409-008-9021-5.

Hacker, D. J., Bol, L., Horgan, D. D., & Rakow, E. A. (2000). Test prediction and performance in a classroom context. *Journal of Educational Psychology, 92*(1), 160–170. doi:10.1037/0022-0663.92.1.160.

Hawkins, S. A. & Hastie, R. (1990). Hindsight: Biased judgments of past events after the outcomes are known. *Psychological Bulletin, 107*(3), 311–327. doi: 10.1037/0033-2909.107.3.311.

Koriat, A. & Bjork, R. A. (2005). Illusions of competence in monitoring one's own knowledge during study. *Journal of Experimental Psychology: Learning, Memory, and Cognition, 31*, 187–194.

Kruger, J. & Dunning, D. (1999). Unskilled and unaware of it: How difficulties in recognizing one's own incompetence lead to inflated self-assessments. *Journal of Personality and Social Psychology, 77*(6), 1121–1134. doi: 10.1037/0022-3514.77.6.1121.

Langendyk, V. (2006). Not knowing that they do not know: Self-assessment accuracy of third-year medical students. *Medical Education, 40*, 173–179.

Lopez, R. & Kossack, S. (2007). Effects of recurring use of self-assessment in university courses. *International Journal of Learning, 14*, 203–214.

Miller, T. M. & Geraci, L. (2011). Training metacognition in the classroom: The influence of incentives and feedback on exam predictions. *Metacognition and Learning, 6*(3), 303–314. doi: 10.1007/s11409-011-9083-7.

Nelson, T. O. & Dunlosky, J. (1991). When people's judgments of learning (JOLs) are extremely accurate at predicting subsequent recall: The "Delayed-JOL Effect." *Psychological Science, 2,* 267–270.

Shaughnessy, J. J. (1979). Confidence–judgment accuracy as a predictor of test performance. *Journal of Research in Personality, 13*(4), 505–514. doi: 10.1016/0092-6566(79)90012-6.

Sinkavich, F. J. (1995). Performance and metamemory: Do students know what they don't know? *Journal Of Instructional Psychology, 22*(1), 77–87.

2 MYTH: STUDENTS LEARN BETTER WHEN TEACHING METHODS ARE MATCHED WITH THEIR LEARNING STYLES

The nature and importance of student learning styles are among the most written about and least agreed upon issues in the educational literature. Broadly speaking, learning styles refer to students' individual preferences for particular educational environments and techniques for learning new information. Scholarly attention to the potential role of learning styles in education began in earnest in the 1970s, but the concept is rooted in much earlier research on cognitive styles (Cassidy, 2004). A long history of research on cognitive styles demonstrates that people do in fact tend to think in different ways. For example, people who are field-dependent prefer to analyze information as part of a larger context, whereas those who are field-independent prefer a more objective analysis of information independent of the surrounding context (Willingham, 2009). Some people prefer to think mainly in concrete terms, while others prefer abstract concepts (see Kozhevnikov, 2007, for a review of cognitive style models). Claiming that such differences in thinking styles do not exist would be akin to claiming that extraversion does not exist.

Students will often report a preference for one type of thinking or another. Debate about learning styles pertains to a separate but related

Great Myths of Education and Learning, First Edition. Jeffrey D. Holmes.
© 2016 John Wiley & Sons, Inc. Published 2016 by John Wiley & Sons, Inc.

claim made by many educators – that instruction tailored to match students' learning preferences leads to more successful learning regardless of the nature of the material to be learned (e.g., Gregorc & Ward, 1977; Dunn, 2000; Zapalska & Dabb, 2002). This idea is very widely endorsed among educators. Nearly four decades ago, Arter and Jenkins (1977) reported that 99% of the teachers they surveyed agreed that "A child's modality strengths and weaknesses should be a major consideration when devising educational prescriptions," and 96% believed that their students learned more when teachers matched their teaching approach to students' modality preferences (p. 290). Recent data suggest that such assumptions have changed little over time. In a survey of primary and secondary school teachers, 94% endorsed the belief that learning is improved when students are taught in a manner consistent with their learning style (Dekker, Lee, Howard-Jones, & Jolles, 2012). Learning style matching is also widely endorsed in higher education and among parents (Pashler, McDaniel, Rohrer, & Bjork, 2009), and college students likewise tend to view their own perceived learning styles as important (Krätzig & Arbuthnott, 2006). Popular websites (e.g., "Overview of learning styles," n.d.) and even the websites of university learning centers (e.g., "Three learning styles," n.d.) assert that people learn in different ways and that matching learning styles with teaching methods improves learning.

The literature on learning styles is extensive, complex, and fragmented. There is no uniformly accepted definition of what a learning style is, nor is there a universally accepted model of specific learning styles. One useful definition that helps to illustrate the broad concept of learning styles is that they refer to "the way people absorb, process, and retain information" (De Bello, 1990: 204), although many other more complex definitions have been offered (see Hyman & Rosoff, 1984; Cassidy, 2004, for reviews). What is perhaps more important is the remarkable proliferation of learning-style models that scholars have devised over the past several decades. In an important review, Coffield, Moseley, Hall, and Ecclestone (2004) identified 71 different learning-style models. Whereas the established idea that people differ in their cognitive styles originated in psychological research, much of the literature on learning styles has been produced outside the field of psychology – specifically in such fields as education and business – which led to a poorly integrated field of research with "complexities and convolutions difficult to comprehend and assimilate" (Cassidy, 2004: 419). Kozhevnikov (2007) blames this lack of coherence on researchers' shift toward using self-report measures to assess conscious learning-style preferences, replacing an emphasis on assessments of abilities. Often there is little attention to whether such perceptions of one's own learning are accurate or important.

Given the proliferation of learning-style models, it is not possible to provide a detailed description of even a meaningful sample of such models here. Several comprehensive reviews are available for readers wishing to better understand the specifics of various models (Cassidy, 2004; Coffield et al., 2004). Instead, this chapter will focus primarily on the evidence for the broad hypothesis that learning is reliably enhanced when teachers attempt to match their style of teaching – irrespective of content – to students' self-reported learning styles. Despite the popularity and widespread endorsement of the learning-styles approach to instruction, many researchers have noted that there are few methodologically sound studies that provide support for its efficacy (Coffield et al., 2004; Pashler et al., 2009). Unlike most fields of research, more than half the available scholarly literature on learning styles comes from doctoral dissertations. Although dissertations often include well-conducted research, they are student projects that are held to a lower threshold of quality than is found in published, peer-reviewed research.

The most broadly researched and applied model of learning styles addresses students' preferences for learning through specific sensory modalities – usually visual, auditory, and kinesthetic (Arter & Jenkins, 1977; Stahl, 1999). In their review of several early studies on student learning preferences, Arter and Jenkins first outlined the type of evidence required to conclude that matching instruction to learning styles actually enhances learning. Such evidence, they explain, must come from experimental rather than correlational research, and must meet several specific methodological criteria. First, the method of categorizing students by learning style must have demonstrated reliability and validity. Second, there must be evidence that students classified as particular types of learners perform differently on corresponding ability measures; for example, students with an auditory learning style must perform significantly better on auditory tests than on visual tests. This criterion helps to demonstrate that learning-style instruments are assessing something other than simple preferences. Third, some students must be taught using methods matched to their preferred style, while others are taught with methods that are contrary to their preferred style. Finally, students in all conditions must be assessed with the same outcome test after instruction. Furthermore, to ensure that the experimental findings have utility, the participants must be representative of classroom populations and the teaching objectives and methods must be consistent with actual educational environments.

Perhaps not surprisingly, Arter and Jenkins (1977) found relatively few studies that met all their criteria. They identified 14 such studies assessing the effects of matching teaching styles to auditory or visual learning styles when teaching reading to schoolchildren. The studies they reviewed were diverse with respect to the age of student participants, the duration and method of instruction, and the type of outcome test used to evaluate learning. Only one of the studies yielded a significant result supporting the matching approach, and Arter and Jenkins identified several methodological limitations that limited the validity of this single study. Tarver and Dawson (1978) conducted a similar review, and likewise found virtually no evidence that matching instruction to learning style improves learning. They concluded that the lack of observed benefit across a variety of instructional and assessment methods supports the conclusion that students' preferences for specific modalities cannot be matched with teaching methods to produce better outcomes.

Kampwirth and Bates (1980) conducted an even more extensive review of 22 studies of elementary school children in which researchers compared learning outcomes when students with preferences for either visual or auditory learning learned via either a matched method or an unmatched method. In only two of the studies was there an effect of matching consistent with learning-styles predictions. In the other 20 studies, there was either no consistent effect of matching or, in some cases, the observed effect was the opposite of what learning-styles models would predict. That is, students in some studies actually learned more when they were taught in their less-preferred modality. Kampwirth and Bates also pointed out that many researchers first screen participants to identify those with a distinct preference for learning via one modality or the other, and exclude from their studies participants with less distinct preferences. This practice would tend to exaggerate the effects of matching, while simultaneously making the results less applicable to real-life educational settings where all students are included.

In 1987, Kavale and Forness touched off a particularly interesting and contentious professional debate about learning styles. These researchers sought to conduct a more rigorous integration of learning-styles research than had previously been conducted. Using a statistical technique called meta-analysis – a method for combining the results of many existing studies – the researchers analyzed data from more than 3,000 elementary and secondary students collected during 39 studies in which learning styles were assessed, teaching materials and techniques were designed to match those styles, and an outcome test was administered. Only 16 of the studies came from published articles; the rest came mostly from dissertations, with a few coming from books. Kavale and Forness found that 13 of the 39 studies revealed some small positive effect of matching. Interestingly, when the researchers classified the 39 studies based on methodological quality using an established procedure, they found that studies of poor quality showed the largest – but still very small – effects of matching, while studies of high quality showed extremely small effects not statistically different from no effect at all. They also reported that more than one-third of students receiving matched instruction performed more poorly on outcome tests than control students who did not receive customized instruction. Kavale and Forness concluded that there was no support for the hypothesis that matching improves learning.

Kavale and Forness's (1987) analysis and conclusions were met with derision by one of the staunchest advocates of matching instruction to students' learning styles. Dunn (1990) was highly critical of Kavale and Forness for including studies in their meta-analysis that Dunn claimed were methodologically flawed. Ironically, Kavale and Forness attempted to account for methodological quality and found that the studies that were most flawed were those that provided the strongest support for matching. Dunn cited 10 studies that she claimed provided support for matching instruction to learning style, but 9 of the 10 studies came from unpublished dissertations – mostly from her own institution. As noted above, most dissertation research has the distinct limitation of lacking rigorous peer review.

A few years later, Dunn and her colleagues (Dunn, Griggs, Olson, Beasley, & Gorman, 1995) published their own meta-analysis of 36 studies conducted on Dunn's own model of learning styles. The researchers concluded that there was an overall average positive effect whereby students performed better after instruction that was consistent with their learning style than with instruction that was inconsistent. Again, however, the quality of the data included in the analysis is indeterminate. Of the 36 studies, 35 came from unpublished dissertations. Dunn and colleagues also eliminated several studies that they claimed had serious methodological flaws, but provided few details on the nature of either the included or excluded studies. It is particularly difficult to evaluate the validity of the researchers' conclusions when nearly all the data came from unpublished sources. Furthermore, it is difficult to comprehend why research seemingly demonstrating the validity of such an important educational principle has largely failed to appear in peer-reviewed sources. The evidence supporting other learning-style models likewise suffers from the limitation of consisting nearly entirely of unpublished projects not subject to peer review (Stahl, 1999).

A few years after the publication of Dunn and colleagues' (1995) analysis, Kavale and colleagues (Kavale, Hirshoren, & Forness, 1998) provided a critique. They concluded that Dunn et al. could not have conducted a comprehensive review of research on the Dunn learning-styles model, as evidenced by the fact that nearly all included studies were dissertations and that many relevant databases were not searched. The critics also pointed out that Dunn and colleagues reported average effects of matching, but did not report variability around those averages as is customary in meta-analyses and is necessary for interpreting the findings. Kavale and colleagues cite some evidence from Dunn et al.'s report suggesting that the omitted information could potentially invalidate the findings. They also criticized Dunn for including studies that were likely to be statistical outliers, as evidenced by effect sizes so large as to be unrealistic given the nature of the research. Kavale and colleagues bluntly concluded that the meta-analysis had "all the hallmarks of a desperate attempt to rescue a failed model of learning style" (p. 79).

Harsh critiques aside, recent research evaluating the benefits of matching instruction to students' preferred learning modality have continued to yield little positive evidence. For example, Massa and Mayer (2006) conducted two experiments comparing visually-oriented learners with verbally-oriented learners in terms of learning from a multimedia lesson that emphasized either verbal or visual presentations of content. In one experiment involving college students and a replication involving non-college-educated adults, the researchers used self-report measures to categorize participants as either visualizers or verbalizers. Participants were then randomly assigned to study a computerized lesson in electronics under training conditions emphasizing either verbal or visual learning. The researchers observed no interaction between student learning preference and the type of instruction in determining performance on any of four composite learning measures. The researchers then analyzed effects on separate components of the composite tests. Among 51 specific outcome measures, significant matching effects occurred in only two cases, which is less than the number of positive effects that would be expected due to chance. Moreover, nearly half of the effects were in the opposite direction to what would be predicted by the matching hypothesis. Massa and Mayer concluded that they had found no support for the claim that learners with visual and verbal orientations will benefit from different methods of instruction.

Other recent research further calls into question the premises of the matching hypothesis with respect to various learning modalities. For example, Constantinidou and Baker (2002) had adults ranging in age from 19 to 77 complete a learning-styles instrument to assign scores for visual and verbal learning preferences. Participants attempted to learn lists of objects presented under one of three conditions: an auditory condition in which participants heard the words out loud, a visual condition in which participants saw drawings of the objects, and a combined condition in which participants saw a drawing and heard the name of the object at the same time. Constantinidou and Baker found no correlation between preferences for a visual learning style and performance under any of the three methods of instruction. Interestingly, preferences for auditory learning did not correlate with performance on the auditory memory task as would be predicted by the matching hypothesis, but did correlate with performance on the visual memory task – contradicting the matching hypothesis.

In a similar study, Krätzig and Arbuthnott (2006) had university students complete an established inventory to assign scores for visual and auditory leaning preferences, as well as kinesthetic preferences. In addition, participants separately reported which of the three learning styles they believed best fitted them. Finally, they completed measures of visual, auditory, and kinesthetic memory. There were no significant positive correlations between scores on the learning style inventory and objective measures of memory associated with the corresponding modality. That is, a preference for visual learning was not associated with better visual memory, nor were auditory and kinesthetic preferences associated with performance on relevant memory tests. The same pattern of findings emerged when researchers used participants' self-categorizations of learning style. Importantly, only 29 of the 65 participants were classified the same way by the learning-styles inventory and their own self-classification. The researchers repeated their analysis using only the data for those participants who were categorized the same way using both assessments, and still there was no support for the learning-styles hypothesis. Krätzig and Arbuthnott state that, contrary to the predictions associated with learning-style models, they found no evidence that visual, auditory, or kinesthetic learners learn better in their preferred modality.

In the most recent test of the assumptions associated with the matching hypothesis, Rogowsky, Calhoun, and Tallal (2014) had 121 college-educated adults complete an established leaning-styles survey assessing preference for auditory or visual learning, as well as actual aptitude measures assessing auditory comprehension and visual comprehension. The 61 participants who could be definitively categorized as having a specific learning style were randomly assigned to learn content from a nonfiction book by either reading an ebook or listening to an audiobook. They then answered questions assessing their comprehension of the content immediately after exposure and again two weeks later. Across all participants, preference for an auditory learning style was not associated with better performance on a listening comprehension test than on a reading comprehension test; similarly, a preference for visual learning was not associated with better performance on a reading comprehension test than it was on a listening comprehension test. Moreover, self-reported visual learners scored higher than auditory learners on both listening and reading aptitude tests. With respect to the modes of instruction implemented among participants with the most distinctive learning preferences, there was no significant interaction indicating that participants with a particular learning style learned more – in terms of either immediate performance or longer-term comprehension – from a particular instructional method. Rogowsky and colleagues found that only the general comprehension aptitude measures – and not the learning style measures – were associated with how much participants learned.

As noted at the beginning of this chapter and illustrated by the research described thus far, learning styles associated with specific sensory modalities – visual and auditory and to a lesser extent kinesthetic – have been the most widely studied preferences, and the existing research yields little support for matching instruction to these preferences. Research on other learning-style models leads to very similar conclusions. For example, Lundstrom and Martin (1986) tested the matching hypothesis based on Gregorc's (Gregorc & Ward, 1977) model in which learners are categorized into one of four learning styles based on their preferences for concreteness versus abstraction and sequentialness versus randomness. Based on Gregorc's model, the researchers predicted that students with certain styles would perform better studying independently and students with other styles would learn more as part of a group. The researchers had college students complete a learning-styles instrument as well as achievement tests and measures of attitudes toward the styles of instruction. Students then participated either in an instructional method involving individual study or one involving interactions between groups of students. There was no interaction between any of the learning styles and either of the instructional methods in affecting either student achievement or attitude toward instruction.

Bostrom (1990) reviewed four studies investigating learning-style matching for purposes of software training. The studies all tested the efficacy of matching on a learning-styles model proposed by Kolb (1984), whereby learners are categorized as having one of four possible styles depending on their preference for concrete versus abstract experiences, and for active versus reflective learning activities. Of the four studies, only the single published study yielded significant results.

Nonetheless, Bostrom interpreted all four studies as having a "consistent pattern of findings" supporting the importance of these learning styles (p. 101). This is a curious conclusion given that even for the single published study, only one out of three tested effects was significant according to accepted standards and all effects were extremely small.

Hayes and Allison (1993) reviewed 17 studies investigating the effects of matching based on several different learning-styles models. They reported that 10 of the 17 studies provided some support for the effectiveness of matching, but that the findings were inconsistent. Often the findings supported matching for one particular learning style within a model and not for other styles; some studies revealed support for matching when learning was measured in one way, but not when it was measured in another. Moreover, positive effects tended to be very small in magnitude – suggesting that matching was associated only with very weak effects or no effects at all.

In one of the most recent tests of the effects of matching instruction to learning styles, researchers investigated yet another model (Cook, Thompson, Thomas, & Thomas, 2009). Cook and colleagues used a learning-style measure to assess medical students' preference for a sensing learning style emphasizing applied learning such as data collection and experimentation, versus an intuitive learning style emphasizing broader patterns and theories. The researchers predicted that participants with a sensing learning style would prefer and learn more from an instructional approach where applied problems were presented in advance of didactic information, and that intuiting learners would prefer and learn more when didactic information was presented in advance of applied problems. Medical residents each completed web-based learning modules containing both didactic content and medical case problems to be solved; all modules contained identical content, but varied in terms of whether the didactic information or case problem was presented first. Participants completed two modules from each format presented in randomized order; they completed a test of applied knowledge after each module and a cumulative final exam at the end of the academic year. Cook and colleagues found no significant effect where sensing or intuitive learners learned more from instructional methods designed to match their learning preferences. There was also no evidence that learning styles predicted faster learning when a matched instructional method was used. The researchers conducted additional analyses of other learning-style dimensions assessed by the instrument they used, and found no evidence that any of the dimensions were associated with improved learning either independently or in conjunction with particular teaching methods.

Researchers have proposed many explanations for why matching teaching methods to learning styles does not have the benefits that most teachers assume. From a measurement perspective, many tests used to identify students' learning styles have poor reliability which may indicate that students' preferences are not necessarily stable across time (Stahl, 1999). Stahl also argues that inventories purportedly assessing learning styles often are actually assessing abilities. For example, some students classified as auditory learners might prefer auditory presentations simply because they have poor reading skills, so emphasizing auditory teaching methods could deprive them of opportunities to improve their reading comprehension skills. Accordingly, Stahl recommends tailoring teaching methods to students' developmental skill level rather than to their supposed learning styles.

Many researchers have also criticized advocates of learning-style models for failing to consider the nature of the content being taught (Snider, 1992; Pashler et al., 2009). Hyman and Rosoff (1984) cited this failure as a major weakness of the learning-styles concept, stating that effective teaching requires attention to the subject matter being learned. For example, learning to read a map requires a visual representation rather than an auditory explanation only (Willingham, 2009). Snider puzzled over the question of why people agree that one cannot learn to play basketball solely through discussion, but believe that students can learn to read solely through visual or kinesthetic methods. Reading, she insists, requires some skills that are neither kinesthetic nor visual. Cook and colleagues (2009) agree that teaching methods should be tailored to learning objectives rather than to students' learning styles.

Arter and Jenkins (1979) proposed that learning-style models simply may not describe students' characteristics accurately, the assessed characteristics may not have a meaningful effect on learning, or the effect may be weak compared with the effect of other factors. Accordingly, a very large number of studies indicate that there are many techniques that improve student learning more powerfully and consistently than matching teaching to learning styles (see Walberg, 1984; Kavale et al., 1998). Kavale and Forness (1987) explained that learning-style assessment itself is problematic because when people are assessed and categorized in this way, there is a great deal of overlap across groups in their actual preferences. In other words, most people's preferences do not follow a clean categorical model where one style is preferred strongly and consistently above all others. Kavale and Forness state that for students with less differentiated preferences – which is most of them – learning preferences make very little difference in comparison with many other factors that affect learning.

Pashler and colleagues (2009) question the very notion that students differ greatly in the ways in which they learn. They assert that although many factors may affect the type of teaching that is most effective for individual students, the assumption that there are vast differences between students in terms of the way they learn can distract from the application of empirically supported principles that can improve learning across the board. Willingham (2009) agrees stating, "Children are more alike than different in terms of how they think and learn" (p. 113). He goes on to explain that although people differ in memory ability associated with specific senses, most memories are stored based on meaning rather than the specific sensory mode through which the information was absorbed. Therefore, having strong auditory memory or strong visual memory does not help when the objective is to learn meaning, because the meaning is not stored based on sense-specific information such as visual and auditory details.

Other researchers have pointed out additional ways that learning-style models neglect important details about how the brain works. Geake (2008) emphasized that that "focusing on one sensory modality flies in the face of the brain's natural interconnectivity" (p. 130). In general, neither learning nor teaching practices can be cleanly differentiated according to learning-style assumptions, so it is likely all modalities are important for learning (Kavale and Forness, 1987; Arter & Jenkins, 1979). Accordingly, teaching that integrates multiple modalities simultaneously tends to produce greater learning gains across all students than teaching that is tailored to specific modalities (Massa & Mayer, 2006; Tight, 2010). Finally, researchers have questioned the utility of any learning model that neglects or denies – as learning-style models do – the role of intelligence (Hyman & Rosoff, 1984).

Clearly, there is a disconnect between what most teachers assume about students' learning styles and the experimental evidence supporting such assumptions – a disconnect that Pashler and colleagues (2009) characterized as "striking and disturbing" (p. 117). Researchers have provided a number of explanations for this disconnect. Pashler and colleagues noted that learning-style models are appealing because they classify people into neat categories and focus on treating students as individuals. The models are also consistent with the idea that everyone can learn very effectively if only the right individualized teaching method is used, and justify blaming the educational system rather than any lack of ability if a child is not succeeding academically. Willingham (2009) suggests that the vast majority of teachers believe in the importance of learning styles because the concept is so widely accepted that it seems that it must be true, and because confirmation bias causes people to interpret ambiguous data as confirming their expectations. Other researchers have elaborated by pointing out that teachers do not usually systematically collect data comparing the effectiveness of different teaching methods so they may tend to remember times when matching seemed to work, interpret what they observe primarily in terms of what they expect to see, or misattribute students' progress to learning-style matching when many other factors could have been at play (Arter & Jenkins, 1977).

Those who criticize the practice of matching instruction to learning styles assert neither that all students are the same nor that all teaching methods will be equally effective across all students and all situations. However, given the pressure on teachers to assess learning styles and develop lesson plans to match those styles (Rogowsky et al., 2014), as well as the commercial interests helping to drive such an agenda (see Pashler et al., 2009), it is important to determine whether such efforts are in the best interest of students. Arter and Jenkins (1977) adeptly pointed out that if matching does not yield benefits under controlled research conditions, it is even less likely to be beneficial in classrooms. Pashler and colleagues noted that even if a study provided the necessary experimental evidence, it would support only a specific type of classification rather than learning-style models in general. Furthermore, they argue, the benefits of implementation would need to be evaluated in the context of the increased cost – in terms of teacher training and other factors – of assessing styles and customizing teaching methods. Others fear that students may be hindered by being told that they have one learning style rather than the ability to learn in a variety of ways (Henry, 2007). It would certainly appear to be good news that, as researchers have found, students can learn via many modes and can shift to learning strategies other than those they most prefer when the situation or content demand it (Krätzig & Arbuthnott, 2006; Constantinidou & Baker, 2009). Arter's and Jenkins' admonition regarding learning-style matching made nearly 40 years ago is no less apropos today: "no matter how strongly a given model of learning may appeal to conventional wisdom, that model's validity and utility is still an empirical question" (p. 282).

References

Arter, J. A. & Jenkins, J. R. (1977). Examining the benefits and prevalence of modality considerations in special education. *Journal of Special Education, 11,* 281–298.

Arter, J. A. & Jenkins, J. R. (1979). Differential diagnosis–prescriptive teaching: A critical appraisal. *Review of Educational Research, 49*, 517–555.

Bostrom, R. P. (1990). The importance of learning style in end-user training. *MIS Quarterly, 14*, 101–119.

Cassidy, S. (2004). Learning styles: An overview of theories, models, and measures. *Educational Psychology, 24*, 419–444.

Arter, J. A. & Jenkins, J. R. (1977). Examining the benefits and prevalence of modality considerations in special education. *Journal of Special Education, 11*, 281–298.

Cook, D. A., Thompson, W. G., Thomas, K. G., & Thomas, M. R. (2009). Lack of interaction between sensing–intuitive learning styles and problem-first versus information-first instruction: A randomized crossover trial. *Advances in Health Science Education, 14*, 79–90.

Constantinidou, F. & Baker, S. (2002). Stimulus modality and verbal learning performance in normal aging. *Brain and Language, 82*, 296–311.

De Bello, T. C. (1990). Comparison of eleven major learning styles models: Variables, appropriate populations, validity of instrumentation, and the research behind them. *Journal of Reading, Writing, and Learning Disabilities, 6*, 203–222.

Dekker, S., Lee, N. C., Howard-Jones, P., & Jolles, J. (2012). Neuromyths in education: Prevalence and predictors of misconceptions among teachers. *Frontiers in Psychology, 3*, 1–8.

Dunn, R. (1990). Bias over substance: A critical analysis of Kavale and Forness' report on modality-based instruction. *Exceptional Children, 56*, 352–356.

Dunn, R. (2000). Capitalizing on college students' learning styles: Theory, practice, and research. In: R. Dunn & S. A. Griggs (Eds.), *Practical approaches to using learning styles in higher education* (pp. 3–18). Westport, CT: Bergin & Garvey.

Dunn, R., Griggs, S. A., Olson, J., Beasley, M., & Gorman, B. S. (1995). A meta-analytic validation of the Dunn and Dunn model of learning-style preferences. *Journal of Educational Research, 88*, 353–362.

Geake, J. (2008). Neuromythologies in education. *Educational Research, 50*, 123–133.

Gregorc, A. F. & Ward, H. B. (1977). A new definition for individual, *NAASP Bulletin, 61*, 20–26.

Hayes, J. & Allinson, C. W. (1993). Matching learning style and instructional strategy: An application of the person–environment interaction paradigm. *Perceptual and Motor Skills, 76*, 63–79.

Henry, J. (2007). Professor pans "learning style" method. *The Telegraph*. Available at: http://www.telegraph.co.uk/news/uknews/1558822/Professor-pans-learning-style-teaching-method.html.

Hyman, R. & Rosoff, B. (1984). Matching learning and teaching styles: The jug and what's in it. *Theory into Practice, 23*, 35–43.

Kampwirth, T. J. & Bates, M. (1980). Modality preference and teaching method: A review of the research. *Academic Therapy, 15*, 597–605.

Kavale, K. A. & Forness, S. R. (1987). Substance over style: Assessing the efficacy of modality testing and teaching. *Exceptional Children, 54*, 228–239.

Kavale, K. A., Hirshoren, A., & Forness, S. R. (1998). Meta-analytic validation of the Dunn and Dunn model of learning style preferences: A critique of what was Dunn. *Learning Disabilities Research & Practice, 13*, 75–80.

Kolb, D. A. (1984). *Experiential Learning: Experience as the source of learning and development.* Upper Saddle River, NJ: Prentice Hall.

Kozhevnikov, M. (2007). Cognitive styles in the context of modern psychology: Toward an integrated framework of cognitive style. *Psychological Bulletin, 133*, 464–481.

Krätzig, G. P. & Arbuthnott, K. D. (2006). Perceptual learning style and learning proficiency: A test of the hypothesis. *Journal of Educational Psychology, 98*, 238–246.

Lundstrom, K. V. & Martin, R. E. (1986). Matching college instruction to student learning style. *College Student Journal, 20*, 270–274.

Massa, L. J. & Mayer, R. E. (2006). Testing the ATI hypothesis: Should multimedia instruction accommodate verbalizer–visualizer cognitive style. *Learning and Individual Differences, 16*, 321–335.

Overview of learning styles (n.d.). Available at: from http://www.learning-styles-online.com/overview.

Pashler, H., McDaniel, M., Rohrer, D., & Bjork, R. (2009). Learning styles: Concepts and evidence. *Psychological Science in the Public Interest, 9*, 105–119.

Rogowsky, B. A., Calhoun, B. M., & Tallal, P. (2014). Matching learning style to instructional method: Effects on comprehension. *Journal of Educational Psychology, 107*, 64–78.

Snider, V. E. (1992). Learning styles and learning to read: A critique. *Remedial and Special Education, 13*, 6–18.

Stahl, S. A. (1999). Different strokes for different folks: A critique of learning styles. *American Educator, 23*, 27–31.

Tarver, S. G. & Dawson, M. M. (1978). Modality preference and the teaching of reading: A review. *Journal of Learning Disabilities, 11*, 17–29.

Three learning styles (n.d.). Available at: http://blc.uc.iupui.edu/Academic-Enrichment/Study-Skills/Learning-Styles/3-Learning-Styles.

Tight, D. G. (2010). Perceptual learning style matching and L2 vocabulary acquisition. *Language Learning, 60*, 792–833.

Walberg, H. J. (1984). Improving the productivity of America's schools. *Educational Leadership, 8*, 19–27.

Willingham, D. T. (2009). *Why students don't like school.* San Francisco: Jossey-Bass.

Zapalska, A. M. & Dabb, H. (2002). Learning styles. *Journal of Teaching in International Business, 13*, 77–97.

3 MYTH: LECTURING IS BROADLY INFERIOR TO OTHER TEACHING METHODS

Lecturing has become a much maligned teaching method in recent decades. One need only perform a brief Internet search or attend a teaching conference to understand the frequency with which the lecture format is criticized in the educational field. Many educators and administrators strongly emphasize small-group learning and other interactive techniques, and educational accrediting agencies sometimes place explicit limits on the amount of class time devoted to lecturing (Gunderman, 2013; Walthausen, 2013). Matheson (2008) summarizes a variety of common criticisms of lecturing, including that it is an outdated method, that it is ineffective due to students' limited attention spans, and that student passivity during lectures is unlikely to promote effective learning. However, Matheson also points out that claims about the relative effectiveness of various teaching techniques are often based on little evidence. It is possible that alternatives to lecturing are more effective for achieving certain learning outcomes or educating certain types of students, but research findings fail to justify a broad indictment of the lecture method.

One particular difficulty in evaluating the relative effectiveness of teaching methods is the inherent lack of experimental control possible when conducting classroom research. Perhaps the most noteworthy obstacle is the difficulty in defining exactly what lecturing means. The term "lecture" may call to mind ideas about a person standing at a podium reading from a written speech, rather than a teacher who is

Great Myths of Education and Learning, First Edition. Jeffrey D. Holmes.
© 2016 John Wiley & Sons, Inc. Published 2016 by John Wiley & Sons, Inc.

dynamic, engaging, and interactive. Although many instructors work from a lecture model, what actually happens in the classroom varies widely. It is therefore difficult to standardize procedures for research comparisons because there are so many variables to control. Burkill, Dyer, and Stone (2008) noted that people tend to envision lecturing as instructors talking to students in a unidirectional fashion, but that in fact there are many ways for lectures to be interactive. They surveyed 106 academic lecturers in the United Kingdom. Nearly all the respondents agreed that good lectures should include student discussion, and that students in lecture courses should be encouraged to participate. More than 90% of the respondents reported that they try to activate student interest, increase student motivation, and encourage student participation. Most of the instructors reported that their teaching approach – even in lecture courses – is student-centered. These findings raise questions about the assumption that lecture classes are by nature unidirectional and focused exclusively on the transmission of information. Therefore, the line between lecturing and other teaching approaches is far from clear.

Research comparing lecturing with alternative teaching methods is nothing new. Two reviews provide evidence that statements regarding the broad inferiority of lectures relative to other methods may be exaggerated. Dubin and Taveggia (1968) reviewed findings from 36 studies, published between 1924 and 1965, in which researchers compared lecture to discussion methods in terms of students' performance on examinations. They found virtually no overall differences between the methods in terms of exam performance; students taught via lecture performed better in 51% of the comparisons, and students taught via discussion performed better in 49% of the comparisons. The authors also reported that the average difference in outcome scores between methods was not significantly different from zero – leading them to conclude that the two methods tend to produce equivalent learning outcomes. Dubin and Taveggia also compared lecture-only techniques to techniques that combined lecture with discussion. Again, they found that the average difference between the methods was not significantly different from zero.

Approximately 30 years after Dubin and Taveggia's review, Bligh (2000) published an updated and more sophisticated analysis of experimental findings on the effectiveness of lectures relative to other methods such as discussion. Bligh reported that when the learning objective is acquisition of information, most comparisons showed no significant difference between teaching methods. When differences were observed, they were as likely to favor lectures as they were to favor alternative methods. Bligh also noted that existing published research probably represents an underestimate of how frequently data reveal no differences between methods, because studies showing no difference are less likely to be published. Bligh concluded from his review that lectures are as effective as other methods for teaching content. However, he suggested that discussion techniques may be more effective for encouraging students to think about content. He reviewed several studies showing that students tend to be more thoughtful during discussions than during lectures, and noted that it is difficult to use lectures to get students to think. Nonetheless, Bligh's review further demonstrates that the lecture method is not universally inferior to alternative methods.

Research conducted since Bligh's (2000) review has led to similarly mixed conclusions regarding the relative effectiveness of teaching methods. For example, Schwerdt and Wupperman (2011) examined data from nearly 9,000 students at hundreds of schools who took a national math and science exam given to many eighth grade students in the United States. The classroom teachers reported the proportion of time they spent teaching via traditional lecture versus having students work on problems. Schwerdt and Wupperman controlled for variables such as school and class size, as well as numerous teacher variables such as certification, motivation, age, and years of training. The researchers reported that students in classes with teachers who devoted more time to lecture tended to score higher on the math exam than students whose teachers emphasized actively working on problems – with or without guidance. Differences in scores on the science exam were not significant. The authors asserted that simply encouraging teachers to devote more time to active problem-solving is unlikely to increase student learning and may even detract from it.

In another recent study (Costa, van Rensburg, & Rushton, 2007), undergraduate students in medical training were randomly assigned to either 12 formal lectures or 12 discussion classes covering the same content and utilizing the same textbook. Students in the discussion condition performed slightly better than those in the lecture condition on a written exam, although the researchers emphasized that the difference was small. There were no differences between the methods when the assessed outcome was performance on an oral exam.

One contemporary technique that has been offered as an active-learning alternative to lecturing is known as problem-based learning, in which students engage in active problem-solving with instructor facilitation. In a study of problem-based learning, Beers (2005) compared the learning outcomes of students in two sections of a nursing course. Students in one course were taught specific content via lecture, and students in the other course were taught the same content via problem-based learning. There were no significant differences between the two groups of students in terms of their scores on either a pre-test or post-test of the course material. Smits and colleagues (2003) conducted a similar study, but this time physicians receiving specialized training were randomly assigned either to problem-based learning or to a lecture course. Although there was no difference in acquired content knowledge as a function of teaching method, physicians trained using problem-based learning showed slightly better performance on a measure of actual task-relevant job performance. This finding is consistent with assertions that lecturing may be as effective as alternative methods for communicating content, but that some alternative methods may be preferable for teaching applied skills (Bligh, 2000).

Yet another alternative teaching technique that has emerged in recent years is known as interteaching – which involves classroom interactions between students working in pairs. The students engage in instructor-facilitated discussions of course materials provided in advance (Saville, Zinn, Neef, Van Norman, & Ferreri, 2006). Saville and colleagues conducted two studies comparing interteaching to lecture, and found that students in the interteaching conditions performed somewhat better on content exams than students who heard lectures. Interestingly, the difference in outcome was greater in their first study in which the measure of effectiveness was scores on brief quizzes than it was in their second study in which the outcome measure was scores on more comprehensive exams. This pattern could indicate some role for measurement error in the observed differences. Since measurement error tends to decrease as the length of a test increases, the larger observed differences on the short quizzes may in part reflect imprecision in measurement.

Saville et al. (2006) provide an excellent analysis of the components of interteaching that might be responsible for its apparent effectiveness, but they also note that interteaching has many components that, thus far, have not been independently evaluated. Interestingly, one of these components is lecture. In a follow-up study (Saville, Cox, O'Brien, & Vanderveldt, 2011), Saville and colleagues investigated the role of lecture as part of interteaching – noting that lecture generally takes up about one-third of interteaching class time and specifically targets content with which students report having difficulty. The researchers compared exam scores for students taught via interteaching with or without a lecture component. Students whose interteaching experience included a lecture component scored significantly higher across all five exams than students who experienced interteaching without lecture.

In one of the most important and influential recent studies evaluating the benefits of alternatives to the lecture method, Freeman and colleagues (2014) used meta-analysis – a method for combining existing studies to reveal more reliable patterns – to integrate 398 published and unpublished studies comparing traditional lecture to a variety of active-learning strategies for teaching undergraduates in science, technology, engineering, and math (STEM) courses. They found that students enrolled in STEM courses in which some type of active learning was employed earned grades, on average, one-half letter grade higher than students in lecture-only courses. Moreover, students in courses with an active-learning component were much less likely to fail compared with students in lecture-only courses. The authors asserted that that their findings support the objective of "abandoning traditional lecturing in favor of active learning" (p. 8410).

Although Freeman and colleagues provide important data to inform teaching strategies, several caveats must be noted. First, the average failure rate was indeed lower in active learning than in lecture courses, but the failure rate in both types of courses was extraordinarily high – with one in five active learning and one in three lecture students failing. The apparent reduction in failure rates is impressive, but the high failure rate in both types of classes makes it unclear to what extent the students were representative of college students in general. Second, although active learning provided average benefits in classes of all sizes, the benefits decreased as class size increased. This finding is grist for arguments in favor of reducing class sizes, but represents a limitation when smaller classes are not an option. Third, the instructors participating in all studies in the analysis volunteered to teach an active-learning course, so it is likely that they valued the method. As the researchers note: "It is an open question whether student performance would increase as much if all faculty were required to implement active learning approaches" (p. 8412). Finally, Freeman and colleagues defined lecturing as a practice in which an instructor speaks continuously to students and does not encourage discussion or interact with students aside from answering an occasional question. In comparison, the active-learning studies they analyzed included a wide variety of activities – some vague and some specific, taking as little as 10% and as much as 100% of class time. The researchers reported that the available data were insufficient to determine whether some activities were more effective than others, or whether incremental increases in time spent on active-learning exercises were associated with incremental learning benefits. Moreover, the distinction between lecturing and its alternatives as represented in the reviewed studies may not reflect the way that many courses are taught. Based on the categorization of studies for the meta-analysis, it appears that a course taught by an instructor who employs a lecture format but punctuates the lectures with interactive questions and discussion would be classified as an active-learning course – likely increasing student learning beyond what is typical in a lecture environment. As noted earlier, most lecturers report that they already do this. Freeman and colleagues certainly provide evidence that active-learning exercises are likely to enhance student learning, but such activities are part of many lecture-based courses so the distinction drawn for research purposes may be blurred in practice.

The relative merits of any teaching method cannot be adequately evaluated in isolation from student preferences and individual differences. In one recent study (Venkatesh et al., 2012), researchers surveyed more than 15,000 students and more than 2,600 instructors from universities in Quebec regarding their preferences for traditional lecture methods versus interactive instructional techniques. For instructors, perceptions of effective student learning were positively associated with interactive methods and negatively associated with a lecture format. In contrast, effective lecturing was the strongest predictor of perceived course effectiveness among students. It appears therefore that instructors' views about the merits of traditional lecture do not necessarily match up with students' views.

Baer (2010) speculated on a possible aptitude–treatment interaction whereby students' preferences for particular teaching methods may be a function of their ability level. Based on his review of past research, Baer suspected that the structured nature of lectures might be more beneficial for lower-performing students, whereas higher-performing students could benefit more from student-centered methods. However, he noticed that students he had observed at Yale University – virtually all of whom presumably have high ability – were much more likely to attend lectures than they were to attend discussion sessions. This pattern occurred despite the fact that attendance was taken during discussion sessions but not during lectures. Baer conducted a series of four studies of college students to investigate student preferences as a function of ability. In general, students reported liking group work better than lectures, but they believed they learned more from lectures. High-achieving students liked lectures more than low-achieving students did, and higher grade point average was associated with stronger perceptions of the superiority of lectures over group work. Baer speculated that high-ability students may not believe that group work with lower-ability students will be beneficial. He noted that his study did not assess actual learning outcomes, so it is possible that students are simply wrong about what methods are most effective. Nonetheless, students do not agree that lectures are ineffective – a finding that Baer finds especially compelling given that students' greater enjoyment of group work would seem to bias them toward thinking group work is more effective. The preference for the lecture format among high-achieving students has emerged in other studies as well (Beers, 2005). Baer emphasizes that presumably the strongest students know something about how best to learn, so instructors should pay attention to these students' opinions.

Some research does suggest that certain types of students may benefit more from group work than from lecture. Opdecam, Everaert, Van Keer, and Buysschaert (2014) studied nearly 300 students taking an advanced accounting class who were allowed to select either a lecture course or a team-learning course in which students prepared materials beforehand and discussed the content during class. The researchers went to great lengths to be sure the team-learning strategy included many important elements for effective group interaction based on group process research. Consistent with earlier research, lower-performing students were more likely to choose the team-learning format. The average grade point average (GPA) of those who opted for the lecture format was significantly higher than the GPA of those who chose team learning; those opting for team learning also had earned lower grades in the previously-taken introductory accounting course. By the end of the advanced course, however, team learning students' scores on an advanced accounting exam were similar to the scores of students who had chosen the lecture class and who initially were higher achieving. It should be noted that the difference in observed effectiveness between the two methods was small. Further, it does not appear that the lecture format was detrimental to learning, but rather that the team-learning approach helped lower-performing students to catch up.

Anderson and Scott (1978) found that students with low aptitude and poor opinions of their own academic abilities showed greater academic involvement during discussion and group work than during lecture. High-achieving students showed high involvement in both class formats, but during group work spent more time off-task than they did when being taught by lecture. Accordingly, Baer (2010) advises college instructors to be cautious about making pedagogical decisions based primarily on the needs of low-performing students – noting that eliminating lectures might mean high-achieving students learn less.

It is worth noting that ability level is not the only student factor that helps predict the effectiveness of various teaching methods. Dowaliby and Schumer (1987) studied college students' performance in an introductory psychology course as a function of trait anxiety levels. Students low in anxiety learned more in a discussion class than in a lecture class. In sharp contrast, students high in anxiety learned more in a lecture class than in a discussion class. Perhaps forcing anxious students to participate in group work actually has a negative effect on their ability to learn. Dowaliby and Schumer suggest that in regard to research on the effectiveness of various teaching methods, "Perhaps there are no 'main effects' to be found and significant treatment effects will be evidenced only when successful attempts are made to account for individual differences" (p. 130). In other words, there may not be a single teaching technique that is most effective regardless of student characteristics.

Most instructors, especially at the college level, do not receive formal training in effective lecturing. Instead, they tend to base their approach on their experiences as students (DeGolia, 2013). Cooper and Foy (1967) had university students and instructors rate the importance of various teacher characteristics that could enhance the effectiveness of lectures. The researchers acknowledged that students' views may not be the best way to evaluate teaching methods, but they asserted that students' attitudes influence the effectiveness of any strategy. Moreover, students and instructors provided quite similar rankings of the importance of various teacher characteristics. Fortunately, many of the characteristics rated as most important had to do with clear and logical presentation of content. Only further down on the list did personality characteristics, such as the lecturer having a good sense of humor, show up. This suggests that the aspects of lecture most highly valued by students can be learned by instructors, because they pertain to the quality of the presentation rather than to the personality of the lecturer.

A common criticism of the lecture method is that students' attention spans only last between 10 and 15 minutes, and therefore students are unlikely to retain content delivered in a typical lecture (see Wilson and Korn, 2007, for a review of such criticisms). Wilson and Korn found that these claims are mostly anecdotal, that in fact there are few controlled studies of student attention span, and that a variety of empirical findings are inconsistent with the 10–15-minutes claim. Notwithstanding the limited evidence that students' attention spans prohibit them from learning via lectures, instructors can implement classroom techniques to periodically reset students' attention. For instance, Ruhl, Hughes, and Schloss (1987) found that a strategy as simple as using periodic two-minute pauses during lectures was correlated with increased student recall of course content and improved exam performance. It seems that a small intervention to change the pace of a class can reduce the potential effects of students' waning attention.

Parker (1993) asserted that critics of the lecture model are actually criticizing bad lectures, and that lectures are more effective when they promote information processing. He stated that lectures are particularly appropriate when the objective is for students to increase their knowledge and comprehension of content, and especially when there is a lot of content for students to learn. Based on established information-processing research, Parker recommended several strategies to enhance student learning during lectures. For example, instructors should help students link new content with information already learned. This process is facilitated when instructors state learning objectives at the beginning of class and connect them with students' existing knowledge. Since rehearsal facilitates the transfer of information to long-term memory, instructors should present information repeatedly in addition to linking it with past experience. Instructors can also explicitly draw students' attention to particularly important information, thereby enhancing information processing and retention. Finally, Parker points out that sensory adaptation processes can mean that an instructors' voice becomes less novel to students as a lecture progresses, so instructors can use brief silences, demonstrations, or questioning to reset students' attention. Although much of this advice has not been tested specifically in classrooms, the cognitive principles upon which it is based are well established.

White (2011) questions the idea that instructors must choose between lectures and interactive approaches. He asserts that lectures can include interactive elements – between students and also between students and the instructor. Other researchers agree that it is possible to introduce active-learning techniques – even in large lecture classes (Ebert-May, Brewer, & Allred, 1997). For example, Van Dijk, Van Den Berg, and Van Keulen (2001) studied engineering students who were randomly assigned to one of three teaching conditions – each 90 minutes long and covering the same content. One condition included only traditional lecture, a second condition included lecture combined with students responding to questions via an electronic response system, and the third condition consisted of brief lectures only on key topics along with the electronic response system and peer-to-peer instruction. Van Dijk and colleagues found that, based on a test of the course content, students learned as much from lecture as from interactive methods.

Ernst and Colthorpe (2007) similarly compared students – this time in a physiology course – who were taught either with traditional lecture or an interactive lecture format that included brief activities every 10–20 minutes. Students in the interactive lecture courses performed slightly better on exams than students experiencing only traditional lecture.

However, the classes taught using the two different approaches were also taught in different years, introducing the possibility that the observed differences were not the result of differences in instruction. The evidence is therefore not yet conclusive that introducing interactive components to lectures has a definitive positive effect on learning. Van Dijk and colleagues (2001) suggest that active processing of information is probably more likely when active or interactive techniques are used, but this is not always the case and traditional lecturing does not always lead to passivity or lack of critical thinking.

Instructors seeking guidance to improve their lecture skills have a host of resources available to them (e.g., Bligh, 2000; Di Leonardi, 2007; DeGolia, 2013). For example, DeGolia provides excellent step-by-step guidance for preparing and implementing lectures. She provides strategies for identifying learning objectives, identifying interesting content, understanding the audience, capturing attention and activating students' interest, encouraging participation, establishing rapport, and establishing an effective classroom environment. Much of DeGolia's advice is grounded in empirical research. It is not clear how many instructors seek out such resources in an effort to improve their lecture skills, but training in such skills does not appear to be the norm.

Evidence supporting the general inferiority of the lecture method relative to alternatives in terms of student learning is equivocal. Therefore, it is important to consider additional variables that might affect pedagogical decisions. One advantage of lectures is their efficiency relative to most other approaches. Lectures enable instructors to communicate information to large numbers of students simultaneously. In an ideal world, efficiency of method might not be an important consideration; however, reality has long dictated that educators consider the efficiency of their methods – especially given persistent increases in class size at many institutions (Degering & Remmers, 1939; Dubin & Taveggia, 1968; Weir, 2009; DeGolia, 2013). Bligh (2000) acknowledges that both discussion and lecture can be effective, but he advises against using discussion methods for teaching content because they are more expensive in terms of instructor time and yet are no more effective than lectures. Likewise, in discussing the merits of problem-based learning versus lecture, Beers (2005) suggests that educators choose lecture, because problem-based approaches require greater resources but have not been shown to reliably increase student learning.

Even contemporary techniques designed to introduce peer interaction into lecture courses appear to have limitations in terms of efficiency. A recent test of the interteaching method described earlier included classes consisting of only 15–16 students (Saville et al., 2011). This means that the instructor had to facilitate only seven or eight discussions during a class meeting. The practicality of this method in large classes where the instructor would have 20, 30, 40, or more dyads to manage remains an open question. Many teachers might prefer that all classes have only 10 or 15 students, but this is not the reality in contemporary education. Therefore, any potential advantage of alternatives to lecture must be weighed in terms of efficiency.

Even some ardent critics of lectures acknowledge that lectures are useful for some purposes, such as providing a broader context for course content and demonstrating how an expert evaluates that content (Talbert, 2012). Other scholars have pointed out that lectures allow teachers to inspire students by demonstrating enthusiasm for course content, and help students to understand content that is particularly difficult (Matheson, 2008; White, 2011). Lectures also provide an opportunity to challenge students' assumptions about course content (DeGolia, 2013).

Although some educators assume that student-centered approaches are superior to lecture, Burgan (2006) expresses concern about what students actually do in classes where instructors use these methods. She questions whether advocates of student-centered learning have taught large introductory courses or courses in which many students' main objective is getting a good grade. She also ponders how to prevent unmotivated students from taking advantage of hard-working students when the two must work together. Burgan points out that even at the college level, students are at different levels of cognitive and social development, and therefore it is unlikely that all can benefit equally from alternative teaching methods. She notes, "being clueless in a discussion class is much more embarrassing and destructive of a student's self-confidence than struggling to understand in the anonymity of a lecture" (p. 32). Kotsko (2009) likewise questions the wisdom of subjecting students to class discussion when they do not understand the readings, and also questions the notion that most students have adequate reading skills to comprehend and evaluate material read outside classes. Saville and colleagues (2006) noted that students in the interteaching classes they studied often arrived for class unprepared for peer discussions, which could have impacted their partners' learning. In contrast to claims from one cognitive scientist that people learn best through interaction with the environment (see MacKlem, 2006), Burgan cites a different cognitive scientist who argues that, for most disciplines, a great deal of knowledge cannot be learned in the absence of direct instruction.

Lectures have limitations like any other teaching method, so the nature of the course material may dictate the best teaching approach. Lectures may be less effective than some alternatives in helping students to improve critical thinking or communication skills (Parker, 1993), and having students learn by doing is likely to be more effective when the learning objective is acquisition of specific behavioral skills (Bligh, 2000; White, 2011). Bligh points out that lecturing is likely to be ineffective for teaching applied skills such as performing surgery or using a library, but that even these skills require students first to have background knowledge which they can acquire via lecture.

Evaluating the relative effectiveness of various teaching methods is remarkably difficult. Specific methods are often made up of a variety of techniques, there are many variables that are out of researchers' control, and people who conduct the research often have a bias against certain techniques – especially lectures (Bligh, 2000). Given the lack of experimental control that is possible when conducting classroom research, the potential for experimenter bias should be noted. In a meta-analysis of studies of small-group learning, Springer, Stanne, and Donovan (1999) found that the observed effectiveness of the small-group method was significantly greater for studies where the researcher and instructor were the same person than they were when the study did not indicate that the researcher was directly involved in class teaching. When alternative strategies are compared with lecture, one must consider the quality of the research and the size of the effect in light of the many other variables that affect teaching decisions. Perhaps making broad claims about lecture versus other formats is ill-advised. There are simply too many variables to account for, and no method is likely to be implemented the same way across instructors.

The effectiveness of any teaching strategy is a function of both the method itself and student and instructor preferences. Weir (2009) argues that poor lecturing is likely to result when instructors do not work to refine their lectures because they do not value the method. If an instructor enjoys a particular method and believes that it is effective, he or she will try harder to make it effective. Bligh (2000) asserts that students will engage in thoughtful inquiry during lectures if they are disposed to do so, but the same could be said for any teaching method. Indeed, Burgan (2006) claims that motivated students can probably learn from any teaching method. Moreover, there are certainly high- and low-quality class discussions and group interactions, just as there are high- and low-quality lectures. While criticisms of lecture are widespread, they are far from universal. In fact, some current scholars have argued that lectures have "immense value" (Walthausen, 2013: para. 3), and that removing lectures from education would be a "grave error" (Gunderman, 2013: para. 15). All teaching methods have weaknesses, so no single method represents a perfect tool for promoting student learning. Varied learning environments, learning objectives, and learner characteristics demand varied instructional methods, and lectures are likely to remain important among these methods.

References

Anderson, L. W. & Scott, C. C. (1978). The relationship among teaching methods, student characteristics, and student involvement in learning. *Journal of Teacher Education, 29*, 52–57.

Baer, J. (2010). Lectures may be more effective than you think: The learning pyramid unmasked. *International Journal of Creativity & Problem Solving, 20*, 7–21.

Beers, G. W. (2005). The effect of teaching method on objective test scores: Problem-based learning versus lecture. *Journal of Nursing Education, 44*, 305–309.

Bligh, D. A. (2000). *What's the use of lectures?* New York: John Wiley & Sons.

Burgan, M. (2006). In defense of lecturing. *Change, 38*, 30–34.

Burkill, S., Dyer, S. R., & Stone, M. (2008). Lecturing in higher education in further education settings. *Journal of Further and Higher Education, 32*, 321–331.

Cooper, B. & Foy, J. M. (1967). Evaluating the effectiveness of lectures. *Higher Education Quarterly, 21*, 182–185.

Costa, M. L., van Rensburg, L., & Rushton, N. (2007). Does teaching style matter? A randomised trial of group discussion versus lectures in orthopaedic undergraduate teaching. *Medical Education, 41*, 214–217.

Degering, E. F. & Remmers, H. H. (1939). Effectiveness of regular laboratory work versus lecture demonstrations. *School and Society, 49*, 458–460.

DeGolia, S. G. (2013). How to give a lecture. In: L. W. Roberts (Ed.), *The Academic Medicine Handbook: A Guide to Achievement and Fulfillment for Academic Faculty* (pp. 55–67). New York: Springer.

Di Leonardi, B. C. (2007). Tips for facilitating learning: The lecture deserves some respect. *Journal of Continuing Education in Nursing, 38*, 154–161.

Dowaliby, F. J. & Schumer, H. (1973). Teacher-centered versus student-centered mode of college classroom instruction as related to manifest anxiety. *Journal of Educational Psychology, 64*, 125–132.

Dubin, R. & Taveggia, T. C. (1968). *The teaching–learning paradox: A comparative analysis of college teaching methods.* Eugene: University of Oregon Press.

Ebert-May, D, Brewer, C., & Allred, S. (1997). Innovation in large lectures: Teaching for active learning. *BioScience, 47*, 601–607.

Ernst, H. & Colthorpe, K. (2007). The efficacy of interactive lecturing for students with diverse science backgrounds. *Advances in Physiology Education, 31,* 41–44.

Freeman, S., Eddy, S. L., McDonough, M., Smith, M. K., Okoroafor, N., Jordt, H., & Wenderoth, W. P. (2014). Active learning increases student performance in science, engineering, and mathematics. *PNAS, 111,* 8410–8415.

Gunderman, R. (2013). Is the lecture dead? *The Atlantic.* Available at: http://www.theatlantic.com/health/archive/2013/01/is-the-lecture-dead/272578.

Kotsko, A. (2009). A defense of lecture. *Inside Higher Education.* Available at: http://www.insidehighered.com/views/2009/11/20/kotsko.

MacKlem, K. (2006). Just quit lecturing them. *Maclean's, 119,* 38–39.

Matheson, C. (2008). The educational value and effectiveness of lectures. *The Clinical Teacher, 5,* 218–221.

Opdecam, E., Everaert, P., Van Keer, H, & Buysschaert, F. (2014). Preferences for team learning and lecture-based learning among first-year undergraduate accounting students. *Research in Higher Education, 55,* 400–432.

Parker, J. K. (1993). Lecturing and loving it: Applying the information-processing model. *Clearing House, 67,* 8–11.

Ruhl, K. L., Hughes, C. A., & Schloss, P. J. (1987). Using the pause procedure to enhance lecture recall. *Teacher Education and Special Education, 10,* 14–18.

Saville, B. K., Zinne, T. E., Neef, N. A., Van Norman, R., & Ferreri S. J. (2006). A comparison of interteaching and lecture in the college classroom. *Journal of Applied Behavior Analysis, 39,* 49–61.

Saville, B. K., Cox, T., O'Brien, S., & Vanderveldt, A. (2011). Interteaching: The impact of lectures on student performance. *Journal of Applied Behavior Analysis, 44,* 937–941.

Schwerdt, G. & Wupperman, A. C. (2011). Is traditional teaching really all that bad? A within-student between-subject approach. *Economics of Education Review, 30,* 365–379.

Smits, P. B., de Buisonje, C. D., Verbeek, J. H., van Dijk, F. J., Metz, J. C., & ten Cate, O. J. (2003). *Scandinavian Journal of Work, Environment, & Health, 29,* 280–287.

Springer, L., Stanne, M. E., & Donovan, S. S. (1999). Effects of small-group learning on undergraduates in science, mathematics, engineering, and technology: A meta-analysis. *Review of Educational Research, 69,* 21–51.

Talbert, R. (2012). Four things lecture is good for. Available at: http://chronicle.com/blognetwork/castingoutnines/2012/02/13/four-things-lecture-is-good-for.

Van Dijk, L. A., Van Den Berg, G. C., & Van Keulen, H. (2001). Interactive lectures in engineering education. *European Journal of Engineering Education, 26,* 15–28.

Venkatesh, V., Rabah, J., Fusaro, M., Couture, A., Varela, W., & Alexander, K. (2012). Perceptions of technology use and course effectiveness in the age of web 2.0: A large-scale survey of Quebec University students and instructors.

World Conference on E-Learning in Corporate, Government, Healthcare, and Higher Education, pp. 1691–1699.

Walthausen, A. (2013). Don't give up on the lecture. *The Atlantic*. Available at: http://www.theatlantic.com/education/archive/2013/11/dont-give -up-on-the-lecture/281624.

Weir, R. (2009). Boring within or simply boring. *Inside Higher Education*. Available at: http://www.insidehighered.com/advice/instant_mentor/weir5.

White, G. (2011). Interactive lecturing. *The Clinical Teacher, 8*, 230–235.

Wilson, K. & Korn, J. H. (2007). Attention during lectures: Beyond ten minutes. *Teaching of Psychology, 34*, 85–89.

4 MYTH: USING POWERPOINT IN THE CLASSROOM IMPROVES STUDENT LEARNING

It is virtually impossible to calculate the number of PowerPoint presentations given each day. One estimate puts the number at approximately 30 million (Parks, 2012), but the precise number is unimportant. Certainly, electronic presentation software – most notably PowerPoint – has become ubiquitous in education in a relatively short period of time. Although PowerPoint has both advocates and critics, it is difficult to find many critics among students. Nearly all researchers surveying students about their attitudes toward classroom PowerPoint presentations report that the students identify a variety of advantages with the software and believe that PowerPoint leads to more effective learning (Mantei, 2000; Roehling & Trent-Brown, 2011; Hill, Arford, Lubitow, & Smollin, 2012). However, most empirical comparisons to date show no meaningful learning advantage from PowerPoint relative to other methods of presentation. A few studies show small positive effects, but these studies typically have methodological limitations that preclude conclusions about the unique effects of PowerPoint; a comparable number of studies suggest potential negative learning outcomes associated with PowerPoint. Research on the educational effectiveness of PowerPoint, like research in many areas of education, is often hindered by researchers' inability to control all aspects of the learning process in order to isolate the effects of a single factor.

Great Myths of Education and Learning, First Edition. Jeffrey D. Holmes.
© 2016 John Wiley & Sons, Inc. Published 2016 by John Wiley & Sons, Inc.

Nonetheless, it is possible to draw some general conclusions from the existing research.

In one early investigation conducted as PowerPoint was becoming broadly popular for classroom use, Szabo and Hastings (2000) conducted three studies to examine student preferences and learning outcomes associated with the software. Using a survey, they found that the vast majority of undergraduate students believed that lecture classes that include PowerPoint slides are more interesting and maintain student attention better than classes without PowerPoint. The majority of students also believed that PowerPoint enhanced learning over traditional teaching approaches. Szabo and Hastings then collected learning data from 25 students in a research methods course. In each of three class meetings, the students took mock exams testing their learning of content from the class meeting one week earlier. During one class, the instructor used overhead transparencies and wrote on the chalkboard; a second lecture was accompanied by PowerPoint slides; and a third lecture included PowerPoint slides, but students were provided with printouts of the slides prior to the class. The students scored significantly higher on exams when the instructor used PowerPoint than when the instructor used transparencies; there was no difference in performance between the PowerPoint class where students received copies of the slides and the class where they did not. Despite a small positive effect seemingly attributable to PowerPoint, the authors interpreted their findings with caution. They noted that the number of students in the study was very small, and that learning was assessed with mock exams rather than by genuine classroom tests. Furthermore, the study involved comparisons of only a single class meeting for each teaching approach.

In their third study, Szabo and Hastings (2000) failed to replicate the PowerPoint effect they had observed in their previous study. This time they studied college students enrolled in two classes. Each class had one meeting in which the instructor used transparencies and one meeting in which the instructor used PowerPoint. A week after each class meeting, the students took a genuine class quiz to assess learning. The researchers observed no consistent benefit from using PowerPoint, in that one class performed better on the quiz that followed a PowerPoint lecture and the other class performed better following the transparency lecture. Szabo and Hastings speculated that PowerPoint may produce some benefits in certain situations, but concluded that no generalized learning benefit occurs from adding PowerPoint to traditional lectures.

Other studies conducted over brief time periods have similarly failed to reveal learning benefits attributable to PowerPoint. For example, Corbeil

(2007) compared student performance in two college French classes. In one class, the instructor used PowerPoint slides for 180 minutes of class time to explain grammatical concepts. In the other class, the same instructor used the textbook and wrote on the chalkboard to explain these concepts. There was no significant difference between the classes on a pre-test of the information, indicating that the classes had similar knowledge prior to the lessons. There was also no significant difference between the classes on exams assessing students' learning of the grammatical concepts immediately following the instruction or six weeks later. However, all students who completed a survey about the course felt that the PowerPoint slides were effective, helped them to understand the grammatical concepts, and maintained their attention more effectively than the textbook. Corbeil acknowledged that the differences between the classes were not limited to the presence or absence of slides, in that using PowerPoint permitted the instructor to include a greater number of examples and more elaborate explanations for the concepts. Nonetheless, these benefits did not translate to any observed learning advantage.

Subsequent researchers further tested PowerPoint learning effects by comparing teaching methods in real classrooms over extended periods of time. For example, Nouri and Shahid (2005) studied students in two sections of an undergraduate accounting class. In one section, the instructor used transparencies containing only black text. In the other section, the same instructor taught the same content using PowerPoint slides in full color with graphics and animation. The students took quizzes at the end of each class and three exams containing both conceptual and problem-solving items over the course of the semester. The students also completed a survey at the end of the semester evaluating the course and instructor. Students in the PowerPoint class rated the class as more understandable and the instructor as more prepared than did students in the transparency class. However, quiz scores indicated significant differences only twice – once favoring the PowerPoint class, and once favoring the transparency class. In both cases the score difference was small. There were no significant differences between the classes in exam performance on either conceptual or problem-solving items.

Other researchers studying student learning over entire semesters have observed outcomes similar to those reported by Nouri and Shahid (2005). Based on data from four introductory economics courses, there was no significant difference in course achievement between classes where the instructor used PowerPoint slides and courses where the same instructor did not use slides (Rankin & Hoaas, 2001). Daniels (1999) found no significant difference in student performance between an economics class taught one year using only the chalkboard and the same course taught a year later using PowerPoint. Again, the majority of students reported a preference for PowerPoint rather than the chalkboard, and 98% of the students rated the slides as at least somewhat useful.

In a more complex study, Beets and Lobingier (2001) alternated three teaching methods across three introductory accounting classes. All classes were taught by the same experienced instructor using the same textbook. The three methods consisted of the instructor using only the chalkboard to supplement lecture, using overhead transparencies containing text, and using slide presentation software. PowerPoint was not specifically identified, but it was likely the software used. The instructor systematically alternated methods so that each class experienced one-third of the semester with each method. All presentations contained identical content and the students did not receive any additional notes. The students took a short quiz at the end of each class and an exam after each third of the semester. Beets and Lobingier reported no significant differences in quiz or exam scores based on teaching method. Nonetheless, on a survey completed during the last week of class, the majority of students reported a preference for the computerized slides.

Two studies conducted by Susskind (2005; 2008) illustrate even more vividly the effects of PowerPoint use on student beliefs and attitudes despite the absence of any significant increase in learning. Susskind's first study included two introductory psychology courses taught by the same instructor. For the first half of the semester, the instructor taught one section using traditional lecture including notes on a white board, and the other section using the same content but presenting the lecture notes on PowerPoint. For the second half of the semester, the sections were reversed so that both classes experienced both presentation methods. Despite no significant difference in exam performance, the students reported that the class was more interesting, more organized, and more enjoyable when the instructor used PowerPoint. They also reported that they took more and better notes, felt greater self-efficacy, and were more confident about the exam that followed PowerPoint lectures.

Susskind (2008) replicated his first study and demonstrated that PowerPoint use might even affect student perceptions of factors unrelated to classroom events. For the first half of the semester in an undergraduate psychology course, the instructor taught one section using a traditional lecture format, including overhead transparencies of actual PowerPoint slides. The instructor taught the other section using identical slides presented on a computer. For the second half of the semester, the methods were switched between the two sections. Replicating previous research, Susskind (2008) found no differences in exam scores based on whether the course content was presented on transparencies or computerized PowerPoint. However, students again preferred the PowerPoint lectures and rated them as better organized, more interesting, and more enjoyable. Students further reported that that the instructor was more effective, that they took more notes, that their notes were more useful, and that it was easier to understand the material during PowerPoint lectures. As a result, students reported greater confidence in how well they had learned the material. Perhaps most interestingly, Susskind observed a kind of halo effect where PowerPoint use appeared to improve students' perceptions of unrelated aspects of the course. Students rated the course website as more useful during the time that PowerPoint was being used in class – despite the fact that both classes had access to the exact same website. Such varied perceptions are especially noteworthy given that the instructor used identical slides in both classes and only varied the method of projection.

Other researchers have similarly concluded that PowerPoint can affect subjective student perceptions even when it does not improve learning. Apperson, Laws, and Scapansky (2006) collected data from college students in ten separate classes across four academic disciplines. Five instructors taught a course using the chalkboard and transparencies one semester, and the same course using PowerPoint the following semester. The instructors used the same textbook, exams, and lecture materials for both semesters. Students taking PowerPoint classes were more likely to report ease in staying focused on the course content, that the instructor did a good job of maintaining their interest, and, most importantly, that PowerPoint improves student learning. They also rated the professor more positively and were more likely than students in the non-PowerPoint classes to report that they wished to take another class from the same instructor. Replicating the halo effect that Susskind (2008) reported, students in the PowerPoint classes provided higher ratings of how well the instructor explained the importance of the material, felt that the instructor provided more opportunities to apply their learning, made course goals clearer, gave more assignments requiring critical thinking, and provided better and more rapid feedback on tests and assignments. Such subjective differences emerged despite these variables being kept constant and despite the absence of any significant difference in average grades between the PowerPoint and non-PowerPoint classes.

Some researchers have found evidence that PowerPoint may occasionally detract from student learning. Savoy, Proctor, and Salvendy (2009) randomly assigned undergraduate and graduate students in a human factors course to lecture conditions in which two topics were taught using two methods. The instructor presented each topic using either the chalkboard or PowerPoint slides containing both text and tables. Students attended the lectures one week apart and took a quiz two weeks later covering content from both lectures. Savoy and colleagues observed no significant difference in performance between the PowerPoint and non-PowerPoint sections on quizzes assessing content that the instructor had presented visually. Students retained both text and graphic content equally well whether the material had been presented on the chalkboard or on PowerPoint slides. However, for information communicated out loud by the professor, students in the traditional lecture performed 15% better on the quiz than students in the PowerPoint lecture. The researchers interpreted this finding as indicating that the PowerPoint slides had distracted students from the spoken information delivered by the professor. Amazingly, there was no significant difference in quiz performance covering auditory material between students in the PowerPoint lecture and students who did not attend the lecture at all – providing validation for instructors who suspect that students sometimes focus excessively on slide content and fail to attend to the instructor's spoken words.

In another study revealing possible reductions in learning as a function of PowerPoint use, Bartsch and Cobern (2003) examined the effect of utilizing various visual and auditory features of the software. An instructor in an undergraduate social psychology course randomly varied his teaching method in one-week increments throughout the semester. The instructor varied between using transparencies, PowerPoint slides containing only text, and PowerPoint slides that included pictures, sound effects, and variations in text characteristics. Students completed periodic quizzes and a survey after each class asking them to report how much they enjoyed the class and how much they thought they had learned. Students thought that they learned more from PowerPoint lectures than lectures with transparencies. On actual quiz performance, however, there was no significant difference between transparency and text-only PowerPoints, but students scored about 10% lower on quizzes assessing content presented with the elaborate PowerPoint slides. At the end of the semester, students reported enjoying the transparency approach less than the PowerPoint methods, and believed they learned less from the transparency lectures.

In a final study suggesting a possible negative PowerPoint effect, Amare (2006) assessed students in four sections of a technical writing course. The instructor taught two sections using text-only PowerPoint slides and two sections using a more traditional lecture approach that included providing handouts and writing on the chalkboard. Students in all sections studied the same content, completed the same assignments, and took the same exams. Although students were not randomly assigned to the four classes, the students took a pre-test at the beginning of the semester and a post-test at the end so the researcher could evaluate progress over time. Amare reported that students tended to prefer PowerPoint over non-PowerPoint lectures, but that students in the non-PowerPoint sections improved more over the course of the semester than students in the PowerPoint sections.

Some researchers have observed positive learning effects associated with PowerPoint, but most such studies have noteworthy methodological limitations. For example, Erwin and Rieppi (2000) studied more than 300 college students distributed over two sections each of abnormal psychology, development, and statistics courses. In one section of each course an instructor used PowerPoint, and in the other section there were no restrictions on what technologies the instructor could use. Students took the same final exam regardless of the teaching style of the course, and students in the PowerPoint sections scored higher on the exam in all three subjects. However, there was no standardization of content within the specific courses, because each of the six courses was taught by different instructors who each developed their own lecture and presentation materials. The researchers in fact acknowledged that each instructor's general teaching style, rather than any PowerPoint effect, could have led to the observed differences. The instructors were aware of the varying conditions, and it is likely that the students were similarly aware. Furthermore, the PowerPoint lectures included an interactive component that was not available in the non-PowerPoint sections. Although the nature of this interactive component was not fully described by the researchers, any such factor might explain the differences in test performance.

In another study showing positive PowerPoint effects, Blalock and Montgomery (2005) compared students in two sections of an undergraduate economics course which met during consecutive hours during the same semester, taught by the same instructor in the same classroom. The instructor taught the earlier class using only the chalkboard, but based lecture content on PowerPoint slides provided by the textbook publisher; the instructor taught the later class using the actual PowerPoint slides. Students took four identical exams on the same dates. The researchers performed several analyses – some of which indicated that PowerPoint did not have an effect on learning and others that indicated a very small effect. However, the students were not randomly assigned to the two classes, nor was there a pre-test to determine initial equivalence of the students in the two sections. The researchers also noted that students in the earlier class could have communicated test content to some students in the PowerPoint class – leading to slightly higher scores in the later section. It is important to note that even if these limitations were absent, the difference in performance between the two sections had limited practical utility. Students in the PowerPoint section answered an average of four more exam items correctly out of 185 items administered over the semester – a difference in performance of only 2%.

Mantei (2000) compared exam data from ten sections of an undergraduate geology course taught over five years by an instructor who used the chalkboard and transparencies, with data from four sections of the same course taught over two years by the same instructor using PowerPoint along with lecture notes that students accessed online. Students in all sections followed the same policies, completed the same activities, learned the same topics using the same textbook, received the same practice test questions, and completed the same exams. However, the notes provided online for the PowerPoint sections included detailed outlines of the lectures used in the earlier non-PowerPoint sections, along with figures and tables from the textbook. The slides themselves were also available to students, who were instructed to print the slides and lecture notes in advance, review them, and bring them to class. Mantei reported a significant increase in student exam scores beginning in the first semester that PowerPoint was used, and the class average of all PowerPoint sections was about 5% higher than the average of all non-PowerPoint sections. However, since students in the PowerPoint sections had access to lecture notes and slides in advance, it is possible that this was the factor that led to better exam performance. It is therefore not possible to conclude that PowerPoint had an independent effect on learning.

In a subsequent study, Bartlett and Strough (2003) found that using PowerPoint produced no learning benefits that were not attributable to providing students with a course guide containing questions for students to answer and activities to demonstrate class concepts. More than 900 students from seventeen sections of a college psychology course over three semesters were taught using one of three methods: traditional lecture, lecture with the course guide as a supplement, or lecture with both the course guide and PowerPoint. Students in the sections with the course guide earned significantly higher grades than students in sections without the course guide; adding PowerPoint did not result in any additional increase in students' grades. Interestingly, the same effects emerged regarding student evaluations. Students receiving the course guide rated their classes more positively in terms of organization and fairness of exams than students who did not receive the course guide, and PowerPoint was not associated with any additional improvement in student attitudes.

A final study suggesting a possible positive PowerPoint effect was conducted by Lowry (1999), who compared student performance across three consecutive years of an introductory environmental science course. During the first year, the instructor taught the course using transparencies to explain concepts; for complex diagrams, the instructor used multiple layers of transparencies. Students worked on problems outside class and a tutor then worked through the problems in class. In the second and third years of the course, the instructor used PowerPoint to present content that had previously been presented on transparencies. The slides included animations to present the complex diagrams and were partially automated so the tutor could interact individually with students who were struggling. Lowry reported that students scored significantly higher on exams when the instructor used PowerPoint. Although students were not randomly assigned to classes, the apparent improvement in student learning was sustained for two consecutive years. It is important to note that the presentation of information in the course was considerably altered by the switch to PowerPoint. Lowry reported that presenting certain content such as complex, multilayered diagrams had been awkward when using transparencies and that switching to PowerPoint made the process simpler and smoother. The computerized animation also allowed the instructor to interact with struggling students. Although not a precise comparison of PowerPoint versus non-PowerPoint because more than one factor varied across classes, Lowry's data provide some support for the potential advantage of PowerPoint when instructors use it to communicate information that cannot easily be communicated using other methods.

Shapiro, Kerssen-Griep, Gayle, and Allen (2006) completed a very small meta-analysis of both published and unpublished experimental studies on the effectiveness of PowerPoint for increasing student learning. As noted elsewhere in this book, meta-analysis is a method for combining the results of many studies to reduce the effects of limitations associated with smaller individual studies. Although the researchers did not report the specific methods with which PowerPoint was compared in each individual study, they combined 16 comparisons from 12 studies and found a very small average positive effect associated with PowerPoint. Despite the average effect however, nine of the 16 comparisons showed no significant effect, and another comparison showed a difference in favor of traditional instruction over PowerPoint; six comparisons showed an effect in favor of PowerPoint and only four of these were published. Therefore, of 16 comparisons, there were only four published effects in favor of PowerPoint. The researchers concluded that caution is warranted when interpreting their findings, given the very small average effect associated with PowerPoint use and the impossibility of controlling for numerous other variables that could have affected the results of the individual studies.

Existing research suggests that learning benefits associated with PowerPoint, as they have been investigated thus far, are either very small or nonexistent. This pattern echoes a conclusion reached by Clark (1983), who completed a review of media learning research years before PowerPoint became a fixture in educational environments. Clark reviewed a large body of literature on the effect of various media on learning. He concluded "that media are mere vehicles that deliver instruction but do not influence student achievement any more than the truck that delivers our groceries causes changes in our nutrition" (p. 445). Clark argued that only content can affect learning and that researchers are unlikely to find clear evidence of learning that can be uniquely credited to any specific type of media.

Despite Clark's (1983) admonitions, conclusions regarding PowerPoint effectiveness must remain tentative. Kosslyn, Kievit, Russell, and Shephard (2012) noted that there is little research on how to most effectively design PowerPoint presentations, but they developed a set of recommendations based on broader research regarding how people learn. For example, they emphasized that slides should promote encoding by drawing learners' attention to important information. Since people notice things that stand out from the background, slide designers can use animations and high contrast text to emphasize important details. Designers must also recognize that human working memory is very limited in capacity, so slides must not overwhelm learners' ability to process information. Finally, effective learning requires that new information must become linked with knowledge already in the learner's long-term memory, so the presenter must connect the content with what the audience already knows and avoid unfamiliar jargon. Kosslyn (2007) provides additional guidance for slide design grounded in principles of cognitive psychology, and other scholars have provided guidance informed by human factors research (Durso, Pop, Burnett, & Stearman, 2011).

Kosslyn and colleagues (2012) collected a random sample of PowerPoint presentations from the Internet and had two judges use specific guidelines to independently rate the presentations for violations of the identified principles. The slide shows violated an average of six out of nine principles, and no slideshow in the sample had zero flaws. The researchers also conducted a survey of more than 200 people who regularly view

PowerPoint presentations and found that audience members often notice – and are distracted by – violations of principles for optimal slide design. Kosslyn and colleagues concluded that important guidelines are often missed or ignored by people developing PowerPoint presentations. It is possible, therefore, that researchers have found little evidence that PowerPoint enhances learning because they have thus far failed to distinguish good PowerPoint presentations from bad PowerPoint presentations.

There is no shortage of PowerPoint critics who have identified reasons why PowerPoint could be detrimental to learning. Perhaps most notably, Tufte (2003) argued that PowerPoint promotes a particular way of thinking characterized by linear understanding of complex material, fragmentation of information into a format consistent with individual slides and bullets, and an emphasis on format over content. Adams (2006) argued that PowerPoint encourages teachers to present information in certain limited ways, such as in the form of bulleted lists, a format that Tufte fears "can make us stupid" (p. 5). Adams partially blames the software's default settings, which she feels deter teachers from presenting information in other ways and encourages them to focus on content that can be presented on a single slide rather than more complex information. Another critic of PowerPoint has similarly lamented the "bulletization of education," asserting that PowerPoint conveys the idea that only what is presented on slides is important (Isseks, 2001: 74).

Just as there are compelling intuitive reasons why PowerPoint might hinder learning, there are also reasons why it might enhance learning. Daniels (1999) points out that PowerPoint makes it possible for instructors to include animations during class, that the software helps with organization and permits instructors to include more content or activities using the time they would otherwise be writing on the chalkboard, that PowerPoint's color and transition features might enhance instructors' ability to maintain student attention and interest, and that instructors can provide slides to students in advance to improve note-taking. Furthermore, Doumont (2005) disagrees with Tufte's (2003) broad indictment of PowerPoint, stating that Tufte criticizes the software for ineffectiveness in accomplishing objectives it was not designed to accomplish. Doumont asserts that Tufte demonstrates only that "inappropriate use yields inappropriate results" (p. 67), and argues that "what comes out of PowerPoint depends largely on what goes into it, and the tool will likely neither improve poor thinking nor corrupt sound reasoning" (p. 69).

To date, there is little direct evidence that using PowerPoint in educational settings has any broad consistent effect – positive or negative – on student learning. However, most researchers provide little or no specific description of how PowerPoint slides are designed for various studies, so it is often impossible to identify how the slides were actually used in classes (Levasseur & Sawyer, 2006). Susskind (2005) suggests that, given the overall lack of effect, researchers might be wise to examine more specific features of PowerPoint such as animation, video, graphics, and other features to determine if there are specific properties that can enhance learning. Several researchers have speculated that PowerPoint may provide unique advantages and benefits when an instructor seeks to teach complex concepts using graphs, charts, or diagrams that cannot easily be drawn on a chalkboard (Bartsch & Cobern, 2003; Savoy et al., 2009).

Based on the research to date, PowerPoint appears to affect students' subjective attitudes about classes, while having little impact on their actual learning (Apperson et al., 2006; Susskind, 2008). Some researchers have gone so far as to speculate that PowerPoint may enhance student entertainment rather than student learning (Szabo & Hastings, 2000), and that "multimedia technology may consist of more flash than substance" (Bartlett & Strough, 2003: 337). However, Apperson and colleagues note that improving students' attitudes about their courses and their education is a nontrivial outcome and that this benefit on its own may be quite powerful.

References

Adams, C. (2006). PowerPoint, habits of mind, and classroom culture. *Journal of Curriculum Studies, 38,* 389–411.

Amare, N. (2006). To slideware or not to slideware: Students' experience with PowerPoint vs. lecture. *Journal of Technical Writing and Communication, 36,* 297–308.

Apperson, J. M., Laws, E. L., & Scapansky, J. A. (2006). The impact of presentation graphics on students' experience in the classroom. *Computers & Education, 47,* 116–126.

Bartlett, R. M. & Strough, J. (2003). Multimedia versus traditional course instruction in introductory social psychology. *Teaching of Psychology, 30,* 335–338.

Bartsch, R. A. & Cobern, K. M. (2003). Effectiveness of PowerPoint presentations in lectures. *Computers & Education, 41,* 77–86.

Beets, S. D. & Lobingier, P. G. (2001). Pedagogical techniques: Student performance and preferences. *Journal of Education for Business, 76,* 231–235.

Blalock, M. G. & Montgomery, R. D. (2005). The effect of PowerPoint on student performance in principles of economics: An exploratory study. *Journal for Economics Educators, 5,* 1–7.

Clark, R. E. (1983). Reconsidering research on learning from media. *Review of Educational Research, 53*, 445–459.

Corbeil, G. (2007). Can PowerPoint presentations effectively replace textbooks and blackboards for teaching grammar? Do students find them an effective learning tool? *CALICO Journal, 24*, 631–656.

Daniels, L. (1999). Introducing technology in the classroom: PowerPoint as a first step. *Journal of Computing in Higher Education, 10*, 42–56.

Doumont, J. (2005). The cognitive style of PowerPoint: All slides are not evil. *Technical Communication, 52*, 64–70.

Durso, F. T., Pop, V. L., Burnett, J. S., & Stearman, E. J. (2011). Evidence-based human factors guidelines for PowerPoint presentations. *Ergonomics in Design, 19*, 4–8.

Erwin, T. D. & Rieppi, R. (2000). Comparing multimedia and traditional approaches in undergraduate psychology classes. *Teaching of Psychology, 26*, 58–61.

Hill, A., Arford, T., Lubitow, A., & Smollin, L. M. (2012). "I'm ambivalent about it": The dilemmas of PowerPoint. *Teaching Sociology, 40*, 242–256.

Isseks, M. (2011). How PowerPoint is killing education. *Educational Leadership, 68*, 74–76.

Kosslyn, S. M. (2007). *Clear and to the point: 8 psychological principles for compelling PowerPoint presentations*. New York: Oxford University Press.

Kosslyn, S. M., Kievit, R. A., Russell, A. G., & Shephard, J. M. (2012). PowerPoint presentation flaws and failures: A psychological analysis. *Frontiers in Psychology, 3*, 1–22.

Levasseur, D. G. & Sawyer, K. (2006). Pedagogy meets PowerPoint: A research review of the effects of computer-generated slides in the classroom. *Review of Communication, 6*, 101–123.

Lowry, R. B. (1999). Electronic presentation of lectures – effect upon student performance. *University Chemistry Education, 3*, 18–21.

Mantei, E. J. (2000). Using Internet class notes and PowerPoint in the physical geology lecture. *Journal of College Science Teaching, 29*, 301–305.

Nouri, H. & Shahid, A. (2005). The effect of PowerPoint presentations on student learning and attitudes. *Global Perspectives on Accounting Education, 2*, 53–73.

Parks, B. (2012). Death to PowerPoint. *Bloomberg Businessweek*. Available at: http://www.businessweek.com/articles/2012-08-30/death-to-powerpoint.

Rankin, E. L. & Hoaas, D. J. (2001). The use of PowerPoint and student performance. *Atlantic Economic Journal, 29*, 11.

Roehling, P. V. & Trent-Brown, S. (2011). Differential use and benefits of PowerPoint in upper level versus lower level courses. *Technology, Pedagogy, and Education, 20*, 113–124.

Savoy, A. Proctor, R. W., & Salvendy, G. (2009). Information retention from PowerPoint and traditional lectures. *Computers & Education, 52*, 858–867.

Shapiro, E. J., Kerssen-Griep, J., Gayle, B. M., & Allen, M. (2006). How powerful is PowerPoint? Analyzing the educational effects of desktop presentational programs in the classroom. In: B. M. Gayle, R. W. Preiss, N. Burrell, & M. Allen (Eds.), *Classroom communication and instructional processes: Advances through meta-analysis* (pp. 61–75). Mahwah, NJ: Lawrence Erlbaum.

Susskind, J. E. (2005). PowerPoint's power in the classroom: Enhancing students' self-efficacy and attitudes. *Computers & Education, 45,* 203–215.

Susskind, J. E. (2008). Limits of PowerPoint's power: Enhancing students' self-efficacy and attitudes but not their behavior. *Computers & Education, 50,* 1228–1239.

Szabo, A. & Hastings, N. (2000). Using IT in the undergraduate classroom: Should we replace the blackboard with PowerPoint? *Computers & Education, 35,* 175–187.

Tufte, E. R. (2003). *The cognitive style of PowerPoint.* Cheshire, CT: Graphics Press.

5 MYTH: MINIMALLY GUIDED INSTRUCTION IS SUPERIOR TO TRADITIONAL DIRECT INSTRUCTION

Minimally guided teaching strategies have become popular over the past several decades. Minimally guided methods include a variety of techniques that involve students working on problems or discussing issues without specific instruction on how to solve the problems, and sometimes even without instruction about what they are supposed to accomplish. In contrast, direct instruction involves teachers providing students with all the information they need to learn (Clark, Kirschner, & Sweller, 2012). Minimally guided techniques are based in constructivist learning philosophy, proponents of which assume that learning involves construction of knowledge and that people learn most effectively when they engage in the discovery of knowledge rather than having knowledge imparted to them. Many authors advocate for the effectiveness of constructivist teaching methods, and many assume the superiority of these methods over direct instruction (Steffe & Gale, 1995; Mayer, 2004). Such methods are quite popular and are a central component of the Common Core educational standards that have been adopted by nearly all states in the United States.

Great Myths of Education and Learning, First Edition. Jeffrey D. Holmes.
© 2016 John Wiley & Sons, Inc. Published 2016 by John Wiley & Sons, Inc.

Bruner's (1961) article is often cited as the origination point of minimally guided instruction – often referred to as discovery learning – although the philosophical roots extend back at least to the work of Dewey (1897; 1902). Bruner distinguished between methods that are essentially teacher-centered, wherein the teacher sets the pace of instruction and decides on the mode of teaching, and those that are student-centered, wherein teachers and students are more collaborative and students take an active role in the learning process. He hypothesized that the process of students learning by discovery might have unique benefits over traditional instructional processes, speculating that "discovering for oneself teaches one to acquire information in a way that makes that information more readily viable in problem-solving" (p. 26).

Around the same time that Bruner (1961) expressed his hypotheses regarding the effectiveness of discovery as a learning method, Piaget (1965) summarized trends he had observed in education over the preceding 30 years. He noted a growing emphasis on the idea that students should discover knowledge and learn concepts independently rather than having someone else impose that knowledge. He further emphasized the importance of active learning, although he noted that classroom activities are not ends in themselves, but instead become valuable to the extent that they promote cognitive activities such as reflection and abstract thinking. Piaget was critical of methods where students are provided with concepts rather than discovering them, arguing that direct instruction methods are less likely to lead to learning that transfers to broader contexts.

Over the subsequent decades, the hypotheses of Bruner (1961) and Piaget (1965) formed the backbone of various constructivist teaching approaches. Jonassen (1991; 1998) describes constructivist perspectives of learning as based on the assumption that knowledge cannot be transmitted to learners, but rather must be constructed by them based on individual experiences with the world. Jonassen contrasts constructivist views, where reality is assumed to exist primarily in individuals' minds, to objectivist views that assume an external reality that students can come to understand through direct instruction.

The literature on minimally guided instruction is particularly challenging to summarize because many terms are used inconsistently which makes it difficult to clearly understand what teachers actually do when they apply various techniques. Conducting research on minimally guided learning is likewise difficult because there is no consistently applied definition of what it is (Klahr & Nigam, 2004; Alfieri, Brooks, Aldrich, & Tenenbaum, 2011). As a consequence, there is surprisingly little direct experimental research comparing fully guided and minimally guided instruction. Many claims concerning the effectiveness of different methods are based on interpretations of related educational research rather than on direct experimental comparisons. Moreover, there is much disagreement among educational researchers concerning what broad techniques even qualify as minimally guided. Since teachers virtually never provide students with a problem to solve or a topic to discuss without any guidance at all (Brunstein, Betts, & Anderson, 2009), the distinctions between differing levels of guidance quickly become blurred.

One of the few well-controlled direct comparisons of discovery learning with direct instruction was conducted by Klahr and Nigam (2004), who compared the techniques in terms of both initial learning and transfer of learning to other tasks. The researchers randomly assigned third and fourth grade students to learn to design experiments via either direct instruction or discovery learning. In both conditions, students engaged in active learning by developing experiments to test scientific questions pertaining to the motion of balls of different materials rolling down ramps varying in steepness, length, and roughness. In the direct instruction condition, the teacher presented and explained examples of good and bad experimental designs; in the discovery condition, students spent the same amount of time designing experiments, but without any explanations or examples. Immediately after this phase, students each designed four new experiments; a week later, they each evaluated science fair posters produced by sixth grade students from a different school. The data were collected by an experimenter who was blind to the experimental conditions, and the students' responses were coded by independent evaluators.

Klahr and Nigam (2004) found that students in the direct instruction condition improved far more in their ability to design quality experiments – ultimately performing twice as well as students in the discovery condition. The majority of students (77%) in the direct instruction condition achieved mastery of the learning task, whereas only 23% of the students in the discovery condition achieved mastery. Direct instruction led to much greater success for students at all levels of initial performance. Moreover, students' ability to critique science posters did not vary as a function of the learning method. Mastery of the learning task was the critical variable determining students' ability to evaluate the posters – whether students had achieved that mastery through direct instruction or discovery learning. In sum, direct instruction led to greater learning overall, and discovery learning did not lead to greater transfer of learning to another context.

In an interesting partial replication of Klahr's and Nigam's (2004) study, Dean and Kuhn (2006) compared discovery with direct instruction over a longer time frame. They randomly assigned fourth grade classes to one of three conditions with the same learning objective used by Klahr and Nigam. Students in a practice condition worked on computerized problems without teacher guidance for 12 sessions over 10 weeks. Students in a second condition engaged in the same 12 practice sessions preceded by a single direct instruction session at the outset where a teacher presented two good and two bad examples of experiments along with explanations. The length of this direct instruction session was not reported, but it appears from the procedure that it was quite brief. Students in a third condition received only the single direct instruction session with no subsequent practice. When students were tested seven weeks after the last session, those who had received both practice and direct instruction were no better off than students who had only practiced. The authors concluded that, at least in this case, direct instruction was not a necessary part of the learning process.

There are several reasons to be wary of this conclusion. First, the single direct instruction session was apparently very brief and was followed by 12 practice sessions for both groups. It is perhaps not surprising that the effect of the direct instruction session would be diluted after students' participation in 12 practice sessions. Second, students in the practice only condition still received guidance in the form of an introductory session where the learning activities were explained, as well as reminders during some practice sessions of information from earlier sessions. This would further dilute any direct instruction effect since students in all groups were in fact receiving guidance. Finally, the researchers did not compare equivalent amounts of unguided practice and direct instruction. The finding that very minimal direct instruction increased learning only slightly beyond a great deal of practice is of uncertain value.

In another test of learning with minimal guidance, Rittle-Johnson (2006) assigned children in grades three through five to two conditions in which the students solved math problems. In the instruction condition, the experimenter directly taught students a specific strategy for solving the problems; in the discovery condition, the experimenter provided no instruction and told students to think of a way to solve the problems. Students then solved a series of problems, each of which was followed by feedback and the correct answer. They then took an immediate post-test and another post-test two weeks later. When solving the initial problems, students who received direct instruction averaged nearly twice as many correct answers as those in the discovery condition – despite the fact that all students received feedback on their performance as they worked through the problems. Students who had received direct instruction also did better on both the immediate and delayed tests, which included problems that were analogous to those they had seen previously, as well as problems that had some similarities but were different from what the students had seen before. Rittle-Johnson concluded that direct instruction was a more reliable way of teaching students the correct way to solve problems. She also noted that many students in the discovery condition – but no students in the instruction condition – used incorrect strategies, and she found no evidence that the discovery method led to greater transfer of learning.

Alfieri and colleagues' (2011) meta-analysis provides a broad perspective on the relative effectiveness of discovery learning versus guided instruction. These researchers emphasized that a host of varying techniques have been included under the heading of discovery learning, but that the term is most commonly used to refer to methods in which students must acquire knowledge and understanding independently rather than having it provided to them. Alfieri and colleagues integrated the findings from more than 100 studies comparing minimally guided discovery methods with explicitly guided techniques. Overall, guided instruction led to greater learning, although the effects varied widely in strength due to the wide variety of samples, learning objectives, and research methods. Interestingly, studies published in top-tier journals demonstrated larger benefits of direct instruction over unguided instruction than studies published in lower-tier journals. Although the superiority of guided instruction was observed across learning domains, it was stronger when students learned verbal and social skills than when they learned math and science topics. Some types of explicit instruction were more effective than others, but all were more effective than unguided discovery. The researchers concluded that unguided discovery is not an effective strategy in terms of student learning, and that techniques such as direct teaching, having students do worked examples where they have access to all steps in the problem-solving process, and providing students with explicit feedback on their performance are much more effective. They further concluded that direct instruction is usually necessary to teach students problem-solving approaches before discovery methods can be employed, and that optimal teaching methods all involve some kind of meaningful guidance, instruction, or feedback.

There is evidence that student learning can sometimes be enhanced under conditions of minimal guidance. Brunstein et al. (2009) argue that discovery learning and direct instruction represent ends of a continuum ranging from one extreme at which students are told what to learn, to the other extreme at which they must figure out what to learn. However, Brunstein and colleagues also point out that all discovery learning methods involve some guidance and that pure discovery can therefore be distinguished from guided discovery. They randomly assigned undergraduate students to use a computerized tutoring program to solve complex math problems under one of four conditions: receiving verbal instructions, receiving a direct demonstration of how to solve the problems, receiving both verbal instructions and a demonstration, and receiving neither instruction nor a demonstration – which was intended as a discovery learning condition. The researchers reported that students in the minimally guided condition were ultimately most successful in that they completed a lengthy problem set more quickly. However, Brunstein and colleagues noted that in fact their discovery condition did provide guidance by providing general instructions on the purpose of the problems to be solved, limiting the options that students had for exploring possible solutions, and providing feedback on student performance. They speculated that additional instruction throughout the process would likely have led to similar success and even greater efficiency. The researchers concluded that students may sometimes be able to learn with minimal guidance but only when they search within a limited number of possible solutions, and engage in extended practice, on tasks that are not too cognitively demanding.

There are several reasons why instruction with minimal guidance tends not to have the dramatic advantages that advocates expect. First, the emergence of minimally guided instructional philosophy and techniques occurred prior to the publication of much of the existing research on human cognitive processing, and the techniques are in some ways inconsistent with that research (Kirschner, Sweller, & Clark, 2006; Sweller, 2009). Perhaps most relevant are the now well-known limitations of human short-term memory (Miller, 1956), which are particularly striking when a person is trying to actively work with the information in his or her immediate consciousness rather than merely maintaining it in memory (see Cowan, 2000, for a review). Sweller argues that educational methods that require teachers to deliberately withhold knowledge from students so that the students can discover it themselves are problematic because they ignore the limitations of working memory.

In his review of cognitive load theory, Artino (2008) similarly concluded that students will learn less effectively when teaching methods place excessive demands on their working memory. He cites the perils of teaching approaches characterized by extraneous cognitive load, which he defines as the extra load placed on working memory when students have to engage in cognitive tasks unrelated to the material or skills to be mastered. He argues that good teaching should minimize such extraneous demands on working memory, and that teachers can accomplish this by directly providing students with the background information they need to solve a particular problem, and then giving students the opportunity to solve increasingly complex problems. He questions the wisdom of employing minimally guided techniques with students learning novel information, because such techniques are likely to overwhelm students' working memory. Other researchers agree that direct instruction places fewer demands on working memory, because students can focus their attention on relevant information and need only understand the problem and how to solve it rather than having to expend cognitive energy searching for the problem itself (Clark et al., 2012). Artino asserts that any teaching method must be adapted to the current knowledge level of the students involved. When students are learning truly novel material, they will likely need direct instruction; as their knowledge of the topic deepens, they will be able to perform more complex tasks with greater autonomy. This perspective is consistent with Bjork's and Bjork's (2011) description of what they term desirable difficulties relevant to learning. They explain that engaging in tasks that make learning seem more difficult – such as varying the methods used to learn – can lead to more effective learning, but only if the learner has "the background knowledge or skills to respond to them successfully" (p. 58). In the absence of such knowledge, they state, the same methods create difficulty that is detrimental to learning.

The full relevance of this progression from novice to expert, and its implications for instructional methods, is evident when one considers the cognitive skills necessary to demonstrate true expertise in any particular domain. Kirschner et al. (2006) cite evidence that people who become very effective at solving problems in a specific domain are successful because they have a great deal of relevant past experience stored in long-term memory. Novices have access only to the information immediately available to them, and their ability to process that information is greatly restricted due to the limitations of working memory. In contrast, experts can draw on the vast experience stored in their long-term memory, making working memory limitations far less pertinent. Experts can therefore quickly determine how to solve a problem because they can recognize similarities to past problems. Kirschner and colleagues assert that minimally guided teaching approaches require novice students to tax their working memory capacity by trying to identify relevant information and an effective problem-solving strategy, thereby leaving students with less working memory capacity to transfer information to long-term memory. Without relevant knowledge, students can only "blindly search for possible solution steps" (Clark et al., 2012: 10).

Neglecting to consider the limitations of working memory may have especially dire consequences for low-achieving students. Clark (1982) reviewed nine studies examining the interaction between teaching method and student ability in determining student achievement. In the majority of studies, lower ability students learned more effectively from less cognitively demanding methods characterized by greater structure and guidance. High ability students tended to learn more from methods that provided less guidance and therefore imposed greater cognitive demands. Paradoxically, students reported greater enjoyment of teaching methods from which they learned less – although they were not aware that they were learning less. High ability students tended to report greater enjoyment of structured methods characterized by lower cognitive load, whereas low ability students preferred unstructured methods that imposed greater cognitive load. Three decades after Clark's review, he and his colleagues continued to express concern that minimally guided approaches pose the risk that only high-achieving students will discover knowledge, and other students will become frustrated and disinterested (Clark et al., 2012). Even Bruner (1961), an early advocate of discovery learning, asserted that "Discovery ... favors the well-prepared mind" (p. 22).

A second factor that may limit the effectiveness of minimally guided approaches is the nature of the material taught as part of formal education. Sweller (2009) cites a number of constructivist arguments regarding the human ability to learn many skills outside formal educational environments and with little or no conscious effort. For example, most children learn to speak and engage in meaningful social interaction simply by being around others who are engaging in those behaviors. However, there are important distinctions between these type of skills and the skills that teachers typically want students to learn. Geary (2012) argues that skills that were relevant to daily survival throughout human evolutionary history develop with little effort on the part of learners. He considers skills such as speaking and social interaction to be examples of such biologically primary knowledge. In contrast, Geary categorizes skills such as reading, writing, solving math problems, and critically evaluating evidence as biologically secondary knowledge because these skills have existed only for a tiny portion of human evolutionary history. Developing these skills requires conscious effort and explicit instruction. Geary asserts that children are inherently motivated to learn primary knowledge but not secondary knowledge, stating "We would not need modern schooling, or at least not 12 or more years of it, if children found the activities that promote secondary learning as engaging as they find interacting with friends, and secondary learning as effortless as native-language learning" (p. 613).

Finally, minimally guided approaches often inappropriately equate cognitive activity with behavioral activity. In his critique of minimally guided techniques, Mayer (2004) agrees with other critics (Kirschner et al., 2006; Sweller, 2009) that the constructivist educational philosophy indeed has merit due to its emphasis on active student involvement, student construction of knowledge, and practical application of knowledge. However, Mayer takes issue with the assumption that active learning requires actual behavioral activity and unguided discovery. He questions constructivist assumptions that teaching methods such as interactive activities and group discussions are effective, whereas supposedly passive methods such as reading books and listening to lectures are ineffective. He refers to this assumption as the constructivist teaching fallacy because it "equates active learning with active teaching," and notes that discussing a problem guarantees neither active cognitive processing, nor a solution (p. 15). His critique parallels Piaget's (1965) observations from four decades earlier – that cognitive activity is a far more important factor in the learning process than behavioral activity. Mayer acknowledges that it is difficult to develop strategies that treat behavioral activity as a means to facilitate cognitive activity rather than an end in itself. Nonetheless, he emphasizes that thinking, rather than behavioral activity, is the most important factor in the learning process and that "guidance, structure, and focused goals" are critical for promoting thinking (p. 17).

It is important to note that there is much disagreement among researchers regarding what specific teaching methods are appropriately defined as minimally guided. For example, Kirschner et al. (2006) place discovery learning, inquiry learning, constructivist learning, and problem-based learning all under the heading of minimally guided techniques, calling them "essentially pedagogically equivalent approaches" (p. 75). Artino (2008), likewise, refers to all these techniques as similar to one another in their withholding of direct instruction. Other researchers disagree that techniques such as problem-based learning are in fact minimally guided (Hmelo-Silver, Duncan, & Chinn, 2007; Schmidt, Loyens, Van Gog, & Paas, 2007). Schmidt and colleagues agree that minimally guided instruction is not effective for teaching students novel information. However, they argue that problem-based learning – where students work in small groups on problems that include a description of an event that students must attempt to understand – is actually characterized by flexible and adaptive guidance. They note that group members usually study relevant background material on their own between discussions, and that discussions are often guided by a tutor who may at times provide information to assist the process. Hmelo-Silver and colleagues agree, arguing that in both problem-based learning and inquiry learning, teachers sometimes provide necessary information – although only after students' need to have such information becomes apparent.

Kirschner and his colleagues responded to these advocates by citing evidence that problem-based learning is by definition self-directed because students must search for possible solutions rather than being directly taught how to reach solutions (Sweller, Kirschner, & Clark, 2007). They assert that requiring students to search for solutions strains working memory resources and inhibits learning in ways that would not occur if students were simply provided with the necessary information. Interestingly, they also argue that collaboration itself taxes working memory resources because students must cope with the cognitive demands of group interaction. Hmelo-Silver and colleagues (2007) claim that scaffolding in the form of providing information to students when necessary can increase the effectiveness of problem-based and inquiry learning. Kirschner and colleagues criticize this view as ignoring the most obvious and direct form of scaffolding which begins with providing students with a problem and teaching them how to solve it.

Based on the educational research to date, as well as related research on human memory and cognitive processing, there appears to be little basis for claims that minimally guided teaching methods are more effective than guided approaches. Importantly, many critics of withholding guidance do not find fault with discovery-based learning when such learning includes direct instruction. Mayer (2004) cites several studies dating to the 1950s suggesting that guided discovery is more effective than unguided discovery. Moreover, Alfieri and colleagues (2011) provided evidence through their meta-analysis that guided discovery may in fact lead to greater student learning than either unguided discovery or explicit instruction. Mayer concludes that students will benefit most from a balance of appropriate guidance to help them identify what must be learned, and appropriate freedom to become engaged with the learning process and to actively work to make sense of what they are learning. Other scholars agree that such a balance is desirable, but note that it is challenging to implement because it is difficult to know when it is best to teach students a solution and when it is best to let them discover a solution (Brown & Campione, 1994).

Withholding guidance from students may have negative consequences beyond ineffective learning. Researchers have cited evidence that minimally guided approaches can lead students to discover false information, which results in confusion and the establishment of misconceptions (Brown & Campione, 1994; Kirschner et al., 2006; Clark et al., 2012). Students may also become frustrated when they are unsure what to do. Brunstein and colleagues (2009) reported that in one of their studies, half of the discovery learning students – but none of the direct instruction students – quit the experiment because "they felt totally lost and did not want to continue" (p. 798). Minimally guided methods may also lead to expanded achievement gaps between groups of students. Von Secker and Lissitz (1999) cited US National Education Standards that advocate student-centered learning, assert that active learning must involve interaction between students, and deemphasize the importance of teachers presenting information in favor of students discovering knowledge. To investigate the wisdom of these standards they studied US Department of Education data on a sample of more than 2,000 tenth graders who were representative of a much larger US student sample and found that a shift away from teacher-centered instruction did not lead to any significant improvement in average student achievement, and actually increased gender and ethnicity achievement gaps. The researchers concluded that using student-centered methods rather than teacher-centered methods will not improve student learning unless students first acquire some basic knowledge so that self-directed activities and group collaboration can be effective.

It is interesting to note that one of the most frequently cited articles ostensibly advocating minimally guided methods actually contains a more balanced perspective than secondary sources imply. Bruner (1961) presented many of his ideas in the form of hypotheses and did not make broad claims about the effectiveness of discovery methods. For example, as noted earlier, he stated that "discovering for oneself teaches one to acquire information in a way that makes that information more readily viable in problem-solving" (p. 26), but he followed immediately with the infrequently cited statement, "So goes the hypothesis. It is still in need of testing" (p. 26). It is also apparent from Bruner's article that he, like other scholars, had difficulty describing exactly what various proposed discovery methods would look like in practice.

Critics of minimally guided instruction generally do not question the potential value of having students engage in independent work to practice skills they have been taught, but rather the belief that knowledge students gain via minimally guided approaches is somehow more valuable or more useful than knowledge that teachers present in a direct fashion (Sweller, 2009; Clark et al., 2012). Indeed, it remains to be empirically demonstrated that teachers can enhance student learning by deliberately withholding information from students. Sweller et al. (2007) make this point effectively, and point out that the superiority of discovery methods over direct instruction has been a dominant assumption in education for many years, and has proven to be "sufficiently attractive to be impervious to the near total lack of supporting evidence from randomized, controlled experiments" (p. 120). There may be conditions under which specific minimally guided techniques are superior to direct instruction for particular learning objectives assuming particular student characteristics, but such parameters have not been adequately identified and tested. Consequently, there is little evidence to conclude that minimal guidance in general is superior to direct teaching methods.

References

Alfieri, L., Brooks, P. J., Aldrich, N. J., & Tenenbaum, H. R. (2011). Does discovery-based instruction enhance learning? *Journal of Educational Psychology, 103,* 1–18.

Artino, A. R. (2008). Cognitive load theory and the role of learner experience: An abbreviated review for educational practitioners. *AACE Journal, 16,* 425–439.

Bjork, E. L. & Bjork, R. A. (2011). Making things hard on yourself, but in a good way: Creating desirable difficulties to enhance learning. In: M. A. Gernsbacher, R. W. Pew, L. M. Hough, & J. R. Pomerantz (Eds.), *Psychology and the real world: Essays illustrating fundamental contributions to society* (pp. 55–64). New York: Worth.

Brown, A. L. & Campione, J. C. (1994). Guided discovery in a community of learners. In: K. McGilly (Ed.), *Classroom lessons: Integrating cognitive theory and classroom practice* (pp. 229–270). Cambridge, MA: MIT Press/Bradford Books.

Bruner, J. S. (1961). The act of discovery. *Harvard Educational Review, 31,* 21–32.

Brunstein, A., Betts, S., & Anderson, J. R. (2009). Practice enables successful learning under minimal guidance. *Journal of Educational Psychology, 101,* 790–802.

Clark, R. E. (1982). Antagonism between achievement and enjoyment in ATI studies. *Educational Psychologist, 17,* 92–101.

Clark, R. E., Kirschner, P. A., & Sweller, J. (2012). Putting students on the path to learning: The case for fully guided instruction. *American Educator, 36,* 6–11.

Cowan, N. (2000). The magical number 4 in short-term memory: A reconsideration of mental storage capacity. *Behavioral and Brain Sciences, 24,* 87–185.

Dean, D. & Kuhn, D. (2006). Direct instruction vs. discovery: The long view. *Science Education, 91,* 384–397.

Dewey, J. (1897). *My pedagogic creed.* New York: E. L. Kellogg.

Dewey, J. (1902). *The child and the curriculum.* Chicago: University of Chicago Press.

Geary, D. C. (2012). Evolutionary educational psychology. In: K. R Harris, S. Graham, T. Urdan, C. B. McCormick, G. M. Sinatra, & J. Sweller (Eds.),

APA educational psychology handbook, vol. 1: Theories, constructs, and critical issues (pp. 597–621). Washington, DC: American Psychological Association.

Hmelo-Silver, C. E., Duncan, R., G., & Chinn, C. A. (2007). Scaffolding and achievement in problem-based and inquiry learning: A response to Kirschner, Sweller, and Clark (2006). *Educational Psychologist, 42*, 99–107.

Jonassen, D. H. (1991). Objectivism versus constructivism: Do we need a new philosophical paradigm? *Educational Technology Research & Development, 39*, 5–14.

Jonassen, D. H. (1998). Designing constructivist learning environments. In: C. M. Reigeluth (Ed.), *Instructional theories and models*, 2nd edn. (pp. 215–239). Mahwah, NJ: Lawrence Erlbaum.

Kirschner, P. A., Sweller, J., & Clark, R. E. (2006). Why minimal guidance during instruction does not work: An analysis of the failure of constructivist, discovery, problem-based, experiential, and inquiry-based teaching. *Educational Psychologist, 41*, 75–86.

Klahr, D. & Nigam, M. (2004). The equivalence of learning paths in early science instruction. *Psychological Science, 15*, 661–667.

Mayer, R. E. (2004). Should there be a three-strikes rule against pure discovery learning? The case for guided methods of instruction. *American Psychologist, 59*, 14–19.

Miller, G. A. (1956). The magical number seven, plus or minus two: some limits on our capacity for processing information. *Psychological Review, 63*, 81–97.

Piaget, J. (1965). Science of education and the psychology of the child. In: H. E. Gruber & J. J. Voneche (Eds.), *The essential Piaget* (pp. 695–725). New York: Basic Books.

Rittle-Johnson, B. (2006). Promoting transfer: Effects of self-explanation and direct instruction. *Child Development, 77*, 1–15.

Schmidt, H. G., Loyens, M. M., Van Gog, T., & Paas, F. (2007). Problem-based learning *is* compatible with human cognitive architecture: Commentary on Kirschner, Sweller, & Clark (2006). *Educational Psychologist, 42*, 91–97.

Steffe, L. P. & Gale, J. (Eds.). (1995). *Constructivism in education*. Hillsdale, NJ: Lawrence Erlbaum.

Sweller, J. (2009). What human cognitive architecture tells us about constructivism. In: S. Tobias & T. M. Duffy (Eds.), *Constructivist instruction: Success or failure?* (pp. 127–143). New York: Routledge/Taylor & Francis.

Sweller, J., Kirschner, P. A., & Clark, R. E., (2007). Why minimally guided teaching techniques do not work: A reply to commentaries. *Educational Psychologist, 42*, 115–121.

Von Secker, C. E. & Lissitz, R. W. (1999). Estimating the impact of instructional practices on students achievement in science. *Journal of Research in Science Teaching, 36*, 1110–1126.

6 MYTH: REWARDS ALWAYS UNDERMINE STUDENTS' INTRINSIC MOTIVATION

For more than 40 years, many scholars and educators have expressed concern that overtly rewarding students ultimately reduces their intrinsic motivation to engage in activities for which they have been rewarded. According to researchers, intrinsically motivated people engage in activities because they find the activities themselves rewarding (Deci, 1971). Consistent with the philosophy that students should be self-motivated (Workman & Williams, 1980; Eisenberger & Cameron, 1996), it is likely that most educators would prefer that students be intrinsically motivated to learn and would oppose the use of strategies that could undermine that motivation. Early research findings were quickly translated into broad concerns that rewards often "do more harm than good" (Levine & Fasnacht, 1974: 816), and broad indictments against the use of rewards – particularly in education – continue today despite the availability of a remarkably complex and nuanced body of research (Lavorata, 2013; see also Eisenberger & Cameron, 1996; Flora & Flora, 1999). Kohn's (1993) popular book *Punished by Rewards* reflects common concerns about the potential downsides of many kinds of rewards.

Researchers have offered two primary rationales for why rewards might reduce people's intrinsic interest in an activity. According to the overjustification hypothesis, intrinsic motivation for an activity is reduced

Great Myths of Education and Learning, First Edition. Jeffrey D. Holmes.
© 2016 John Wiley & Sons, Inc. Published 2016 by John Wiley & Sons, Inc.

when a person is induced with some external reward because the person no longer sees the activity as its own end (Lepper, Greene, & Nisbett, 1973). In other words, the reward signals that the activity does not have value in its own right and is not worth doing in the absence of an external reward. According to cognitive evaluation theory, rewards reduce intrinsic motivation when people perceive the rewards as controlling their behavior rather than providing information about performance (Deci & Ryan, 1985). Deci and Ryan assert that rewards can reduce people's sense of self-determination which shifts their attributions for a behavior to extrinsic factors rather than intrinsic interest.

Decades of concern about the potential negative effects of rewards began in the 1970s. Deci (1971) performed the first three of what would become well over 100 experiments on the effect of rewards on intrinsic motivation. In his first experiment, Deci had 24 college students work on a puzzle game over three sessions. All students simply performed the task during the first session, half of the students received money for each puzzle they completed during the second session, and all students again performed the task without reward during the third session. At the end of the third session, the experimenter left the room for 8 minutes, during which time participants could do whatever they wanted such as continuing with the puzzle task or reading magazines. Deci assessed students' intrinsic motivation by measuring how long they engaged in the puzzle task during their free time, and their ratings of how enjoyable they found the task to be – two measures of intrinsic interest that researchers have used in scores of subsequent studies. Students who had been paid for completing the task spent less of their later free time on the task than students who had not been rewarded. However, the difference between the conditions was not statistically significant. Moreover, there was no significant difference during any of the three sessions between rewarded and unrewarded participants in the degree to which they rated the puzzle task as interesting and enjoyable.

In his second experiment, Deci (1971) conducted a field study in which four out of eight college students working as headline writers for a student newspaper began to receive 50 cents for each headline they wrote; later this payment was removed. The other four students never received pay. Whereas performance among the rewarded students remained stable, students who were never paid gradually increased the speed at which they wrote headlines, which Deci interpreted as evidence for increased intrinsic motivation. However, final data were unavailable for two of the control participants so this conclusion was based on a sample of just four rewarded participants compared with two unrewarded participants.

Despite the modest findings of Deci's first two experiments, the results have been cited over 3,000 times – often as the foundation for various critiques of the use of rewards in education.

In his third experiment, Deci (1971) foreshadowed the results of numerous subsequent studies, suggesting that any potential negative effect of rewards on intrinsic motivation does not generalize to rewards provided verbally. Deci replicated his first experiment with a different sample of 24 college students engaging in a puzzle game; however, instead of monetary rewards, students in the reward condition received verbal praise during the second session. For students who did not receive praise, the free time spent on the puzzle task declined significantly over the three trials; for students who received praise, free time spent on the task remained steady. Deci noted the contrast to his first experiment in which the intrinsic motivation of unrewarded students did not decline over the three sessions, and speculated that the differing pattern might have been due to differences in the student samples across the two experiments. In any case, Deci stated that praising students seemed to increase their intrinsic motivation relative to students who were not rewarded. However, there was little indication of an actual increase in intrinsic motivation among praised students when their free time spent on the task was compared with their time on task prior to being rewarded. Only when compared with nonrewarded students, whose intrinsic motivation appeared to decline greatly over the three sessions, was there a significant effect. Furthermore, there were again no differences between the groups for any of the sessions in students' ratings of how interesting and enjoyable they found the tasks to be. Deci summarized his three experiments by asserting that money reduces intrinsic motivation but praise does not.

Two years after Deci's (1971) initial studies, Lepper and colleagues (1973) conducted a classroom experiment in which 51 preschool children who initially demonstrated intrinsic interest in a drawing activity were randomly assigned to one of three reward conditions. The researchers told some children that they would receive a certificate and a ribbon as rewards for engaging in the drawing activity; a second group of children received the same rewards, but learned of the rewards only after they had completed the activity; and a third group of children engaged in the activity with no reward. When the children engaged in the drawing activity between one and two weeks later without any rewards, the children who had previously received an expected reward spent less time on the activity than they had two weeks earlier – in contrast to children in the other two groups for whom there was no decline in time on task. Moreover, the drawings produced by children in the expected reward group were of lower quality than the other two groups. Lepper and colleagues concluded that the expected reward decreased intrinsic interest in the drawing activity, but that the same reward did not undermine intrinsic motivation when it was unexpected. This latter finding is particularly noteworthy because it demonstrated early on that although rewards may reduce intrinsic motivation under some conditions, they do not appear to do so under all conditions.

Adding further nuance to early findings on the effects of rewards on intrinsic motivation, Greene, Sternberg, and Lepper (1976) investigated the impact of rewarding fourth and fifth grade math students with credit toward school math awards over an extended period of time rather than in a single session. Some students were rewarded for math activities in which they had previously shown the most interest, some were rewarded for their least preferred math activities, and some were rewarded for math activities of their own choosing. Students in a control condition were rewarded for all activities. After a reward period of 13 days, the researchers withdrew the rewards and monitored the time students spent on each task for 13 more days. Students in all three experimental groups – those rewarded for high interest, low interest, and personally chosen activities – spent less time on rewarded tasks following removal of the rewards than they had during the baseline period, but the effect was significant only for the high interest and choice groups. Students rewarded for activities they had specifically chosen showed the greatest decline in intrinsic interest following removal of rewards. However, students rewarded for high interest activities did not differ from students who were rewarded for all four activities in terms of their time spent on previously rewarded tasks. Moreover, students who were rewarded for all activities actually spent more time on task after reward withdrawal than students who were rewarded only for certain activities. Green and colleagues concluded that reductions in intrinsic motivation following longer-term reward programs emerge "under some conditions" (p. 1229), and acknowledged ambiguities given that students rewarded for high interest activities – who presumably would have demonstrated the greatest reduction in intrinsic interest after being rewarded and having the reward removed – in fact showed no less intrinsic interest than students who were rewarded for all activities.

A significant limitation of Greene and colleagues' (1976) study is that there was no true control group of students who were not rewarded at all, so the researchers could not assess the absolute effect of rewards relative to no rewards. It is possible that the apparent declines in intrinsic interest occurred due to task repetition rather than to the retraction of rewards. Suspecting this to be the case, Mynatt et al. (1978) replicated the study by observing 20 first grade students as the children chose among 30 educational games during two daily free-play periods for 9 days. Following this baseline period, the children were randomly assigned to groups and provided with target games that were either the most popular or least popular during the baseline period. Half of the children in each of these groups were told that they would receive a reward of candy if they played with any of their target games, while the remaining students received no incentive. The children played with the games under these contingencies for 11 days, at which time the children in the reward condition were told that they would no longer receive the rewards. The play sessions continued for another nine days, with both rewarded and nonrewarded children demonstrating a decline in intrinsic interest over time. There was no significant difference in intrinsic motivation between the rewarded and nonrewarded groups. Importantly, among children playing games that held low initial intrinsic interest, there was no change in interest by the end of the experiment, but the reward greatly increased their use of the educational games. Mynatt and colleagues concluded that they had found no evidence of a reduction in intrinsic motivation attributable to rewards, and that any such effect "may be a limited and temporary one" (p. 177).

Despite the equivocal results of early studies, the idea that rewards can undermine intrinsic motivation caught on quickly and resonated with many people concerned about educational strategies. During the 1970s and 1980s, numerous conflicting studies emerged. Eventually two researchers (Cameron & Pierce, 1994) conducted a meta-analysis to better assess the effects of rewards on intrinsic motivation. As noted in other chapters of this book, meta-analysis is a method for combining the results of multiple studies to minimize the limitations of specific studies and provide a more comprehensive picture of research findings in a particular area. Cameron's and Pierce's meta-analysis of 96 published experimental studies turned out to be the opening salvo in a contentious debate. They concluded that rewards generally do not reduce intrinsic motivation as measured by willingness to engage in, enjoyment of, or positive attitudes toward rewarded activities. More specifically, Cameron and Pierce asserted that when intrinsic motivation is assessed by participants' free time spent on a task, verbal praise increases intrinsic motivation, unexpected tangible rewards have no effect on intrinsic motivation, and expected tangible rewards do not undermine intrinsic motivation if they are contingent on the quality of task performance rather than on mere participation in an activity. Interestingly, when the measure of intrinsic motivation is self-reported attitudes and enjoyment of the activity, verbal praise again increases intrinsic motivation and tangible rewards do not undermine intrinsic motivation – even when the rewards are expected and based only on participation. Moreover, rewards for quality performance actually increase intrinsic motivation as measured by participants' self-reported enjoyment. In summary, Cameron and Pierce concluded that the negative effect of rewards is very narrow, in that it emerges only when rewards are expected and not linked with the quality of performance, and when intrinsic motivation is measured by free time on task rather than how much participants actually report that they enjoy the task.

Cameron's and Pierce's (1994) conclusion that "teachers have no reason to resist implementing incentive systems in the classroom" (p. 397), did not sit well with critics. Ryan and Deci (1996), two long-time investigators advocating that rewards generally tend to decrease intrinsic motivation, called the meta-analysis "flawed" (p. 33), and accused Cameron and Pierce of omitting some relevant studies and inappropriately combining others. Cameron and Pierce (1996) countered by criticizing Ryan and Deci for failing to reanalyze the actual data. They further asserted that they had included "all relevant studies" (p. 40) in their meta-analysis, and argued that reanalysis based on Ryan's and Deci's critique would only reveal further limitations to the undermining effect of rewards and would not change the overall conclusions.

In light of such disagreement, Deci, Koestner, and Ryan (1999) conducted their own meta-analysis of 128 experiments – including many published after Cameron's and Pierce's meta-analysis or omitted by Cameron and Pierce because they came from unpublished doctoral dissertations. Deci and colleagues included only studies in which initial task interest was neutral or greater. In contrast to Cameron and Pierce, they concluded that based on free time on task, intrinsic interest was reduced by rewards in general, and that undermining effects were present for rewards that were expected, tangible, and provided for performing a task, completing a task, or doing well on a task. However, when the measure of intrinsic motivation was self-reported interest in the task, the researchers detected no overall negative effect of rewards. Furthermore, they concluded that rewards based on the quality of performance did not reduce intrinsic motivation. Importantly, Deci and colleagues concurred with Cameron and Pierce that, based on both free time and self-report measures, unexpected rewards did not undermine intrinsic motivation and verbal rewards actually increased intrinsic motivation.

The same year that Deci and colleagues published their meta-analysis, Eisenberger, Pierce, and Cameron (1999) published yet another meta-analysis of 50 published and unpublished studies. They again concluded that rewards contingent on quality of performance had no overall effect on intrinsic motivation as measured by free time spent on activities. Interestingly, Eisenberger and colleagues found that in studies where the standard for quality performance was vague – such as when participants were simply told that their objective was to do well on the task – rewards reduced free time spent on the task. In contrast, rewards for meeting specific standards for quality of performance, such as solving a specific number of problems or outperforming a specific proportion of people, increased intrinsic motivation. In terms of self-reported interest, rewards for meeting vague standards had no effect on intrinsic motivation and rewards for meeting specific standards again increased intrinsic motivation.

In a final meta-analysis, Cameron, Banko, and Pierce (2001) attempted to resolve the discrepancies between prior studies by analyzing 145 studies, including 21 from doctoral dissertations. The researchers detected no overall negative effect of rewards on intrinsic motivation, but noted that reporting only this general effect is insufficient to fully understand the effect of rewards. Consistent with Deci and colleagues (1999), they concluded that expected tangible rewards provided simply for engaging in an activity that is already of high interest reduce intrinsic motivation, unexpected tangible rewards have no effect on intrinsic motivation, and verbal rewards increase intrinsic motivation. In contrast to Deci and colleagues, they found that rewards for outperforming other participants in an activity also increase intrinsic motivation, and that rewards based on the number of problems solved in an activity reduces free time spent on the activity but increases self-reported interest. The nuanced results of these dueling meta-analyses demonstrate the complexity of the effects of rewards on intrinsic motivation and should preempt simplistic conclusions that rewards have universal negative or positive effects. Researchers on both sides of the debate agree that there are contingencies under which rewards do not undermine intrinsic motivation; results from specific studies provide important context regarding these contingencies.

In one early study qualifying the negative effect of rewards, researchers observed that the impact of rewards on intrinsic motivation was affected by whether the rewards were contingent on simply performing a task or succeeding at the task. The importance of this distinction, as it turned out, further depended on whether students had performed at a high or low level on the task. Karniol and Ross (1977) taught children a game in which they had to guess which of two images would make a light go on. The game was programmed so that all children were correct on 10 out of 20 trials, but half of the children were told their performance was above average and half were told that their performance was below average. Some children received marshmallows as an expected reward for good performance, whereas some children received the marshmallows simply for performing the task or received no rewards at all. High-performing children receiving rewards merely for engaging in the task later showed less intrinsic interest than those who had been rewarded based on success at the task and those who had not been rewarded at all. However, among low-performing children, rewards based simply on performing the task increased intrinsic motivation relative to rewards contingent on good performance or no rewards. Karniol and Ross were among early observers to suggest that "the detrimental effects of rewards on children's intrinsic motivation may be limited to a narrow set of circumstances" (p. 486).

In a more recent study, researchers investigated whether the effect of rewards would vary depending on the nature of the rewarded activity. Cameron, Pierce, and So (2004) randomly assigned college students to engage in either an easy or difficult version of a task in which they had to identify differences between cartoons. Half the students received an expected $2.00 reward for successfully completing sets of problems, whereas the other half were not rewarded. During a subsequent free choice period, students who had been rewarded for an easy task did indeed spend less free time on the task than those who had not been rewarded. However, those who had been rewarded for a more difficult task spent more free time on the task than those who had not been rewarded.

Several studies clarify such findings that even expected tangible rewards – those most condemned by reward critics – sometimes increase intrinsic motivation. It appears that the most important contingency is that the reward be closely tied to specific levels of task performance. For example, Eisenberger, Rhoades, and Cameron (1999) used the same task employed by Cameron and colleagues (2004) requiring college students to identify differences between cartoons. Half of the students received an expected monetary reward for meeting each performance standard and half received no reward. Students who had been rewarded for their achievement spent more subsequent free time on the task, and reported greater enjoyment and even a greater sense of self-determination in the decision to engage in the task than students who had not been rewarded. These differences occurred despite the fact that all students received the same feedback that they had achieved excellence on the task. Eisenberger and colleagues concluded that providing a reward for success on a task increases intrinsic motivation for the task.

In an even more sophisticated study using the cartoon task, Cameron, Pierce, Banko, and Gear (2005) randomly assigned college students to receive monetary rewards during a learning phase, a test phase, both phases, or to receive no rewards at all. During the learning phase, students worked on nine puzzles and could not advance to a new puzzle until they met each increasingly demanding performance goal; rewarded students received increasingly large rewards as their performance improved. During the test phase, students worked on ten new puzzles. Students who received rewards for successful performance during either the learning or test phases spent more free time on the task and rated it as more interesting and enjoyable than students who had not been rewarded. The researchers even found evidence of transfer of intrinsic interest to different activities, in that rewarded students spent more free time than nonrewarded students on other puzzle solving tasks. In a similar study, Pierce, Cameron, Banko, and So (2003) had Canadian college students engage in a complex puzzle-solving task in which half of the students were randomly assigned to maintain a steady level of performance and half were encouraged to meet increasingly high standards of performance. Furthermore, half of the students received an expected reward of $1 for each puzzle solution and half were told nothing about rewards. Students who received rewards spent more free time engaged in the task than students who had not received rewards. Moreover, those who received rewards for increasingly strong performance spent more free time on the task than students in any other condition.

Researchers have also observed that rewards informing participants about their competency at a task do not tend to diminish intrinsic motivation. Rosenfeld, Folger, and Adelman (1980) randomly assigned college women engaging in a crossword task to receive monetary rewards that either were or were not contingent on the number of tasks they completed, and that either did or did not provide information on each participant's supposed ability level. When the monetary reward communicated to participants that their task-specific ability was superior to others' ability, the reward led to participants spending more free time on the task, as well as to greater self-reported enjoyment and a greater willingness to perform the task in the future. In contrast, monetary rewards not tied to participants' ability led to less free time being spent on the task and reduced interest and willingness to return to the task. The authors concluded that rewards undermine intrinsic motivation when they do not provide information regarding task competence, but increase intrinsic motivation when they do. Nearly 30 years later, Eisenberger and Aselage (2009) similarly found that rewards communicating to college students that they had outperformed their peers increased the students' intrinsic motivation relative to unrewarded students.

Rosenfeld and colleagues (1980) proposed that when rewards do not provide feedback about a person's competence or ability on a task, they merely serve as inducements to act which can ultimately reduce intrinsic motivation. In contrast, rewards providing feedback about competence are not merely inducements and therefore do not reduce intrinsic motivation. Pierce and colleagues (2003) agree and propose that rewards communicating skill or ability preserve a person's focus on his or her own characteristics rather than on external inducements. However, many researchers suggest that providing such information has a potential downside. Cameron and colleagues (2005) pointed out that in their study, they rewarded participants for achievement, but they arranged the experiment so that all participants believed they had succeeded. They proposed that rewards based on achievement might undermine intrinsic motivation when participants – students in particular – do not perform at the highest possible level and therefore do not receive the highest possible reward. Other researchers are likewise particularly wary of rewards that might communicate to students a sense of failure or incompetence by signaling that they did not reach the highest level of performance (Deci et al., 1999).

The authors of one recent study even found that personality characteristics may play a role in the effects of rewards on intrinsic motivation. Replicating an earlier study (Thill, Mailhot, & Mouanda, 1998), Hagger and Chatzisarantis (2011) studied the difference in reward effects between students with an autonomy orientation and students with a control orientation. The researchers explain that people with an autonomy orientation tend to perceive the cause of behaviors as internal to themselves, see themselves as engaging in activities based on their own choice, and have high intrinsic motivation. People with a control orientation tend to perceive their behavior as being caused by external events and are therefore motivated primarily by external factors such as rewards. Based on a questionnaire, Hagger and Chatzisarantis identified 80 college students who scored highly on one orientation or the other. The students engaged in an activity requiring them to solve puzzles, which all students could solve after a few minutes. Half of the students received a monetary reward for each solved puzzle, while the remaining students received no reward. Among students whose personalities were characterized by a control orientation, rewarded students later spent less free time on the task than those who had not been rewarded – supporting the undermining effect of rewards. However, among students with an autonomy orientation, there were no differences in free time on task between the reward and no reward conditions. The researchers concluded that an autonomy orientation offers protection from the negative effects of rewards on intrinsic motivation. In fact, the effect of orientation on intrinsic motivation was stronger than the effect of rewards, and intrinsic motivation was highest among students with an autonomy orientation who received rewards.

Although scores of studies concerning rewards and intrinsic motivation have been conducted over the past four decades, many scholars have questioned the generalizability of many of these studies to applied educational environments. Most researchers have studied the impact of rewards in controlled laboratory environments using short-term procedures and often employing tasks that, although cognitive in nature, do not closely resemble typical academic tasks. In the midst of the early studies, Davidson and Bucher (1978) noted that most studies demonstrating that rewards undermine intrinsic motivation involved scenarios unlike those in which rewards are actually used. They conducted a very small study of preschool children engaging in academic tasks and concluded that rewarding children on a continuous basis as is usually done in educational settings increases intrinsic motivation. Flora and Flora (1999) surveyed college students about their reading habits and found that students who had been rewarded for reading as children spent no less time reading for pleasure and reported no less enjoyment of reading than students who had not received such rewards.

One caveat of virtually all the research on the effects of rewards on intrinsic motivation that is particularly relevant to educational issues is that any undermining effect requires that students initially possess intrinsic motivation. That is, virtually all studies suggesting that rewards can undermine intrinsic motivation involve tasks in which research participants are already interested. Researchers who have included low-interest activities in their studies have generally found that rewards increase students' level of engagement in the activity and even increase intrinsic motivation (e.g., Hall, Lund, & Jackson, 1968; Mynatt et al., 1978; Hitt, Marriott, & Esser, 1992). Although some scholars have cited critiques blaming the educational system for failing to maintain the intrinsic motivation for learning with which students begin their education (e.g., Lepper et al., 1973), others argue that it is false that students are intrinsically motivated by default (e.g., Cameron et al., 2001). Workman and Williams (1980) noted that teachers use rewards as motivators for academic activities in which many children would never engage without some extrinsic reward. Rewards, they explain, would be unnecessary if children could be left to learn whatever most interested them at the time they felt like learning it, but the activities necessary to gain skills such as reading and math are unlikely to be intrinsically motivating for all children. One scholar asserted that "The image of a boundlessly curious child is more of an ethical idea than a result of research," and went so far as to call the work of many researchers "silly," because it involves examining the effects of rewarding behaviors that do not need to be rewarded (Sidorkin, n.d.: 3, 5).

Researchers who question and those who defend the wisdom of using rewards agree that the undermining effects of rewards on intrinsic motivation are circumscribed. There is still vigorous debate about just how circumscribed the effects are, but virtually all established researchers agree that rewards do not always reduce intrinsic motivation. For instance, there is widespread agreement that verbal rewards tend to increase intrinsic motivation. In contrast, the impact of tangible rewards on intrinsic motivation is less clear. Although it may be tempting to assume from the research that praise is superior to tangible rewards, it is important to remember that unexpected tangible rewards do not undermine and, like praise, tend to increase intrinsic motivation. Furthermore, Carton (1996) identified several reasons why existing studies do not permit a fair comparison between verbal and tangible rewards. He pointed out that researchers typically provide tangible rewards just once following the conclusion of task sessions or even weeks later following free time follow-up sessions, whereas praise is usually provided repeatedly during the reward session itself. The apparent benefits of praise relative to tangible rewards may therefore reflect the frequency and immediacy with which the rewards are provided. Even tangible rewards most likely to reduce intrinsic motivation – rewards offered in advance that are not contingent on the quality of task performance – tend to produce weak effects of uncertain practical significance (Cameron 2001; Cameron et al., 2001). It is therefore clear that there is no universal negative effect of rewards on intrinsic motivation.

References

Cameron, J. (2001). Negative effects of reward on intrinsic motivation – a limited phenomenon: Comment on Deci, Koestner, and Ryan (2001). *Review of Educational Research, 71*, 29–42.
Cameron, J. & Pierce, W. D. (1994). Reinforcement, reward, and intrinsic motivation: A meta-analysis. *Review of Educational Research, 64*, 363–423.
Cameron, J. & Pierce, W. D. (1996). The debate about rewards and intrinsic motivation: Protests and accusations do not alter the result. *Review of Educational Research, 66*, 39–51.

Cameron, J., Banko, K. M., & Pierce, W. D. (2001). Pervasive negative effects of rewards on intrinsic motivation: The myth continues. *The Behavior Analyst, 24*, 1–44.

Cameron, J., Pierce, W. D., & So, S. (2004). Rewards, task difficulty, and intrinsic motivation: A test of learned industriousness theory. *Alberta Journal of Educational Research, 50*, 317–320.

Cameron, J., Pierce, W. D., Banko, K. M., & Gear, A. (2005). Achievement-based rewards and intrinsic motivation: A test of cognitive mediators. *Journal of Educational Psychology, 97*, 641–655.

Carton, J. S. (1996). The differential effects of tangible rewards and praise on intrinsic motivation: A comparison of cognitive evaluation theory and operant theory. *The Behavior Analyst, 19*, 237–255.

Davidson, P. & Bucher, B. (1978). Intrinsic interest and extrinsic reward: The effects of a continuing token program on continuing nonconstrained preference. *Behavior Therapy, 9*, 222–234.

Deci, E. L. (1971). Effects of intrinsically mediated rewards on intrinsic motivation. *Journal of Personality and Social Psychology, 18*, 105–115.

Deci, E. L. & Ryan, R. M. (1985). *Intrinsic motivation and self-determination in human behavior*. New York: Plenum Press.

Deci, E. L., Koestner, R., & Ryan, R. M. (1999). A meta-analytic review of experiments examining the effects of extrinsic rewards on intrinsic motivation. *Psychological Bulletin, 125*, 627–668.

Eisenberger, R. & Aselage, J. (2009). Incremental effects of reward on experienced performance pressure: Positive outcomes for intrinsic interest and creativity. *Journal of Organizational Behavior, 30*, 95–117.

Eisenberger, R. & Cameron, J. (1996). Detrimental effects of reward: Reality or myth? *American Psychologist, 51*, 1153–1166.

Eisenberger, R., Pierce, W. D., & Cameron, J. (1999). Effects of reward on intrinsic motivation – negative neutral, and positive: Comment on Deci, Koestner, and Ryan (1999). *Psychological Bulletin, 125*, 677–691.

Eisenberger, R., Rhoades, L., & Cameron, J. (1999). Does pay for performance increase or decrease perceived self-determination and intrinsic motivation? *Journal of Personality and Social Psychology, 77*, 1026–1040.

Flora, S. R. & Flora, D. B. (1999). Effects of intrinsic reinforcement for reading during childhood on reported reading habits of college students. *Psychological Record, 49*, 3–14.

Greene, D., Sternberg, B., & Lepper, M. R. (1976). Overjustification in a token economy. *Journal of Personality and Social Psychology, 34*, 1219–1234.

Hagger, M. S. & Chatzisarantis, N. L. D., (2011). Causality orientations moderate the undermining effect of rewards on intrinsic motivation. *Journal of Experimental Social Psychology, 47*, 485–489.

Hall, R. V., Lund, D., & Jackson, D. (1968). Effects of teacher attention on study behavior. *Journal of Applied Behavior Analysis, 1*, 1–12.

Hitt, D. D., Marriott, R. G., & Esser, J. K. (1992). Effects of delayed rewards and task interest on intrinsic motivation. *Basic and Applied Social Psychology, 13*, 405–414.

Karniol, R. & Ross, M. (1977). The effect of performance-relevant and performance-irrelevant rewards on children's intrinsic motivation. *Child Development, 48*, 482–487.

Kohn, A. (1993). *Punished by rewards: The trouble with gold stars, incentive plans, As, praise, and other bribes*. Boston, MA: Houghton Mifflin.

Lavorata, B. (2013). Undermining intrinsic motivation. *SFU Educational Review, 1*, available at: http://journals.sfu.ca/sfuer/index.php/sfuer/article/viewFile/105/92.

Lepper, M. R., Greene, D., & Nisbett, R. E. (1973). Undermining children's intrinsic interest with extrinsic reward: A test of the "overjustification" hypothesis. *Journal of Personality and Social Psychology, 28*, 129–137.

Levine, F. M. & Fasnacht, G. (1974). Token rewards may lead to token learning. *American Psychologist, 29*, 816–820.

Mynatt, C., Oakley, T., Arkkelin, D., Piccione, A., Margolis, R., & Arkkelin, J. (1978). An examination of overjustification under conditions of extended observation and multiple reinforcement: Overjustification or boredom? *Cognitive Therapy and Research, 2*, 171–177.

Pierce, W. D., Cameron, J., Banko, K. M., & So, S. (2003). Positive effects of rewards and performance standards on intrinsic motivation. *The Psychological Record, 53*, 561–579.

Rosenfeld, D., Folger, R., & Adelman, H. F. (1980). When rewards reflect competence: A qualification of the overjustification effect. *Journal of Personality and Social Psychology, 39*, 368–376.

Ryan R. M. & Deci, E. L. (1996). When paradigms clash: Comments on Cameron and Pierce's claim that rewards do not undermine intrinsic motivation. *Review of Educational Research, 66*, 33–38.

Sidorkin, A. M. (n.d.). *What do we want them to do? Against intrinsic motivation*. White paper. Available at: http://wcet.wiche.edu/wcet/docs/webcasts/BadgesforLearning/WhitePaperonIntrinsicVersusExtrinsicValue.pdf, last accessed March 4, 2015.

Thill, E. E., Mailhot, L., & Mouanda, J. (1998). On how task-contingent rewards, individual differences in causality orientations, and imagery abilities are related to intrinsic motivation and performance. *European Journal of Social Psychology, 28*, 141–158.

Workman, E. A. & Williams, R. L. (1980). Effects of extrinsic rewards on intrinsic motivation in the classroom. *Journal of School Psychology, 18*, 141–147.

7 MYTH: MULTITASKING DOES NOT INHIBIT ACADEMIC PERFORMANCE

Modern life provides many opportunities and incentives for people to multitask; that is, to perform more than one task at a time. Many researchers also consider the related process of task switching – rapidly switching back and forth between tasks – to be a form of multitasking. Despite the incentives, researchers have long known that performance on virtually all tasks that require any kind of conscious thought declines when people attempt to perform multiple tasks simultaneously. Most of the large body of research supporting this conclusion was conducted by researchers using simple, well-controlled laboratory tasks. In recent years, however, researchers have paid increasing attention to the impact of multitasking on more complex outcomes, such as student learning. This broadening of focus has coincided closely with the rapid proliferation of personal technologies, which have dramatically altered many aspects of life, including what students do while studying both inside and outside the classroom.

Given the proliferation of personal technologies over recent decades, it would be reasonable to suspect that multitasking habits might vary with age. Many researchers have investigated this possibility. One group of researchers surveyed more than 1,300 people from three generations ending with those born since 1980, and found that each generation reported significantly more multitasking than the one before (Carrier, Cheevor, Rosen, Benitez, & Change, 2009). Researchers studying a large

Great Myths of Education and Learning, First Edition. Jeffrey D. Holmes.
© 2016 John Wiley & Sons, Inc. Published 2016 by John Wiley & Sons, Inc.

sample of third through twelfth grade students found that young people use "recreational media" such as television, videos, and computers an average of more than six hours per day (Roberts, Foehr, & Rideout, 2005: 36). For at least one quarter of this time students use more than one form of media simultaneously, and more than half of the respondents reported that they multitask most or some of the time while reading. In a subsequent study, Foehr (2006) reported that 35% of the time young people are reading and 60% of the time they are doing homework on a computer, they are also engaged in other tasks such as instant messaging, surfing the web, and watching television. It is interesting to note that the data for these latter two studies indicating frequent multitasking among young people were collected before the majority of young people owned cell phones.

Like their younger counterparts, college students frequently multitask and they often do so while engaged in academic tasks. Judd (2013) evaluated more than 3,000 computer logs from sessions at a university computer lab in Australia and concluded that students multitasked during at least half of the sessions. In a similar study, Judd (2014) found that students multitasked during virtually all computer lab sessions and that Facebook use was a particularly common off-task activity. Calderwood, Ackerman, and Conklin (2014) observed college students studying their own academic material and found that they engaged in off-task behaviors, such as using their cell phones and laptops for activity unrelated to academic work, an average of 35 times during a three-hour session. Finally, Tindell and Bohlander (2012) found that of 269 college students surveyed, 92% reported that they had sent or received text messages in class and 30% said they texted in class daily.

Not only do current students multitask a great deal, they tend to doubt that doing so will have any negative impact on their academic performance. Compared with previous generations, young people today perceive multitasking to be easy (Carrier et al., 2009). Furthermore, they tend to believe that they are proficient at multitasking and that multitasking does not interfere with learning (Karpinski, Kirschner, Ozer, Mellott, & Ochwo, 2013: 1190) or academic performance (Rekart, 2012). In a study of nearly 300 college students, only one in three students doubted his or her ability to engage in texting and follow a lecture simultaneously, and only 29% of the students believed that their academic performance would be affected by texting in class (Clayson & Haley, 2012). Some young people even think that multitasking helps them to concentrate and get schoolwork done (Wallis, 2006). Aagaard (2014) cites claims that because current students grew up with many different technologies, they think differently and are used to doing several things at a time. One scholar even referred to the idea that students can learn effectively while multitasking as a "widely held axiom" (Abaté, 2008: 7). In stark contrast to this axiom, Chabris and Simons (2010) provide numerous examples to illustrate how grossly people tend to overestimate their ability to attend to more than one thing at a time and underestimate the negative effects of divided attention. They demonstrate repeatedly that people often fail to notice or remember seemingly obvious objects and events when their attention is focused elsewhere.

As noted earlier, multitasking occurs when a person performs two or more tasks simultaneously, and task switching occurs when a person switches rapidly between tasks although only a single task is performed at any given moment. For many researchers this distinction is artificial because people are nearly always switching between tasks rather than truly performing multiple tasks at the same time (Pashler, Johnston, & Ruthruff, 2001; Willingham, 2010). Salvucci (2013) accommodated the distinction between multitasking and task switching by conceptualizing multitasking on a continuum along which tasks are located based on how much time people tend to focus on one task before changing to another task. For example, when having a conversation while driving, a person's attention shifts back and forth every few seconds. In contrast, when a person checks email while working on a school project, he or she may spend several minutes on each task between switches. The common effect, as Salvucci emphasizes, is that performance gets worse when people multitask no matter where a particular pair of tasks falls on the continuum. The distinction between multitasking and task switching is so blurry that the American Psychological Association (2006) defines multitasking as the simultaneous performance of two tasks or quickly and repeatedly changing from one task to another. Therefore, the research presented in this chapter addresses both types of processes.

For more than a century, researchers have been studying what happens when people attempt to perform more than one task at a time (Pashler, 1994). Pashler reviewed the work of researchers who had studied how people perform on simple laboratory tasks that usually take less than a second to complete. As one example of this type of research, Rogers and Monsell (1995) conducted four experiments in which participants switched between two simple computerized laboratory tasks: classifying numerical digits as odd or even, or classifying letters as consonants or vowels. The researchers found that switching between these simple tasks – even when participants were well trained and practiced on the individual tasks – caused large increases in the time taken to perform the tasks and in the number of errors committed. Moreover, performance declined even though the switches occurred on a specific schedule so participants knew when they would have to change tasks. Monsell (2003) reviewed additional evidence that switching between simple tasks that are well learned causes people both to slow down and to make more mistakes, and that being forewarned of impending switches does not eliminate the effects on performance. Reviewing research on simultaneous task performance, Pashler (1994) similarly concluded that "people have surprisingly severe limitations on their ability to carry out simultaneously certain cognitive processes that seem fairly trivial from a computational standpoint" (p. 241).

Researchers have proposed many explanations for why performance declines when people multitask. Two of the most commonly cited and broadly supported models have to do with capacity sharing and cognitive bottlenecks (Pashler, 1994). According to Pashler, capacity-sharing models are based on the fact that human beings have limited cognitive processing capacities. Therefore, when people try to do more than one thing at a time, their cognitive resources are divided between the tasks so the capacity devoted to any particular task decreases and performance suffers. In comparison, bottleneck models are based on the observation that for many cognitive processes, it is simply not possible to perform two tasks at the same time. If cognitive processing is devoted to one task, it cannot simultaneously be devoted to another task so performance declines because one task must be put on hold while the other is completed. The decline in performance associated with such bottlenecks is amplified due to a sort of "psychological refractory period," which causes performance to suffer because the process of switching between tasks is itself a task that drains cognitive resources (Pashler et al., 2001: 642).

Until relatively recently it was unclear to what extent the large body of research on multitasking might be relevant to academic learning, which is more complex than most laboratory tasks. Sweller (1988) proposed that off-task activities reduce the cognitive processing capacity available for learning, later asserting that "our limited processing capacity is one of the most important and well known of our cognitive characteristics" (Sweller, 1994: 310). In fact, there is reason to expect that performance declines resulting from multitasking would be even greater for more cognitively complex tasks such as academic learning than for simple laboratory tasks. One group of researchers conducted four experiments using two different types of tasks: classifying simple visual images and solving math problems (Rubinstein, Meyer, & Evans, 2001). They found that multitasking costs increased as task complexity increased. That is, the more complex the task, the more performance declined when people switched between tasks.

In contrast to the perspective that multitasking is likely to inhibit learning, some authors have proposed that current students are in fact less susceptible and perhaps even immune to performance declines due to multitasking. Carrier and colleagues (2009) point out that people born since 1980 grew up with many computerized technologies as integral parts of their lives, and that these young people often report that multitasking is easy. The authors speculate that current young people may have greater cognitive resources for multitasking than members of earlier generations. Other authors likewise claim that since technology is such a major component of daily life, young people have developed the ability to successfully multitask even while learning (see Kirschner & Karpinski, 2010). Recent studies shed light on these claims.

Nearly all of the research specifically addressing the impact of multitasking on academic learning has been published since 2000. However, research conducted somewhat earlier on the effects of watching television while reading and doing homework laid the groundwork for later studies. In experiments in which researchers controlled for a host of variables, including previous academic performance, college placement test scores, and general reading comprehension ability, students who read newspaper articles or completed homework assignments with a television on in the room performed more poorly and took longer to complete their work than students who read in silence (Armstrong, Boiarsky, & Mares, 1991; Armstrong & Chung, 2000; Pool, van der Voort, Beentjes, & Koolstra, 2000; Pool, Koolstra, & van der Voort, 2003a; Pool, Koolstra, & van der Voort, 2003b). These researchers foreshadowed later findings on multitasking, even though they investigated only background television effects and their participants were not required to perform any secondary task related to television viewing.

Recent correlational studies reveal consistent associations between multitasking and poorer academic performance. In a large survey of undergraduate and graduate students in the United States and Europe, Karpinski and colleagues (2013) found that students who reported frequent multitasking had lower grade point averages than students who were not regular multitaskers. Junco (2012; Junco & Cotton, 2012) surveyed more than 1,700 college students and found that more frequent multitasking such as accessing Facebook or texting during class and while studying was correlated with lower overall grade point average – even after controlling for variables such as high school grades and self-reported Internet skills. In a survey of more than 1,100 Canadian college students, those who reported more frequent classroom laptop use for activities unrelated to the course material also reported lower academic satisfaction and lower grade point average (Gaudreau, Miranda, & Gareau, 2014). Fried (2008) observed the same pattern in a sample of US college students after controlling for student ACT scores, high school ranking, and class attendance. Fried also found that in-class laptop use was associated with lower student perceptions of lecture clarity, as well as lower levels of attention and understanding of lectures.

Researchers employing more sophisticated methodologies have similarly found that multitasking is negatively correlated with academic performance. Grace-Martin and Gay (2001) used a proxy Internet server to record the computer browsing activities of 82 college students in two upper-level courses. They found that the amount of time students spent on the Internet during class was negatively associated with final course grades. Kraushaar and Novak (2010) studied college students in a business course in which all students were required to bring laptops to class. Students reported their frequency and type of laptop use during the class and during their classes in general; with their permission, their laptop use was also monitored via spyware installed on their laptops. Students opened an average of 65 computer windows per lecture – nearly two-thirds of which were unrelated to class material. Academic performance was lower among students who opened a greater proportion of distracting windows relative to class-relevant windows than among students with lower proportions of distracting windows. Moreover, the frequency of instant messaging windows was associated with poorer performance on quizzes, exams, and assignments. Similarly, Clayson and Haley (2012) found that the number of text messages that college students sent during class was negatively correlated with their course grades – even after controlling for grade point average and number of absences. Finally, Rosen, Carrier, and Cheever (2013) found that middle school, high school, and college students who accessed Facebook at least once during a brief independent study session had lower grade point averages than students who did not access Facebook.

The authors of these studies generally interpret their results as evidence of the perils of multitasking while engaging in learning activities, but they also acknowledge the correlational nature of their data. Their findings are certainly consistent with the hypothesis that multitasking hinders learning, but the same results would be observed if weak students simply tended to engage in more frequent multitasking than strong students. Perhaps students with weaker academic skills, those who are less satisfied with their educational experience, those who are less academically motivated, and those who struggle to pay attention and understand lectures engage in more multitasking to pass the time and entertain themselves.

Fortunately, a number of recent researchers have used controlled experiments, based on which they can draw conclusions about causality, to investigate whether multitasking actually hinders learning.

One consistent finding from experimental research is that people take longer to complete academic tasks if they are multitasking. Fox, Rosen, and Crawford (2009) randomly assigned college students to study reading comprehension passages from SAT and GRE practice exams either as a single task or while simultaneously exchanging instant messages with a confederate. Students in the multitasking condition took longer to read the passage and to complete the test – even though they exchanged instant messages only during the reading portion and not during the actual test. Another group of researchers (Bowman, Levine, Waite, & Gendron, 2010) randomly assigned college students to read a passage from an abnormal psychology book on a computer screen. Students responded to five instant messages either before or while reading the passage, or read the passages without instant messaging. Again, students who engaged in instant messaging while reading took significantly longer to read the passage than students who messaged before reading the passage, or who did not message at all. Finally, Subrahmanyam and colleagues (2013) had college students read two academic passages; half the students were allowed to multitask by using their cell phones and surfing the Internet while reading, and half were not. Even after controlling for students' working memory capacity which is associated with multitasking ability (see König, Bühner, & Mürling, 2005; Colom, Martínez-Molina, Shih, & Santacreu, 2010), students who multitasked took significantly longer to read the passages than students who did not multitask.

Two important threads run through these experimental studies. First, multitasking students took longer than students who did not multitask to read academic material – even after controlling for the time they actually spent on the secondary tasks. Second, in all of the aforementioned experiments, the multitasking students did not score significantly lower on tests assessing their knowledge of the reading content. In other words, students took longer to study the passages if they were multitasking, but they ultimately appeared to learn as well as non-multitasking students. However, students in all three studies were allowed unlimited time to read the passages. The often large differences in time taken to effectively complete the task (e.g., in the 2010 study by Bowman and colleagues, multitasking students took 22–59% longer to read the passage than non-multitasking students) could become more relevant in real-life environments where students have far more material to master and far greater demands on their time.

In an important series of experiments, Pashler, Kang, and Ip (2013) demonstrated that the impact of multitasking on learning is much greater when time is limited and when learners do not control the pace at which information is presented. In their first experiment, Pashler and colleagues had college students read academic passages on a computer screen with the goal of learning as much information as possible. All students read three passages – each under a different multitasking condition with a secondary task designed to be similar to sending text messages. While reading one passage students performed the messaging task at the end of paragraphs, for the second passage they performed the messaging task at random times within paragraphs, and they read a third passage without interruption. After reading each passage, students completed a test of their passage comprehension. As in previous studies that did not involve time limits, multitasking students took longer to read the text, but there was no significant difference between multitaskers and non-multitaskers in how well they scored on comprehension tests. Pashler and colleagues replicated this experiment using auditory recordings of the passages rather than having students read. When students multitasked, the auditory recording stopped while they completed the messaging task and then resumed when the secondary task was complete. Again, there was no significant difference in scores on comprehension tests of the passage content based on whether students multitasked.

Finally, Pashler and colleagues (2013) conducted a third experiment in which students listened to two passages either without interruption or while engaged in random multitasking. The noteworthy difference in this experiment was that the recorded passages continued to play while students engaged in the secondary messaging task – much like the flow of content during a classroom lecture. In this case, students performed significantly worse on the comprehension test when they had multitasked than when they had listened without interruption. The researchers concluded that multitasking is likely to have a negative impact on learning in settings where the presentation of content is controlled by someone other than the student. However, they were also careful to state that their results do not indicate that multitasking while studying is harmless as long as students can control the pace of presentation. Pashler and colleagues noted that the learning task they used did not require students to integrate information or solve higher-level problems. The researchers speculated that multitasking might have an even more powerful impact on higher-level learning and skill development.

Several other experimental studies substantiate the conclusion that at least in environments akin to classroom settings, multitasking inhibits learning. Some researchers have studied how multitasking affects learning in actual classrooms, while others have used simulated lectures to avoid contamination from extraneous factors that might affect learning in real classrooms. One group of researchers (Ellis, Daniels, & Jauregui, 2010) tested students in a college accounting course who were randomly assigned to listen to a lecture with their cell phones turned off, or to send the professor three text messages at any point during the lecture. Students' scores on a test of the lecture content were significantly lower in the texting condition than in the non-texting condition. It is noteworthy that the methodology in this study was not particularly well controlled to mimic typical student texting behavior. Students could have sent all three texts at one time, and could also have sent other texts in addition to the ones assigned. Nonetheless, students who used their phones during class learned less effectively than students whose phones were turned off. In a similar study, Dietz and Henrich (2014) recruited college students to watch a video of a psychology lecture in a classroom. Even after the researchers controlled for students' self-reported texting ability and level of distraction during the lecture, students randomly assigned to send text messages during the video performed significantly more poorly on a test of the lecture content than students whose phones were turned off.

In a more systematic study of the effects of texting on classroom learning, Rosen, Lim, Carrier, and Cheever (2011) randomly assigned college students in classrooms to receive zero, four, or eight text messages during a video lecture. The text messages required simple responses unrelated to lecture content. Despite the researchers' efforts to systematize the experimental conditions, many students reported that during the lecture they received and responded to texts in addition to those associated with the study. Therefore, the researchers categorized students based on the number of texts sent and received, and found that infrequent texters scored significantly higher on a test of the lecture content than frequent texters. The length of texts also was negatively associated with test scores. Interestingly, although the researchers instructed students to respond immediately when they received the assigned text messages, some waited more than four minutes to respond. These students scored higher on the knowledge test than students who responded to texts more quickly. Conrad and Marsh (2014) likewise studied the impact of systematic messaging interruptions on learning. Paralleling the results from texting studies, students who were interrupted by instant messages during a simulated lecture scored significantly lower on a test of lecture content than students who were not interrupted.

Texting and instant messaging are certainly not the only secondary tasks in which students engage during class. In one relatively early study, Hembrooke and Gay (2003) randomly assigned students in an actual class to listen to a lecture either with or without access to a laptop. During one class meeting, students in the control condition left the room to complete a laboratory activity, while the rest of the students listened to a lecture and were encouraged to use their laptops as they usually would during class. Next, these multitasking students left the room and the control students returned to hear the same lecture, but were instructed to keep their laptops closed. Students in the laptop condition scored significantly lower on a test of lecture content than students whose laptops remained closed. Two months later the researchers replicated their study, but reversed the conditions so that students from the original no-laptop condition used their laptops during a lecture, and those who had used their laptops in the previous lecture kept their laptops closed. Once again, students who used laptops scored significantly lower on a test of lecture content than students who did not use laptops. Interestingly, Hembrooke and Gay acquired information on the specific types of laptop activity in which students engaged during class and found that using laptops for Internet searches related to course content was not associated with better test performance than using laptops for unrelated searches and activities. In other words, laptop use distracted from learning even when students conducted Internet searchers relevant to class material.

In another study conducted in an actual classroom, Wood and colleagues (2012) randomly assigned college students to listen to statistics and research methods lectures under a variety of multitasking conditions. Students assigned to texting, emailing, and instant messaging conditions interacted during class with research assistants following scripts. The researchers also included a condition in which students searched for information in Facebook profiles during class. Students in control conditions took notes on paper, on a laptop, or had no restrictions on their technology use. There were some clear findings such as the observation that Facebook users learned significantly less of the lecture content than students who simply took notes. However, the researchers were limited in the extent to which they could draw conclusions because only 57% of all participants reported fully adhering to the instructions for their condition. Many students used technology when they were not supposed to, or used more than just their assigned type of technology. It is noteworthy that across all conditions, students who reported not using any technology scored significantly higher on the test than those who reported using technology. Moreover, there was no significant difference in test performance between light, moderate, and heavy multitaskers. It appears that any level of multitasking inhibits learning.

The difficulty in getting students to comply with assigned research instructions in real classrooms illustrates the value of using simulated environments, which permit greater experimental control, to study multitasking. In one such study, Risko, Buchanan, Medimorec, and Kingstone (2013) randomly assigned students to watch a video lecture either while performing simple computer tasks such as writing emails, posting on Facebook, and searching the Internet, or to focus only on the lecture. Students who did not engage in the computer tasks spent much more time attending to the lecture and scored significantly higher on a test of lecture content than students who engaged in the computer tasks.

Multitasking during class may even reduce learning among students who do not directly multitask themselves. Sana, Weston, and Cepeda (2013) had college students attend a lecture with all students taking notes using their laptops, but with half randomly assigned to engage in online tasks unrelated to the lecture content. Consistent with other studies, students who multitasked performed significantly more poorly than students who did not multitask on a test assessing their knowledge of simple facts from the lecture as well as their ability to apply their acquired knowledge to novel scenarios. Sana and colleagues then conducted a second experiment in which non-multitasking students were randomly assigned to classroom locations where they either could or could not see the laptops of peers who were multitasking. Despite taking notes of similar quality, students who could see other students multitasking learned significantly less from the lecture than students who could not see other students multitasking. Moreover, seeing others engage in off-task activates had an even greater negative effect on learning than actually engaging in those activities.

One team of researchers who studied multitasking in terms of specific brain functions provided some interesting insight into why many people are unaware that their performance and learning are negatively affected by multitasking. Foerde, Knowlton, and Poldrack (2006) explained that declarative memory requires conscious thought and is relevant to acquiring flexible knowledge, whereas habit memory is relevant to task performance that does not require much conscious thought. They used functional magnetic resonance imaging (fMRI) to scan the brains of participants learning a novel classification task requiring them to predict weather based on patterns of data. Participants learned this exercise either as a single task or while simultaneously performing a task requiring them to count different auditory tones. All participants then performed the classification tasks without any distractions and were assessed on their flexible declarative knowledge about the tasks. Although performance on the classification task itself differed only slightly based on whether or not participants engaged in a secondary task while learning, participants possessed significantly more declarative knowledge after learning the task without distraction. Foerde and colleagues concluded that "performance of the secondary task effectively impaired acquisition of flexible knowledge" (p. 11779). Moreover, their fMRI data showed that the presence of the distractor task during learning led to greater activation in an area of the brain associated with automatic, habitual learning, whereas learning without distraction led to greater activation of areas associated with more flexible declarative knowledge. In other words, learning with distraction led to memorization of content, but not to knowledge that could be applied to novel situations. As Bradley (2011) points out, this pattern may help explain why students who multitask often think they are learning effectively. Since they can remember some information they are less likely to become aware that they are not learning as deeply or as effectively as they could if they avoided multitasking.

Despite life-long exposure to numerous personal technologies and frequent attempts to do more than one thing at a time, there is virtually no evidence that young people are able to successfully multitask in ways that members of previous generations could not (Willingham, 2010; Aagaard, 2014). Bennett, Maton, and Kervin (2008) are critical of the whole concept that young people think differently because they are digital natives, arguing that such claims are not based on scientific evidence. In fact, some evidence suggests that people who multitask more frequently actually suffer greater performance deficits than people who multitask less often. Ophir, Nass, and Wagner (2009) found that although high and low multitaskers did not differ in SAT scores, creativity, or scores on any of five primary personality traits or need for cognition, high multitaskers were more affected by distractors when trying to perform a task. High multitaskers were less able than low multitaskers to ignore irrelevant stimuli both from the environment and from their own memories. In a study directly relevant to classroom learning, Risko and colleagues (2013) found that students who regularly used a laptop during class were no better at laptop multitasking than students who did not usually use laptops in class. At least for complex cognitive tasks, there is little evidence that people can learn to be highly effective multitaskers.

The large body of research demonstrating performance declines when people try to do more than one thing at a time appears to translate well to academic learning. When students engage in secondary tasks while studying independently – and especially when they do so in classrooms – they reduce the amount of working memory and processing capacity that they can devote to academic material and their learning is likely to be less than optimal. Willingham (2010) astutely points out that "we remember what we think about," so everyone performs better when they focus on one task at a time (p. 27). Therefore, dividing attention between academic work and anything else is likely to reduce learning.

References

Aagaard, J. (2014). Media multitasking, attention, and distraction: A critical discussion. *Phenomenology and the Cognitive Sciences*. Advance online publication.

Abaté, C. J. (2008). You say multitasking like it's a good thing. *NEA Higher Education Journal, 24,* 7–13.

American Psychological Association (2006). Multitasking: Switching costs. Available at: http://www.apa.org/research/action/multitask.aspx.

Armstrong, G. B. & Chung, L. (2000). Background television and reading memory in context. *Communication Research, 27,* 327–352.

Armstrong, G. B., Boiarsky, G. A., & Mares, M. (1991). Background television and reading performance. *Communication Monographs, 58,* 235–253.

Bennett, S., Maton, K., & Kervin, L. (2008). The "digital natives" debate: A critical review of the evidence. *British Journal of Educational Technology, 39,* 775–786.

Bowman, L. L., Levine, L. E., Waite, B. M., & Gendron, M. (2010). Can students really multitask? An experimental study of instant messaging while reading. *Computers and Education, 54,* 927–931.

Bradley, K. (2011). Can teens really do it all? Techno-multitasking, learning, and performance. *Independent School, 70,* 92–99.

Calderwood, C., Ackerman, P. L., & Conklin, E. M. (2014). What else to college students "do" while studying? An investigation of multitasking. *Computers and Education, 75,* 19–29.

Carrier, L. M., Cheever, N. A., Rosen, L. D., Benitez, S., & Chang, J. (2009). Multitasking across generations: Multitasking choices and difficulty ratings in three generations of Americans. *Computers in Human Behavior, 25,* 483–489.

Chabris, C. & Simons, D. (2010). *The invisible gorilla and other ways our intuitions deceive us.* New York: Crown.

Clayson, D. E. & Haley, D. A. (2012). An introduction to multitasking and texting: Prevalence and impact on grades and GPA in marketing classes. *Journal of Marketing Education, 35,* 26–40.

Colom, R., Martínez-Molina, A., Shih, P. C., & Santacreu, J. (2010). Intelligence, working memory, and multitasking performance. *Intelligence, 38,* 543–551.

Conrad, M. A. & Marsh, R. F. (2014). Interest level improves learning but does not moderate the effects of interruption: An experiment using simultaneous multitasking. *Learning and Individual Differences, 30*, 112–117.

Ellis, Y., Daniels, B., & Jauregui, A. (2010). The effect of multitasking on the grade performance of business students. *Research in Higher Education Journal, 8*, 1–10.

Dietz, S. & Henrich, C. (2014). Texting as a distraction to learning in college students. *Computers in Human Behavior, 36*, 163–167.

Foehr, U. G. (2006). *Media multitasking among American youth: Prevalence, predictors, and pairings*. Menlo Park, CA: Kaiser Family Foundation.

Foerde, K., Knowlton, B. J., & Poldrack, R. A. (2006). Modulation of competing memory systems by distraction. *PNAS, 103*, 11778–11783.

Fox, A. B., Rosen, J., & Crawford, M. (2009). Distractions, distractions: Does instant messaging affect college students' performance on a concurrent reading comprehension task? *Cyber Psychology & Behavior, 12*, 51–53.

Fried, C. B. (2008). In-class laptop use and its effects on student learning. *Computers and Education, 50*, 906–914.

Gaudreau, P., Miranda, D., & Gareau, A. (2014). Canadian university students in wireless classrooms: What do they do on their laptops and does it really matter? *Computers and Education, 70*, 245–255.

Grace-Martin, M. & Gay, G. (2001). Web browsing, mobile computing and academic performance. *Educational Technology and Society, 4*, 95–107.

Hembrooke, H. & Gay, G. (2003). The laptop and the lecture: The effects of multitasking in learning environments. *Journal of Computing in Higher Education, 15*, 46–64.

Judd, T. (2013). Making sense of multitasking: Key behaviours. *Computers and Education, 63*, 358–367.

Judd, T. (2014). Making sense of multitasking: The role of Facebook. *Computers and Education, 70*, 194–202.

Junco, R. (2012). In-class multitasking and academic performance. *Computers in Human Behavior, 28*, 2236–2243.

Junco, R. & Cotton, S. R. (2012). No A 4 U: The relationship between multitasking and academic performance. *Computers and Education, 59*, 505–514.

Kirschner, P. A. & Karpinski, A. C. (2010). Facebook and academic performance. *Computers in Human Behavior, 26*, 1237–1245.

Karpinski, A. C., Kirschner, P. A., Ozer, I., Mellott, J. A., & Ochwo, P. (2013). An exploration of social networking site use, multitasking, and academic performance among United States and European university students. *Computers in Human Behavior, 29*, 1182–1192.

König, C. J., Bühner, M., & Mürling, G. (2005). Working memory, fluid intelligence, and attention are predictors of multitasking performance, but polychronicity and extraversion are not. *Human Performance, 18*, 243–266.

Kraushaar, J. M. & Novak, D. C. (2010). Examining the effects of student multitasking with laptops during the lecture. *Journal of Information Systems Education, 21*, 241–251.

Monsell, S. (2003). Task switching. *Trends in Cognitive Science, 7*, 134–140.

Ophir, E., Nass, C., & Wagner, A. D. (2009). Cognitive control in media multi-taskers. *PNAS, 106*, 15883–15887.

Pashler, H. (1994). Dual-task interference in simple tasks: Data and theory. *Psychological Bulletin, 116*, 220–244.

Pashler, H., Johnston, J. C., & Ruthruff, E. (2001). Attention and performance. *Annual Review of Psychology, 52*, 629–651.

Pashler, H., Kang, S. H. K., & Ip, R. Y. (2013). Does multitasking impair studying? Depends on timing. *Applied Cognitive Psychology, 27*, 593–599.

Pool, M. M., Koolstra, C. M., & Van der Voort, T. H. (2003a). Distraction effects of background soap operas on homework performance: An experimental study enriched with observational data. *Educational Psychology, 23*, 361–380.

Pool, M. M., Koolstra, C. M., & Van der Voort, T. H. (2003b). The impact of background radio and television on high school students' homework performance. *Journal of Communication, 53*, 74–87.

Pool, M. M., Van der Voort, T. H., Beentjes, J. W. J., & Koolstra, C. M. (2000). Background television as an inhibitor of performance on easy and difficult homework assignments. *Communication Research, 27*, 293–326.

Rekart, J. L. (2012). Taking on multitasking. *Kappan, 93*, 60–63.

Risko, E. F., Buchanan, D., Medimorec, S., & Kingstone, A. (2013). Everyday attention: Mind wandering and computer use during lectures. *Computers and Education, 68*, 275–283.

Roberts, D. F., Foehr, U. G., & Rideout, V. (2005). *Generation M: Media in the lives of 8–18 year-olds*. Menlo Park, CA: Kaiser Family Foundation.

Rogers, R. D. & Monsell, S. (1995). Costs of a predictable switch between simple cognitive tasks. *Journal of Experimental Psychology: General, 124*, 207–231.

Rosen, L. D., Carrier, L. M., & Cheever, N. A. (2013). Facebook and texting made me do it: Media-induced task-switching while studying. *Computers in Human Behavior, 29*, 948–958.

Rosen, L. D., Lim, A. F., Carrier, L. M., & Cheever, N. A. (2011). An empirical examination of the educational impact of text message-induced task switching in the classroom: Educational implications and strategies to enhance learning. *Psicología Educativa, 17*, 163–177.

Rubinstein, J. S., Meyer, D. E., & Evans, J. E. (2001). Executive control of cognitive processes in task switching. *Journal of Experimental Psychology: Human Perception and Performance, 27*, 763–797.

Salvucci, D. D. (2013). Multitasking. In: J. D. Lee & A. Kirlik (Eds.), *The Oxford handbook of cognitive engineering* (pp. 57–66). New York: Oxford University Press.

Sana, F., Weston, T., & Cepeda, N. J. (2013). Laptop multitasking hinders classroom learning for both users and nearby peers. *Computers and Education, 62*, 24–31.

Subrahmanyam, K., Michikyan, M., Clemmons, C., Carrillo, R., Uhls, Y. T., & Greenfield, P. M. (2013). Learning from paper, learning from screens: Impact of screen reading and multitasking conditions on reading and writing among college students. *International Journal of Cyber Behavior, Psychology and Learning, 3*, 1–27.

Sweller, J. (1988). Cognitive load during problem solving: Effects on learning. *Cognitive Science, 12*, 257–285.

Sweller, J. (1994). Cognitive load theory, learning difficulty, and instructional design. *Learning and Instruction, 4*, 295–312.

Tindell, D. R. & Bohlander, R. W. (2012). The use and abuse of cell phones and text messaging in the classroom: A survey of college students. *College Teaching, 60*, 1–9.

Wallis, C. (2006). genM: The multitasking generation. *Time*. Available at: http://content.time.com/time/magazine/article/0,9171,1174696,00.html.

Willingham, D. T. (2010). Have technology and multitasking rewired how students learn? *American Educator, 34*, 23–28, 42.

Wood, E., Zivcakova, L., Gentile, P., Archer, K., De Pasquale, D., & Nosko, A. (2012). Examining the impact of off-task multi-tasking with technology on real-time classroom learning. *Computers and Education, 58*, 365–374.

8 MYTH: PEOPLE ARE EITHER LEFT-BRAINED OR RIGHT-BRAINED

The belief that the two hemispheres of the brain are highly specialized to perform different types of cognitive tasks is well entrenched among educators and the general public. In one survey, 89% of primary and secondary school teachers endorsed the belief that differences in hemispheric dominance across students can help to explain differences in learning (Dekker, Lee, Howard-Jones, & Jolles, 2012). Such beliefs lead educators to categorize students as either left-brained or right-brained based on students' preferences for particular types of task – a process that often leads to the assertion that instruction can and should be tailored to activate processing in one brain hemisphere or the other (e.g., Freed & Parsons, 1998). Although there is a large and fascinating body of research illustrating the relative lateralization of certain specific brain processes, many interpretations of this research reflect extreme oversimplifications and neglect realities of how the brain actually functions.

Researchers often use the term *hemisphericity* to refer to the idea that people tend toward particular ways of thinking based on predominance of function in one brain hemisphere or the other (Beaumont, Young, & McManus, 1984). The most common assumptions associated with hemisphericity are that language and logical analysis are the province of the left hemisphere, whereas the right hemisphere is the nonverbal center for emotional processing, spatial abilities, creative and artistic tasks, and holistic thinking (Corballis, 1999; Lindell & Kidd, 2011). These assumptions have been translated into countless proposals for enhancing learning and education.

Great Myths of Education and Learning, First Edition. Jeffrey D. Holmes.
© 2016 John Wiley & Sons, Inc. Published 2016 by John Wiley & Sons, Inc.

Most proposals focus on enhancing functioning of the nonverbal and holistic right hemisphere, since education is ostensibly biased toward left hemisphere verbal and analytic skills (Klein, 1980; see also Hardyck & Haapanen, 1979). Beaumont (1983) cited many claims that Western educational methods neglect right hemisphere processes and that instruction targeting the right hemisphere would improve learning and human life in many ways. Samples (1975) claimed that "education is contrived to focus on the functions of the left," and that "right cerebral functions and intuition have been demeaned" (p. 23). Prince (1978) echoed this claim, asserting that children are born with the ability to use both hemispheres, but that culturally valued skills cause the left hemisphere to gradually suppress the right hemisphere. Therefore, by adolescence, he claims, people are only using between 5% and 20% of their potential. Although he offered no evidence to support these statistics, he claimed that learning would be greatly improved if people relearned to use their right hemispheres. Harris (1988) cited many more claims that the educational system is too focused on the left hemisphere to the detriment of students' creative abilities, as well as many claims that right-brain training would bring about improvements in math skills, creativity, and even mental health. Such claims have not diminished over the years. Recent researchers cite evidence of belief among teachers that traditional educational strategies emphasize skills relevant to the left hemisphere, but not the creative right hemisphere, and cite many examples of educational interventions designed to improve learning by focusing on the right hemisphere (Bruner, 2008; Lindell, 2011; Lindell and Kidd, 2011).

Some authors took hemisphericity assumptions a step further. Sonnier and Sonnier (1995) interpreted evidence of hemispheric specialization to mean that some people think – from birth – exclusively in either a visual or analytical way, and that most people have a preference for one thinking style over the other. They reasoned that people must also learn in very different ways according to their hemispheric dominance. Other scholars similarly interpreted hemispheric specialization research to indicate that students may learn more if teachers match their instructional style to students' preferences for linguistic and analytical versus spatial and holistic thinking (Wheatley, Frankland, Mitchell, & Kraft, 1978; see also Chapter 2, above, on learning styles for more information on the matching idea). For example, Wheatley and colleagues proposed that students who struggle in math might improve if teachers focused on their spatial abilities. Klein (1980) claimed that some learning-disabled students are simply right-hemisphere dominant and only appear disabled because society disproportionately emphasizes verbal skills. Moreover, educators might assume that students who lack interest or proficiency in creative, artistic, empathic, and nonverbal activities rely too heavily on their left hemispheres or have underdeveloped right hemispheres.

Researchers have traced the origins of the right-brain, left-brain dichotomy to cultural factors long predating modern knowledge about brain function. For thousands of years, most people believed that left-handed people systematically differed from right-handed people in a variety of ways, and associated right and left with divergent types of morality and behavior (Corballis, 1980). Wieder (1984) cites historical examples going back to the Greeks to support his contention that modern assumptions about the distinctions between left and right hemisphere function merely represent a repackaging of an earlier assumed – and debunked – dichotomy between cognition and emotion. Corballis similarly concluded that the concept of hemisphericity is driven more by millennia-old beliefs about right and left than by scientific evidence.

Contemporary views regarding hemisphericity are certainly based on evidence more sophisticated and more scientific than long-standing cultural assumptions. The first major neuropsychological advance relevant to hemispheric specialization was Paul Broca's nineteenth-century report on patients with localized damage in the left hemisphere who largely lost the ability to speak (Berker, Berker, & Smith, 1986). Subsequent research confirmed that a region of the brain necessary for speech that came to be known as Broca's area is nearly always located in the left hemisphere, and that damage to specific areas of the left hemisphere often cause people to lose the ability to read, speak, or comprehend language (Sperry, 1982). According to Sperry, these patterns led to the generalization that the left hemisphere is the dominant, language-based hemisphere whereas the right is nondominant and nonverbal.

Research on hemispheric specialization catapulted into scientific and public consciousness as a result of landmark research conducted in the 1960s on patients who had undergone split-brain operations. In normal brains, the two cerebral hemispheres are connected via a band of nerve fibers called the corpus callosum, as well as several other neural pathways or commissures. These connections allow neural impulses to travel between the hemispheres – allowing the two halves of the brain to communicate. Although such interactivity is usually adaptive, it poses problems for patients with severe epilepsy whose seizures are not adequately controlled by medication. For such patients, the links between the hemispheres provide a conduit for localized seizures to spread throughout the brain. In rare cases, such patients underwent a procedure – almost never used today – in which surgeons cut all neural fibers connecting the cerebral hemispheres in order to control the seizures.

Split-brain operations had been conducted on animals for many years before any humans underwent the procedure. Sperry (1961) described findings from early animal research – most notably observing that the surgeries made it appear in some ways that the animals had two brains because each hemisphere appeared to have no access to the experiences of the other. Later research with humans who had undergone the procedure led to similar conclusions. Each hemisphere appeared to have its own separate memories, perceptions, and experiences, but no awareness of processes occurring in the other hemisphere (Sperry, 1982).

In a series of fascinating tests, Sperry and his colleagues made a variety of remarkable observations regarding the potential localization of certain functions to one hemisphere or the other. The researchers designed laboratory procedures that allowed them to present visual, auditory, or tactile information to a single hemisphere and observe how the patient responded. By far the most noteworthy hemispheric differences involved language. Sperry (1964) reported that when an object was presented only to the right hemisphere of the brain, the patient could recognize the object and respond appropriately, but could not name the object or use language to describe it. In contrast, patients had no difficulty naming objects that were presented to their left hemispheres. Such findings appeared to substantiate existing theories about the localization of language in the left hemisphere. Other research suggested left hemisphere dominance for mathematical calculations as well (Gazzaniga & Sperry, 1967).

Split-brain research findings gave rise to the idea that people with normal brains might in fact have two minds (Samples, 1975; Ornstein, 1977); this idea "proved irresistible" because it fit so well with long-standing cultural beliefs that left and right have different characteristics (Corballis, 1980: 286). Almost immediately a host of authors extrapolated from split-brain studies and earlier research on patients with brain damage to assert the importance of the dichotomous nature of brain function. Some authors asserted that the right hemisphere becomes idle during language tasks and the left hemisphere becomes idle during spatial tasks (Ornstein & Galin, 1976). Other authors concluded that the left hemisphere is expressive, rational, logical, and dominant, whereas the right hemisphere is perceptive, emotional, intuitive, and subordinate (see Dobbs, 1989). Still others asserted that the right hemisphere processes information simultaneously, whereas the left employs a sequential approach (Samples, 1975).

Split-brain research played a profound role in the evolution of hemisphericity assumptions, but it appears that many consumers of the research did not consider the limitations of applying data from split-brain patients to the general population. Split-brain patients by definition do not have normal brains. They have suffered from a life-long brain disorder severe enough to require dramatically invasive brain surgery. In addition to potential effects of the surgery itself, there is some evidence that the patients' life-long brain abnormalities could have caused brain reorganization prior to the surgery – further differentiating their brains from normal brains (Hardyck & Haapanen, 1979). Moreover, the large early literature on split-brain effects was based on extremely small samples – usually only three or four patients who showed up in repeated studies (Beaumont, 1981). Perhaps most importantly, the apparent hemispheric differences observed in split-brain patients were usually not detectable outside the laboratory. Even in his early work, Sperry (1964; Gazzaniga & Sperry, 1967) emphasized that the split-brain operation caused little change in everyday behavior or broad intellectual ability. Sperry observed no substantial effects until patients were tested with specific laboratory procedures while blindfolded, engaged in specialized visual tasks where a word or image is very quickly flashed only to one hemisphere, or when only allowed to use one hand to perform tasks. As fascinating as the effects were, neither the brains of split-brain patients nor the experimental tasks necessary to detect effects of the surgery are particularly relevant to learning or cognitive functioning in normal populations.

Split-brain research is certainly not the only source of evidence for the relative hemispheric lateralization of some cognitive functions. Researchers also have developed laboratory techniques to study lateralization in people with normal brains. In dichotic listening studies, researchers present verbal information to participants via only one ear so that it is first accessible to a single hemisphere rather than both hemispheres simultaneously. In visual field studies, researchers present visual stimuli so that it is initially accessible to only one hemisphere. Researchers employing such strategies assess the speed with which participants respond to various kinds of stimuli presented to each hemisphere. For example, responses to verbal stimuli sometimes occur more rapidly when the information is presented to the left hemisphere, which people often interpret as evidence for broad left hemisphere dominance for language (e.g., Wheatley et al., 1978). Researchers have also used electroencephalograms (EEG) and, more recently, brain imaging technologies to assess brain function while participants perform different types of tasks. The findings emerging across these diverse methodologies demonstrate that brain function does not conform to a simple right–left dichotomy.

The most broadly cited hemispheric differences in brain function involve language tasks. As noted above, many scholars have concluded that language is a left-hemisphere function and that the right hemisphere is primarily or even exclusively nonverbal (see Beaumont, 1981). However, a thorough review of the research indicates a far more nuanced picture. Lindell (2006) provides perhaps the best summary of this nuance in her review of the role of the right hemisphere in language. She cites a great deal of evidence from brain-imaging research that both hemispheres play important roles in both speech production and comprehension. She concluded that while the left hemisphere is dominant for speech intended for deliberate, rational communication, the right hemisphere is highly influential for automatic speech that does not communicate new ideas such as counting, reciting memorized rhymes, and reciting the days of the week. Lindell also cited evidence that the right hemisphere helps process the broader meaning of linguistic information. She explains that interpreting the meaning of language requires not only the ability to understand words, but also to understand the links between many phrases and sentences. The right hemisphere is therefore critical for integrating various components of language into a meaningful whole. Lindell also points out that when the right hemisphere is damaged, a person's ability to interpret language in nonliteral ways (e.g., understanding metaphor, sarcasm, or humor) also suffers. Furthermore, the right hemisphere plays a major role in altering the pitch and rhythm of speech to communicate different meanings using the same words. Accordingly, it also dominates in comprehending paralinguistic information; people with right hemisphere damage often do not recognize emotions conveyed by tone of voice. Amazingly, Lindell cited evidence that hemispheric dominance for language processing even varies as a function of the specific visual characteristics of the message. When language is presented in the form of handwriting, script-like text, or unfamiliar fonts, the right hemisphere appears dominant for processing the information; however, when the fonts are simple and familiar, the left hemisphere appears dominant.

Other researchers have similarly questioned the exclusivity of the left hemisphere's role in language. Even in their early work on split-brain effects, Gazzaniga and Sperry (1967) explained that the language deficits in the right hemisphere are mostly expressive rather than receptive. That is, the right hemisphere can comprehend both written and spoken language – even language that is complex – but cannot produce speech (see also Sperry, 1982). Gazzaniga and Sperry speculated that findings that the right hemisphere has little or no language ability may be attributable to the use of insufficient experimental tests. Researchers have also noted that although typical brain development usually results in left dominance for many language functions, the right hemisphere has the potential to develop such abilities if the left is damaged early in life – indicating that there is no inherent biological limitation that makes the right hemisphere nonverbal (Corballis, 1999). Even Broca, who more than 100 years ago discovered an area of the left hemisphere associated with speech production, asserted that his findings did not indicate that language was exclusively a left-hemisphere function (Lindell, 2006).

In contrast to claims about left-hemisphere function, abilities supposedly associated with the right hemisphere are more diverse and include spatial skills, visual perception, musical perception, and creativity (Corballis, 1980; Runco, 2004). Similar to presumed left-hemisphere skills, the evidence is sparse that any complex cognitive processes involve near or complete right-hemisphere dominance. Lindell (2011) reviewed numerous studies investigating hemispheric dominance in creativity – usually defined in research as the ability to produce original, useful ideas. She cited several studies suggesting that the right hemisphere is often somewhat more active during creative verbal tasks such as divergent thinking and producing original stories, as well as nonverbal tasks such as mentally improvising a dance routine or creating drawings. However, she also cited several studies in which researchers using fMRI, EEG, and measures of cerebral blood flow found that creative thinking requires integrated activation of both hemispheres, and that better hemispheric integration is associated with greater creativity. Interestingly, highly creative people show activation across both hemispheres when solving problems, whereas the brain activity in people low in creativity is more lateralized to the right hemisphere (Carlsson, Wendt, & Risberg, 2000). Lindell proposes that "enhanced integration enhances creativity," because creativity requires the ability to access a broad array of memories, as well as the ability to conceptually link many divergent ideas (p. 487). She explains that the discrepancy between studies showing right dominance during creative tasks and those showing that hemispheric integration is more important may be due to the use of very different creativity and brain activation measures across studies. She also noted that the relative activation of the hemispheres would vary based simply on the point during the task when activation measurements are taken. It is likely that for many creative tasks, areas of the right hemisphere would be dominant at some stages of the task, whereas the left hemisphere would be dominant at other stages.

Other researchers have similarly concluded that creativity is anything but a predominantly right-brain process. Katz (1997) asserted that "The claim that creativity is located 'in' the right hemisphere should be dispelled with at once" (p. 204). He cited a host of studies indicating that creativity requires the integration of numerous cognitive processes in both hemispheres, and pointed out that the evidence that does exist for hemispheric specialization of some very specific creative tasks is based on very few studies. He further noted that the dominant hemisphere for creative endeavors may depend on the specific domain. For example, the processes necessary for artistic creativity are likely different from those necessary for mathematical creativity. Moreover, creativity is not purely intuitive but requires logic (Runco, 2004). Therefore "any creative act, from solving a puzzle to composing an aria, requires the integration of processing in both hemispheres" (Lindell, 2011: 485).

One particularly interesting example of how empirical evidence has not conformed to assumptions about hemispheric dominance pertains to musical abilities. Common conceptualizations of hemispheric dominance usually include the assumption that musical abilities are localized in the right hemisphere. Bever and Chiarello (1974) cited research suggesting that people are more proficient at recognizing melodies presented only to the right hemisphere than melodies presented only to the left hemisphere. However, Bever and Chiarello adeptly observed a noteworthy exception to this pattern in a study of musicians. They conducted their own study and found that while nonmusicians performed better on a melody recognition task when the melodies were presented to the right hemisphere, musicians performed better when the melodies were presented to the left hemisphere. The researchers suggested that trained musicians process melodies as a sequence of interrelated components, whereas nonmusicians process melodies holistically. In contrast to the assumption that the right hemisphere is dominant for musical abilities, the researchers concluded that the left hemisphere plays an increasingly significant role in music processing as musical skill increases.

In a more technologically sophisticated study conducted 35 years later, researchers used brain imaging to compare the brain activation of musicians and nonmusicians on a divergent thinking task (Gibson, Folley, & Park, 2009). The task did not involve musical ability, but rather required participants to think of possible uses for a variety of objects. During the task, nonmusicians showed greater left-hemisphere activation – not right-hemisphere activation as many would expect to occur during a creative task. Moreover, the brain activity of musicians was more integrated across hemispheres. The researchers suggested that since playing a musical instrument requires integrated cooperation of both hemispheres – coordinated movement of both hands – musicians must draw on both hemispheres simultaneously, which, over time, might increase integration. In any case, neither musical ability nor creativity are exclusively right-brain processes.

Visual–spatial abilities constitute another type of skill often attributed to the right hemisphere. Kalbfleisch and Gillmarten (2013) define visual–spatial abilities as those reflecting mental processing and manipulation of images and patterns, and holistic approaches for solving problems. They reviewed many studies revealing slightly greater right-hemisphere activation when people completed visual–spatial tasks, but noted that the relative differences in hemispheric activity are slight and too weak to suggest right-hemispheric dominance. Moreover, they cited additional studies showing activation across both hemispheres during visual–spatial tasks, and even some studies indicating left-hemisphere dominance. Kalbfleisch and Gillmarten further observed that when the right hemisphere is damaged, the left hemisphere can learn to perform visual–spatial tasks usually associated with the right hemisphere – further demonstrating that lateralization is flexible and that the left hemisphere is not inherently deficient with regard to spatial abilities. Bruner (2008) agrees that "It makes no sense to claim that spatial reasoning is a right hemisphere task" (p. 56).

Perhaps most interestingly, Kalbfleisch and Gillmarten (2013) reported that greater hemispheric lateralization is generally observed in people of low cognitive ability, but not in those with normal or higher ability. They concluded that giftedness with respect both to visuospatial ability and general mental ability is associated with greater hemispheric integration rather than lateralization. Other researchers have similarly observed that compared with average students, gifted students' brains are characterized by greater integration across hemispheres for both verbal and spatial tasks, which may actually help to explain their advanced cognitive abilities (Alexander, O'Boyle, & Benbow, 1996; Singh & O'Boyle, 2004). Singh and O'Boyle compared gifted middle-school students with middle-school students of average ability and also with college students. The participants performed a visual processing task in which information was variously flashed either to the right or left hemisphere, or was divided between the hemispheres so that interaction was required in order to respond correctly. Some trials required global pattern recognition usually dominant in the right hemisphere, and some trials required analysis of fine detail usually dominant in the left hemisphere. The researchers found that across all the tasks, gifted students' brains operate in a more coordinated fashion than other groups' brains, and this greater coordination is associated with better performance.

As illustrated thus far, the research showing hemispheric dominance for cognitive tasks has always been extremely nuanced and equivocal. Despite this fact, researchers have developed a variety of techniques meant to identify people's presumed hemispheric dominance. Beaumont

(1983; Beaumont et al., 1984) summarized a number of these techniques which include monitoring lateral eye movements given the assumption that the direction in which a person gazes indicates activation in the opposite cerebral hemisphere, using questionnaires assessing preferences for different types of thinking, and interpreting differential performance on tests of verbal and nonverbal skills as indicating hemispheric differences. Beaumont points out that all these techniques are problematic because there is little evidence that any of them are actually associated with predominant processing in one hemisphere or the other; rather, they require that researchers assume at the outset the validity of the right-brain, left-brain dichotomy.

Hemisphericity advocates have also proposed many strategies intended to activate one hemisphere or the other. Alferink and Farmer-Dougan (2010) cited claims that students must read or write to activate the left hemisphere, and must create their own visual images to activate the right hemisphere. Harris (1988) cited numerous supposed strategies for enhancing right-hemisphere functioning such as observing art, listening to music, adding visual elements to supposedly left-brain academic material, adding activities such as yoga and meditation to school curricula, moving the eyes in certain prescribed directions, and many others. Perhaps most intriguing is the claim that a person can "energize" a chosen hemisphere by lying down on the opposing side of the body or breathing only through the opposing nostril (Ostrander, Schroeder, & Ostrander, 1994: 180).

Unfortunately, the findings from research on brain function simply do not conform to the right brain–left brain dichotomy. As reported above, language and creativity, as well as musical and spatial abilities, all are heavily influenced by processing in both hemispheres. Very few consistent patterns have emerged from research on hemisphericity, and the literature is plagued with countless contradictions. For example, Harris (1988) cited some studies showing that the right hemisphere is the center for negative emotions, while the left is dominant for positive emotions, along with contrary studies showing the exact opposite pattern, and still others suggesting that the right hemisphere is dominant for all emotional processing. More recently, researchers conducting a meta-analysis of brain-imaging studies similarly concluded that lateralization of brain activity pertaining to emotions is far more complex than a simple right–left dichotomy suggests (Wager, Phan, Liberzon, & Taylor, 2003). Such nuanced findings correspond well with Sperry's (1982) assertion that it is inaccurate to attribute emotional processing to the right hemisphere because emotional processing spreads very quickly between the hemispheres, and also with Wieder's (1984) observation that both emotional and cognitive processing involve reasoning.

A particularly vivid example of the inconsistency that characterizes hemisphericity research comes from two studies conducted by the same team of researchers. Fink and colleagues (1996) cited research suggesting that the left hemisphere is dominant for processing the details of a stimulus, whereas the right hemisphere is dominant for holistic processing. They conducted an experiment using brain imaging to assess brain function while participants focused either on specific details of a letter-based image – a single large letter made up of different small letters – or on the holistic characteristic of the image. They found that attending to the details of the image activated a particular area of the left hemisphere, whereas attention to the stimulus as a whole activated a different area of the right hemisphere. Fink and colleagues concluded that they had found "direct evidence for hemispheric specialization in global and local perception" (p. 626). However, just one year later the same researchers attempted a replication of their study (Fink et al., 1997). Instead of a letter-based image, this time they used the outline of a single large cup made up of a large number of small anchor shapes. The authors again found evidence of lateralization, but in the opposite direction to that of their previous study. This time, focusing on the holistic context resulted in greater activation in the left hemisphere, whereas focusing on details produced greater activation in the right hemisphere. Fink et al. (1997) concluded that the degree to which there are hemispheric differences in detailed versus holistic processing depends on the specific nature of the stimuli being perceived.

The findings of an earlier study even more directly contradict typical claims that people are left- or right-brained. Arndt and Berger (1978) cited evidence that although some relative differences in hemispheric activation are associated with different types of tasks, the differences are not associated with different types of people. In other words, hemispheric differences that do arise reflect task differences rather than differences in people's brains. Therefore, engaging in certain verbal tasks tends to activate the left hemisphere more than the right, but people who are particularly good at verbal tasks do not get their expertise from greater left-hemisphere activation relative to people who are poor at such tasks. Arndt and Berger had adult men complete several cognitive tests to determine whether they performed better on verbal–analytic tasks suggesting left hemisphere dominance, or spatial–holistic tasks suggesting right hemisphere dominance. Next, the participants completed a discrimination task assessing their reaction time when letters or faces were presented to either the left or right hemisphere only. Across all participants, the right hemisphere was faster at discriminating faces and the left hemisphere was faster at discriminating letters. However, there was no interaction where participants who were initially categorized as right- or left-hemisphere dominant were more proficient at processing information presented to the corresponding hemisphere. The researchers concluded that there was no evidence to assert that a person's mode of thinking – proficiency on what are often thought of as right- or left-hemisphere tasks – actually reflects individual differences in lateralized brain function. Researchers conducting a recent study of brain-imaging data reached virtually the same conclusion (Nielsen, Zielinski, Ferguson, Lainhart, & Anderson, 2013). Nielsen and colleagues analyzed fMRI scans from more than 1,000 people and concluded that lateralization exists for specific types of abilities, but that there is no evidence that people are left- or right-brained in a global sense. Moreover, most people have some relative strengths usually associated with the right hemisphere and some strengths associated with the left (Dobbs, 1989).

Perhaps the most critical fact that hemisphericity advocates tend to overlook is the remarkable structural and functional integration of the brain. Normal human brains have "massive cross-hemisphere connections," and brain-imaging research demonstrates that the hemispheres work in an integrated fashion when performing all types of cognitive tasks (Goswami, 2004: 11). Geake (2008) asserted that not only can the hemispheres communicate, they cannot help but communicate. Lindell and Kidd (2011) argued that the degree of integration in normal brains "renders any claims for dichotomous brain function baseless" (p. 124). Many other researchers have likewise noted that the hemispheres always work together (Harris, 1988; Banich, 1998; Hellige, 2000), and even the pioneers of split-brain research recognized decades ago that in normal brains, the hemispheres work as an integrated whole (Sperry, 1982).

The right-brain–left-brain dichotomy arose in part from misinterpretation and overgeneralization of laboratory research. Virtually all studies of brain lateralization are highly controlled laboratory studies designed to isolate minute components of cognitive functioning. Out of experimental necessity, the tasks that researchers use in such studies bear virtually no resemblance to cognitive or educational tasks in which people engage every day. Hardyck and Haapanen (1979) note that there is little evidence that hemispheric differences in function occur outside these laboratory environments. They note that "in our speech, our communicative acts, our reading, we do not encounter such limited amounts of information and make such simple judgments" (p. 228). Following an extensive review of research on hemispheric specialization, Hellige (1993) concluded that for any cognitive task beyond the most simple, "it is usually impossible to state in simple terms that one hemisphere is superior" (pp. 63–64). When laboratory studies reveal hemispheric differences, the differences constitute relative patterns; they do not show that all processing takes place in one hemisphere, but rather that there is somewhat more activation in one hemisphere than the other (Corballis, 1980; Geake, 2008). Since observed hemispheric differences are relative, categorizing people as right-brained or left-brained inadequately accounts for individual differences in complex thought (Hiscock & Kinsbourne, 1987).

Just as the scientific evidence does not support the right-brain–left-brain dichotomy, there is little justification for the application of hemispheric specialization research to inform educational methods. There is no evidence that traditional educational methods selectively favor the left hemisphere, that individuals favor one hemisphere or the other, or that teaching methods can selectively activate or educate a single hemisphere (Alferink & Farmer-Dougan, 2010; Lindell & Kidd, 2011). Researchers have asserted that right-brain–left-brain distinctions are based on folk theory that is "too crude and imprecise to have any scientific, predictive, or instructional value" (Bruner, 2008: 61), and that hemisphericity is "irrelevant to curriculum planning" (Hiscock & Kinsbourne, 1987: 139). Numerous authors have lamented that people advocating the application of neuroscientific research to education usually have no training in neuroscience and are therefore ill equipped to recognize or communicate the limitations of the research (see Dobbs, 1989; Jorgenson, 2003; Lindell & Kidd, 2011). Goswami (2004) noted that beliefs about right- and left-brain capacities illustrate how easily neuroscientific research can be misinterpreted when applied to education.

More than 30 years ago, Beaumont (1983) questioned why hemispheric specialization should be considered relevant to education since there is no evidence that different ways of thinking reflect differences in hemispheric function. He suggested that any references to neuropsychological processes lend "some added aura of validity and respectability," but are really only distractions (p. 216), and he called hemisphericity assumptions "misleading and dangerous" because they appear to legitimize unjustified educational interventions (p. 222). Corballis (1999) agreed, asserting that assumptions regarding the scientific validity of the right-brain–left-brain distinction represent a "legitimizing force that gives scientific credence to dubious practices" (p. 40). In an even more blunt assessment, Bruner (2008) referred to the idea that people are right-brained or left-brained simply as "one of those popular ideas that will not die" (p. 54).

It is easy to focus on apparent differences between the hemispheres while overlooking their functional overlap, and it may be reassuring to think that the deliberate activation of one hemisphere or the other could release hidden abilities or lead to greater learning (Corballis, 1980; 1999). The literature on differential hemispheric function is remarkably vast and cannot be fully described in any single source. On the first page of his 400-page book published more than two decades ago, Hellige (1993) acknowledged that he could not "provide anything even remotely close to an exhaustive review" of the existing research. Accordingly, the simplistic dichotomization of people as right-brained or left-brained belies the fact that "very little about the brain is ever straightforward" (McCrone, 1999: 29).

References

Alexander, J. E., O'Boyle, M. W., & Benbow, C. P. (1996). Developmentally advanced EEG alpha power in gifted male and female adolescents. *International Journal of Psychophysiology, 23,* 25–31.

Alferink, L. A. & Farmer-Dougan, V. (2010). Brain-(not) based education: Dangers of misunderstanding and misapplication of neuroscience research. *Exceptionality, 18,* 42–52.

Arndt, S. & Berger, D. E. (1978). Cognitive mode and asymmetry in cerebral functioning. *Cortex, 14,* 78–86.

Banich, M. T. (1998). Integration of information between the cerebral hemispheres. *Current Directions in Psychological Science, 7,* 32–37.

Beaumont, J. G. (1981). Split brain studies and the duality of consciousness. In: G. Underwood & R. Stevens (Eds.), *Aspects of consciousness, vol. 2.* London: Academic Press.

Beaumont, J. G. (1983). How many brains for how many minds? Hemisphericity and education. *Educational Psychology, 3,* 213–226.

Beaumont, J. G., Young, A. W., & McManus, I. C. (1984). Hemisphericity: A critical review. *Cognitive Neuropsychology, 1,* 191–212.

Berker, E. A., Berker, A. H., & Smith, A. (1986). Translation of Broca's 1865 report: Localization of speech in the third left frontal convolution. *Archives of Neurology, 43,* 1965–1972.

Bever, T. G. & Chiarello, R. J. (1974). Cerebral dominance in musicians and nonmusicians. *Science, 185,* 537–539.

Bruner, J. T. (2008). In search of … brain-based education. In: *The Jossey-Bass reader on the brain and learning.* San Francisco, CA: Jossey-Bass.

Carlsson, I., Wendt, P. E., & Risberg, J. (2000). On the neurobiology of creativity. Differences in frontal activity between high and low creative subjects. Neuropsychologia, *38,* 873–885.

Corballis, M. C. (1980). Laterality and myth. *American Psychologist, 35,* 284–295.

Corballis, M. C. (1999). Are we in our right minds? In: S. Della Sala (Ed.), *Mind Myths: Exploring popular assumptions about the mind and brain.* Chichester: John Wiley & Sons.

Dekker, S., Lee, N. C., Howard-Jones, P., & Jolles, J. (2012). Neuromyths in education: Prevalence and predictors of misconceptions among teachers. *Frontiers in Psychology, 3,* 1–8.

Dobbs, S. (1989). Some second thoughts on the application of left brain/right brain research. *Roeper Review, 12,* 119–121.

Fink, G. R., Marshall, J. C., Halligan, P. W., Frith, C. D., Frackowiak, R. S. J., & Dolan, R. J. (1996). Where in the brain does visual attention select the forest and the trees? *Nature, 382,* 626–628.

Fink, G. R., Marshall, J. C., Halligan, P. W., Frith, C. D., Frackowiak, R. S. J., & Dolan, R. J. (1997). Hemispheric specialization for global and local processing: The effect of stimulus category. *Proceedings of the Royal Society of London B: Biological Sciences, 264,* 487–494.

Freed, J. & Parsons, L. (1998). *Right-brained children in a left-brained world.* New York: Simon & Schuster.

Gazzaniga, M. S. & Sperry, R. W. (1967). Language after section of the cerebral comissures. *Brain, 90,* 131–148.

Geake, J. (2008). Neuromythologies in education. *Educational Research, 50,* 123–133.

Gibson, C., Folley, B. S., & Park, S. (2009). Enhanced divergent thinking and creativity in musicians: A behavioral and near-infrared spectroscopy study. *Brain and Cognition, 69,* 162–169.

Goswami, U. (2004). Neuroscience and Education. *British Journal of Educational Psychology, 74,* 1–14.

Hardyck, C. & Haapanen, R. (1979). Educating both halves of the brain: Educational breakthrough or neuromythology? *Journal of School Psychology, 17,* 219–230.

Harris, L. J. (1988). Right-brain training: Some reflections on the application of research on cerebral hemispheric specialization to education. In: D. L. Molfese & S. J. Segalowitz (Eds.), *Brain lateralization in children: Developmental implications.* New York: Guilford.

Hellige, J. B. (1993). *Hemispheric asymmetry: What's right and what's left.* Cambridge, MA: Harvard University Press.

Hellige, J. B. (2000). All the king's horses and all the king's men: Putting the brain back together again. *Brain and Cognition, 42,* 7–9.

Hiscock, M. & Kinsbourne, M. (1987). Specialization of the cerebral hemispheres: Implications for learning. *Journal of Learning Disabilities, 20,* 130–143.

Jorgenson, O. (2003). Brain scam? Why educators should be careful about embracing "brain research." *The Educational Forum, 67,* 364–369.

Kalbfleisch, M. L. & Gillmarten, C. (2013). Left brain vs. right brain: Findings on visual spatial capacities and the functional neurology of giftedness. *Roeper Review, 4,* 265–275.

Katz, A. N. (1997). Creativity and the cerebral hemispheres. In: M. Runco (Ed.), *The creativity research handbook, vol. one* (pp. 203–226).Cresskill, NJ: Hampton Press.

Klein, P. S. (1980). The overlooked or misused talents of learning disabled children. *Creative Child and Adult Quarterly, 5*, 30–34.

Lindell, A. K. (2006). In your right mind: Right hemisphere contributions to language processing and production. *Neuropsychology Review, 16*, 131–148.

Lindell, A. K. (2011). Lateral thinkers are not so laterally minded: Hemispheric asymmetry, interaction, and creativity. *Laterality, 16*, 479–498.

Lindell, A. K. & Kidd, E. (2011). Why right-brain teaching is half-witted: A critique of the misapplication of neuroscience to education. *Mind, Brain, and Education, 5*, 121–127.

McCrone, J. (1999). Left brain, right brain. *New Scientist, 2193*, 26–30.

Nielsen, J. A., Zielinski, B. A., Ferguson, M. A., Lainhart, J. E., & Anderson, J. S. (2013). An evaluation of the left-brain vs. right-brain hypothesis with resting state functional connectivity magnetic resonance imaging. *Plos One, 8*, 1–11.

Ornstein, R. E. (1977). *The psychology of consciousness*. New York: Harcourt Brace Janovich.

Ornstein, R. E. & Galin, D. (1976). Physiological studies of consciousness. In: P. Lec, R. E. Ornstein, D. Galin, A. Deichman, & C. Tart (Eds.), *Symposium on consciousness*. New York: Viking Press.

Ostrander, S., Schroeder, L., & Ostrander, N. (1994). *Superlearning 2000*. New York: Delacorte Press.

Prince, G. (1978). Putting the other half of the brain to work. *Training, 15*, 57–61.

Runco, M. A. (2004). Creativity. *Annual Review of Psychology, 55*, 657–687.

Samples, B. (1975). Educating for both sides of the human mind. *Science Teacher, 42*, 21–23.

Singh, H. & O'Boyle, M. W. (2004). Interhemispheric interaction during global–local processing in mathematically gifted adolescents, average-ability youth, and college students. *Neuropsychology, 18*, 371–377.

Sonnier, I. L. & Sonnier, C. B. (1995). Nurturing hemispheric preference through affective education. *Journal of Instructional Psychology, 22*, 182–185.

Sperry, R. W. (1961). Cerebral organization and behavior. *Science, 133*, 1749–1757.

Sperry, R. W. (1964). The great cerebral commissure. *Scientific American, 210*, 42–52.

Sperry, R. (1982). Some effects of disconnecting the cerebral hemispheres. *Science, 217*, 1223–1226.

Wager, T. D., Phan, K. L., Liberzon, I., & Taylor, S. F. (2003). Valance, gender, and lateralization of functional brain anatomy in emotion: A meta-analysis of findings from neuroimaging. *Neuroimage, 19*, 513–531.

Wheatley, G. H., Frankland, R. L., Mitchell, R., & Kraft, R. (1978). Hemispheric specialization and cognitive development: Implications for mathematics education. *Journal for Research in Mathematics Education, 9*, 20–32.

Wieder, C. G. (1984). The left-brain/right-brain model of mind: Ancient myth in modern garb. *Visual Arts Research, 10*, 66–72.

9 MYTH: THERE ARE MANY INDEPENDENT VARIETIES OF INTELLIGENCE

Defining and measuring human intelligence are probably more broadly researched and written about than any other topics in either psychology or education (Roberts & Lipnevich, 2012). The literature on intelligence consists of many thousands of studies, as well as countless books, chapters, and popular articles. This broad base of information reflects the reality that the topic of intelligence is extraordinarily complex and often interwoven with strongly held social, political, and educational ideologies. According to most traditional theories going back more than 100 years, intelligence includes a single unifying mental ability that underlies all specific types of abilities. In contrast, according to some contemporary and popularized views, intelligence is made up of several essentially separate mental abilities with little or no role played by a central underlying component. The debate has numerous implications for educational practice and policy. Many scholars and educators favor the perspective that there are different varieties of intelligence because the theory seems more egalitarian and optimistic than a focus on core mental ability (Hunt, 2011; Roberts & Lipnevich, 2012). However, reconciling theories positing multiple intelligences with the enormous body of existing intelligence research has proven to be difficult.

Interest in formally measuring human intelligence began with the work of Francis Galton (1869) whose early work on the potential heritability of mental ability laid the groundwork for a great deal of controversy that lingers to this day. In the more than 100 years since Galton's work, researchers and scholars have faced chronic difficulty in achieving consensus about what intelligence actually is. The complexity of human thought makes it challenging to develop a definition that encompasses the core aspects of mental ability while satisfying the perspectives of a myriad of stakeholders from a variety of disciplines. Despite the varying definitions that have been proposed, a few common threads run though most conceptualizations of intelligence. Nearly all scholars who study intelligence agree that intelligence involves "the ability to reason, solve problems, think abstractly, and acquire knowledge" (Gottfredson, 1997: 93).

For the past 100 years, the prevailing models of human intelligence have emphasized a single central characteristic, referred to as general intelligence, that links and perhaps powers all other cognitive abilities. Galton (1869) was the first to propose that intelligence consists of a broad general component, and general intelligence was first identified statistically by Charles Spearman (1904; 1927). Spearman observed that people's performance on cognitive test items tended to correlate with their performance on similar items. Perhaps few observers were surprised that test-takers who did well on one type of math item tended to do well on other math items. However, Spearman also found that performance on one type of task tended to predict performance on very different types of tasks. For example, people who did well on math items also tended to do well on items measuring language skills.

Spearman found that scores on a wide variety of cognitive ability tests were positively correlated: people who did well on one type of test tended to do well on others. In his first major publication on the topic, Spearman (1904) analyzed data from children completing a variety of sensory and cognitive tests. He found positive correlations between the scores on the various tests – even in cases where the tests were very different in nature. For example, he reported that scores on a test of simple auditory discrimination – the ability to identify two sets of tones as the same or different – correlated with tests of academic ability and common sense. Spearman hypothesized that correlations between measures of different sensory and cognitive abilities are due to a "common intellective function" (p. 272). He initially proposed this idea somewhat tentatively, noting that the idea of a unifying cognitive component was so radical that a great deal more corroborating evidence needed to accumulate before more definitive conclusions could be drawn.

Spearman invented a now well-known statistical technique called factor analysis that enabled psychometricians – those who measure psychological characteristics – to reduce a large number of measured variables to a smaller and more useful number of underlying elements. For example, one could begin with the responses from a large number of people to a large number of mental ability test items and determine whether there were broader common abilities underlying people's performance on different types of items. This technique allowed Spearman and subsequent researchers to conduct a much more sophisticated evaluation of the cognitive components underlying performance on ability tests. Spearman observed that there was nearly always one main factor that emerged tying together all the diverse cognitive tasks – explaining the correlations between very different types of skills. He referred to this factor as general mental ability, or *g*. On intelligence tests, this general factor is represented by IQ scores. Spearman also noted that differences between people on the general ability factor did not account for all the differences in test performance. He therefore concluded that performance on any particular type of test is a factor of both general mental ability and some more precise ability or talent specific to the particular test.

To explain how a core general ability could affect performance on a broad array of diverse mental tasks, Gottfredson (1997) asserted that overlapping higher-order thinking skills underlie success across cognitive tasks regardless of the specific test content. She further states that the more complex the task, the more the ability to engage in higher-order thinking will affect performance. In a metaphorical illustration, Kaplan and Saccuzzo (2013) use the analogy of a power station providing electricity for a city. They explain that although some lights in some places are brighter than others, a change in the amount of power from the main station would affect the brightness of all the lights in the city. Similarly, greater or lesser *g* would affect the functioning of all specific mental abilities. Spearman himself (1927) likened *g* to a kind of mental energy that powers a variety of more specific abilities.

Over the 100 years since Spearman claimed the existence of a broad general factor of human intelligence and psychologists began formally measuring intelligence, researchers have conducted thousands of studies supporting the existence of the general ability factor. Two recent examples from this long history serve to illustrate the durability of the finding that some common factor underlies performance on different types of tests. In the first of these studies (Johnson, Bouchard, Krueger, McGue, & Gottesman, 2004), researchers had 436 American adults complete a total of 42 ability subtests from three test batteries. The subtests varied in terms of the skills emphasized (verbal knowledge, nonverbal reasoning, inductive reasoning, pattern recognition, etc.) and also in format (multiple-choice versus free response). Johnson and colleagues separately factor analyzed the subtests associated with each of the three test batteries. Consistent with hundreds of previous studies, they found a common factor underlying performance on each battery. Moreover, they found that the general factors underlying the three batteries correlated virtually perfectly with each other despite divergent test content and response formats. The researchers concluded that this pattern constituted the "most substantive evidence of which we are aware that psychological assessments of mental ability are consistently identifying a common underlying component of general intelligence" (p. 104). In a replication of their study, Johnson and colleagues (Johnson, te Nijenhuis, & Bouchard, 2007) analyzed data from 500 adults who had completed 46 separate ability tests from five batteries. All the tests were different from those used in their 2004 study. The researchers again found that the g components from the five batteries correlated highly with each other – again suggesting the existence of a single factor underlying performance both within and across diverse cognitive test batteries.

The statistical evidence for the existence of general mental ability might not be particularly compelling if it was limited to correlations between different types of tests. Just as there is a long history of research suggesting the presence of a general factor underlying human intelligence, there is likewise a great deal of research indicating the importance of this general factor in predicting positive outcomes in a host of domains. To name just a few, g is positively associated with income, health behaviors, longevity, and job performance; g is negatively correlated with criminal behavior (Lubinski, 2004). General mental ability is also more highly correlated with occupational level than any other variable (Jensen, 1986). With respect to job performance in particular, g is correlated with performance on jobs at all levels of complexity (Gottfredson, 2002; Schmidt & Hunter, 2004). Schmidt and Hunter also reported that g is associated with performance in job training programs because people with greater general mental ability learn more and learn faster. They also noted longitudinal data indicating that g is associated with later income even after researchers control for other variables such as family socioeconomic status, neighborhood characteristics, and school quality. In fact, general mental ability measured in childhood is positively correlated with income more than 30 years later.

Most researchers agree that specific abilities exist along with g, but research suggests that none approach g in terms of their role in a variety of life circumstances (Jensen, 1986; Gottfredson, 1997). For example, tests of specific abilities designed to predict performance on specific jobs tend to provide no useful predictive information beyond what is indicated by general mental ability (Schmidt & Hunter, 2004). That is, specific ability tests may measure both specific abilities and g, but it is g that is predicting job performance. Jensen cited further evidence that if it were possible to develop an ability test that did not measure general mental ability, the test would not predict performance in any domain and would therefore be useless. More conceptually, Traub (Gardner & Traub, 2010) asserts that to conclude that there is no general intelligence would mean claiming that the brain has "little or no executive capacity to direct and integrate the mind's activity" (p. 46).

The preceding evidence on general mental ability provides the backdrop with which alternative models of human intelligence are compared. Gottfredson (2002) referred to g as "probably the best measured and most studied human trait in all of psychology" (p. 25). Reviewing many decades of research, Jensen (1986) reasserted that all varieties of mental tests – no matter how diverse the actual tasks – are positively correlated, which indicates that they are all – at least in part – measures of some common intellectual component. He referred to this pattern of correlations among tests as "about as inexorable as gravitation" (p. 305). Jensen further pointed out that the central g factor accounts for more variation in test performance than any other factor, and often for more variation than all other factors together.

Throughout the history of intelligence research there have been critics of the idea that human cognitive ability is characterized by a central common element. Thanks in part to the work of Galton (1869) and subsequent researchers studying the heritability of intelligence, the concept of g long ago acquired connotations of biologically determined and environmentally immutable notions of intelligence. As time went on, concerns about fairness and social justice grew – particularly regarding racial disparities in test performance – causing people to question the reality of g. Critics correctly claimed that g cannot account for all aspects of human cognitive ability and performance. This claim in itself does not contradict the evidence for the existence of g; Spearman himself (1927) emphasized that performance on any particular task is affected by both general and specific abilities. However, there is quite a distinction to be made between this defensible viewpoint and the claim that there is simply no such thing as general mental ability, or that g is not important except with respect to a narrow range of academic tasks – claims that often coincide with models positing independent types of intelligence (e.g., Gardner & Moran, 2006).

Among the many models portraying cognitive ability as consisting of multiple independent varieties of intelligence while downplaying the idea of general mental ability, a few in particular stand out. One of the earliest models was developed by Thurstone (1938), who proposed that intelligence was made up of thirteen separate abilities – although in subsequent models he reduced the number to seven. Later Guilford (1967) proposed a model of intelligence consisting of 120 abilities that operate independently. However, the multiple intelligence model that has been most influential was proposed by Howard Gardner (1983). Perhaps the most noteworthy difference between Gardner's model and those of Thurstone and Guilford is that Gardner's model includes several abilities that most researchers – and perhaps most laypeople – do not generally consider to be part of intelligence. This conceptual expansion is the source of much of the difficulty in reconciling multiple intelligence models with the concept of general mental ability.

Gardner defined intelligence as "a biopsychological potential to process information that can be activated in a cultural setting to solve problems or create products that are of value in a culture" (1999: 33–34). He proposed seven distinct types of intelligence with the labels linguistic, logical-mathematical, spatial, musical, bodily-kinesthetic, interpersonal, and intrapersonal (Gardner, 1983). The first three abilities in this list are consistent with skills assessed on traditional intelligence tests, as is Gardner's eighth intelligence – naturalistic – proposed in a later edition of the model (Gardner, 1999). The remaining intelligences consist of abilities that are not usually included in definitions of intelligence (see Table 1 for Gardner's description of each intelligence).

In developing his theory, Gardner (1983) drew on literature from a variety of disciplines, including psychology, biology, sociology, anthropology, and even the humanities. By his own acknowledgment (Gardner, 2011), he was not trained in psychometric principles when he developed his model of intelligence. This fact might be seen as a strength or a liability depending on one's point of view. He also acknowledges that his choice to use the term "intelligences" was "primarily strategic" in order to garner attention for the model (Gardner, 2011: 128). Other researchers have suggested that Gardner's work was in part motivated by his moral objection to what he perceives to be Western society's emphasis on a narrow definition of what it means to be intelligent (Barnett, Ceci, & Williams, 2006).

Gardner (1983) identified eight criteria to determine whether a particular characteristic constituted a separate form of intelligence. These criteria include localization in a particular area of the brain as indicated by the potential for the ability to be destroyed in isolation by brain damage, and the existence of "prodigies" or "idiot savants" (p. 63) who

Table 1 Gardner's eight intelligences

Linguistic	The "sensitivity to spoken and written language, the ability to learn languages, and the capacity to use language to accomplish certain goals," demonstrated in the skills of those such as "lawyers, speakers, writers, and poets."
Logical-mathematical	The "capacity to analyze problems logically, carry out mathematical operations, and investigate issues scientifically," demonstrated in the skills of those such as "mathematicians, logicians, and scientists."
Spatial	The "potential to recognize and manipulate the patterns of wide space as well as more confined areas," demonstrated in the skills of those such as "navigators and pilots," as well as "sculptors, surgeons, chess players, graphic artists, or architects."
Musical	"Skill in the performance, composition, and appreciation of musical patterns," demonstrated in the skills of those such as "composers, conductors, and musical performers."
Bodily-kinesthetic	The "potential of using one's whole body or parts of the body to solve problems or fashion products," demonstrated in the skills of those such as "dancers, actors, and athletes," as well as craftspersons, surgeons, bench-top scientists, mechanics and many other technically oriented professionals."
Interpersonal	The "capacity to understand the intentions, motivations, and desires of other people and, consequently, to work effectively with others," demonstrated in the skills of those such as "salespeople, teachers, clinicians, religious leaders, political leaders, and actors."
Intrapersonal	The "capacity to understand oneself, to have an effective working model of oneself – including one's own desires, fears, and capacities – and to use such information effectively in regulating one's own life," as demonstrated in "those who excel in introspection."
Naturalistic	"Expertise in the recognition and classification of the numerous species of his or her environment," demonstrated in the skills of those such as "hunters, farmers, and those who study the natural world."

Note: Content quoted from Gardner (1999: 41–43, 48; 2011: 126).

display widely varying abilities – often to the extent that a single ability is exceptionally high while the rest are exceptionally low. Gardner has at times implied that all eight of the criteria must be met to demonstrate that an ability reaches the status of a separate intelligence (1983; Gardner & Moran, 2006), but has sometimes asserted that an intelligence must meet "all or a healthy majority" of the criteria (2006a: 7). Roberts and Lipnevich (2012) argue that such inconsistency serves to "strip the process of selection of its scientific rigor" (p. 44), and assert that most of the criteria are easy to meet so there is potentially no limit to the number of characteristics that could be identified as intelligences. They suggest that such a slippery slope of inclusion might mean that intelligences such as bodily-kinesthetic would need to be further divided into even more specific intelligences such as football, golf, and dance intelligence. To do otherwise, they suggest, would be to assume that someone who is good at football could have been just as good at dancing.

Gardner's theory resonated with educators – many of whom were disenchanted with the concept and presumed implications of general mental ability (Waterhouse, 2006; Roberts & Lipnevich, 2012). Kincheloe (1999) advocated rethinking the concept of intelligence based on a more inclusive view of education that validates alternative forms of intelligence to those currently recognized by psychology. He proposed that doing so would increase inclusiveness by "admitting new members to the exclusive community of the talented" (p. 1). Hunt (2011) asserts that multiple intelligence theory was "an easy sell to educators" (p. 117) because it was so optimistic. According to Hunt, the theory is consistent with the way many people think about intelligence: that there are many separate types of ability and that everyone is good at something. The multiple intelligence model therefore seems more egalitarian than the general intelligence model. Roberts and Lipnevich note the appeal of being able to refer to a child who does poorly in math but is a good musician as having musical intelligence. The model became popular with both teachers and parents because it supported the assumption that "all children are special" (Lohman, 2001: 221). Lohman also points out the potential risk of equating different abilities. Having low musical or bodily-kinesthetic intelligence would be very different in terms of likely life circumstances than having low general intelligence.

Despite its popularity among educators, multiple intelligence theory has been the subject of a great deal of debate and criticism from intelligence researchers. Indeed, the idea that there are many distinct and independent forms of intelligence is difficult to reconcile with the large body of empirical research indicating the existence of general mental ability. Gardner does not deny that statistical analyses of cognitive tests reveal a central factor emerging from correlations between test scores, but he claims that this g factor emerges primarily because the tests share similar formats, and are all affected by a very limited array of abilities – specifically verbal and logical-mathematical skills (Gardner, 2006a).

He also claims that *g* predicts little outside traditional school performance (Gardner & Moran, 2006). In response to such propositions, Lohman (2001) bluntly states that "even the most cursory examination of human abilities literature shows that every one of these claims at best overstates and at worst is simply false" (p. 221). Moreover, there has been little research directly investigating the validity of multiple intelligence theory (Gregory, 2011).

In perhaps the only attempt to directly test the validity of the multiple intelligence framework relative to the general intelligence model, Visser, Ashton, and Vernon (2006a) administered a variety of tests to 200 undergraduate and graduate students, university employees, and friends and relatives of the undergraduates. The participants ranged in age 17–66. The researchers used a variety of established tests to measure abilities corresponding to each of Gardner's eight intelligences – two tests for each intelligence. To ensure that shared verbal demands would not inflate the correlations between tests, Visser and colleagues included nonverbal measures in their study. Some tests were completely nonverbal, and for others the verbal demands were so minimal as to preclude the possibility that they could lead to inflated correlations – particularly among such an educated sample. Many of the tests involved tasks beyond those required on traditional paper-and-pencil tests such as identifying routes on a map, folding paper for a spatial ability test, and performing physical dexterity tasks. The researchers also administered a well-established measure of general intelligence.

Visser and colleagues (2006a) found that most of the correlations between tests assessing traditional cognitive abilities akin to Gardner's linguistic, spatial, logical-mathematical, naturalistic, and even interpersonal intelligences were positive and significant, and all five of these abilities were substantially correlated with a separate measure of general mental ability. Tests assessing abilities not typically considered part of intelligence because they are heavily affected by noncognitive factors – specifically musical, intrapersonal, and bodily-kinesthetic skills – were not significantly correlated with the test of general mental ability. However, a factor analysis of all 16 tests revealed a first ability component that accounted for far more variation between test takers than any other factor.

Visser and colleagues (2006a) concluded that the correlations between diverse tests, the emergence of the general factor, and the correlations of specific tests with a separate measure of general intelligence are inconsistent with multiple intelligence theory. They also emphasized that common verbal influences across tests could not account for the results because the tests minimized verbal influences; even the spatial ability tests – which were almost entirely nonverbal – were positively associated with g. This pattern is consistent with the established evidence going back to the work of Spearman a century ago that "A test's relative standing on g could not be inferred from its superficial characteristics, such as the sensory or response modality involved, whether verbal or nonverbal, numerical or figural, paper-and-pencil test or performance test, or other formal features" (Jensen, 1986: 310). Jensen asserts that tests measure g to the extent that they require complex cognitive processing or mental manipulation – regardless of the specific nature of the test itself.

Not surprisingly, these conclusions were met with skepticism from Gardner (2006b), who criticized Visser and colleagues for using tests emphasizing skills traditionally thought of as cognitive. He stated that the spirit of multiple intelligence theory is to expand the definitions of cognition and intelligence. He further argued that the common factor linking various abilities might arise because the tests all in some way reflect a narrow set of cognitive skills emphasized in traditional schools. In a response to Gardner's critique, Visser, Ashton, and Vernon (2006b) cited evidence that many tasks containing no academic content – such as putting blocks together to copy particular shapes – are highly associated with general mental ability. They went on to cite evidence that g is correlated with biological processes such as cerebral glucose metabolism. Researchers have also found that g is correlated with speed of neural transmission (McRorie & Cooper, 2004), clearly a factor not taught in schools. Perhaps most compelling, Jensen (1986) summarized research linking measures of average brain wave activity with general mental ability. He cited research using a paradigm where participants' brain wave activity is measured via electrodes on the scalp while the participant sits in a reclined chair listening to random auditory clicks, making no voluntary responses whatsoever. Average brain wave measurements taken during this task are strongly correlated with general mental ability – despite the fact that the task requires no conscious problem-solving or cognitive response.

Researchers have also taken issue with Gardner's (1983, 1999) criterion that separate intelligences reflect localized neural processing in specific brain regions, and his claim (Gardner, 2006a) that evidence for multiple intelligences is provided by the fact that brain damage can cause the loss of some skills and not others. Roberts and Lipnevich (2012) point out that most cognitive abilities cannot be localized to specific parts of the brain, referring to this fact as a "major problem with Gardner's view" (p. 45).

Waterhouse (2006) cites evidence that not only cognitive abilities, but even motor abilities such as walking and gesturing are not localized to specific regions of the brain but rather involve multiple brain regions. Barnett and colleagues (2006) further assert that the loss of certain abilities due to brain damage and the localization of certain abilities in the brain do not suggest that those abilities are different intelligences, nor does it disprove the existence of some central ability that drives performance on all cognitive tasks. White (2004) agrees, noting that the loss of specific functions due to brain damage demonstrates only that some physiological condition necessary to perform the function is absent – not that there are distinct types of intelligence.

It often appears that the contrasting conclusions reached by scholars agreeing that intelligence consists of a general ability and those favoring a model of intelligence consisting of multiple independent components are due primarily to differing perspectives on the nature of intelligence and the nature of scientific evidence. Hunt (2011) argued that Gardner's approach to identifying support for his theory is heavily weighted by subjective reasoning and reflection, which differs from the more purely data-driven approach favored by most intelligence researchers. Indeed, Gardner (2006a) provides interesting anecdotal examples for each intelligence that would be compelling to some students of the theory but not to others. His opinion that "it is up to educators to decide whether ideas derived from, inferred from, or catalyzed from MI theory are useful to them" (Gardner & Moran, 2006: 229) appears to reveal a willingness to accept subjective impressions as evidence. Other researchers have argued that Gardner's model is not based on statistical evaluation, but rather on Gardner's subjective view of how human abilities are organized (Roberts & Lipnevich, 2012). Even Gardner's definition of intelligence differs from traditional definitions centered on cognitive abilities in that it includes several largely noncognitive capacities. In some ways, those favoring *g* and those favoring multiple intelligences are not even talking about the same thing.

Intelligence scholars have often been harsh in their criticism of the multiple intelligence model, with many concluding that there is no evidence for the theory (Waterhouse, 2006; Hunt, 2011; Roberts & Lipnevich, 2012). One particular difficulty is that Gardner has not articulated specific ways that each of the intelligences could be measured. He is unapologetic about this fact, stating that multiple intelligence theory is a work of "scientific synthesis" (Gardner, 2006b: 505) that does not lend itself to traditional testing, but is revised as new findings from various disciplines emerge (Gardner & Moran, 2006). This approach renders the theory somewhat immune to direct empirical evaluation. Gardner and Moran go on to refer to paper-and-pencil measurement as an "intrusion," advocating instead for "intelligence-fair" assessments where abilities are assessed as they are naturally expressed (p. 230). Lohman (2001) questions this assertion, pointing out that the types of assessment advocated by Gardner can assess knowledge and skills beyond those on standardized tests, but they overlap greatly with standardized tests in terms of what they measure, they are more time-consuming, and they are more expensive. Barnett and colleagues (2006) likewise question the wisdom of using broader, long-term ability assessments not only because they demand far greater resources, but because such unstandardized measures preclude appropriate comparisons of students or programs because they are vulnerable to so many subjective judgments and personal biases. Moreover, Gardner's (1999) insistence on real-life assessment, coupled with his assertion that real-life tasks often require a combination of intelligences, would seem to make it difficult or impossible to satisfactorily assess the separate intelligences (Visser et al., 2006a).

Although Gardner has not involved himself with assessing multiple intelligences, he is not opposed to others attempting to do so (Gardner & Moran, 2006). However, most tests that have been developed to assess the intelligences are self-report measures rather than true ability tests. In other words, researchers collect data by having participants rate themselves on the various intelligences (e.g., Furnham, 2009). This method is problematic because self-report measures of ability tend to correlate only modestly with actual ability measures (Visser et al., 2006a). One study showed that participants' self-ratings of their ability on each of Gardner's eight intelligences correlated weakly with ability tests selected to assess the intelligences – with correlations ranging from 0 to .38 (Visser, Ashton, & Vernon, 2008). Such findings suggest that self-report measures are exceptionally imprecise indicators of actual ability.

Through his work on his multiple intelligence theory, Gardner has certainly made many important points about the nature of intelligence. Barnett and colleagues (2006) note that although Gardner has not provided sufficient evidence for his theory's validity, his work has had the valuable effect of drawing attention to the topic of intelligence and the limitations of traditional models. He has emphasized the diverse nature of mental abilities, pointed out that no two people exhibit the exact same pattern of cognitive abilities, advocated that teachers should nurture a variety of student talents, and questioned the idea of selecting people for opportunities based only on a measure of general mental ability (Gardner,

1999; 2006a). Importantly, there is nothing inherent in the theory of general intelligence that conflicts with any of these concerns. Virtually all scholars of general intelligence from Spearman onward agree that performance on any mental task is affected both by general intelligence and specific abilities. They simply deny that the different abilities operate in isolation from a common factor of ability. Hogan (2007) notes that the emphasis on maximizing all students' potential may be appropriate in education, but is not a sufficient basis for intelligence models.

There is no question that Gardner's model of intelligence has been quite influential in educational settings. There are many programs in schools across the world – in both Western and non-Western countries – whose developers based their work on the multiple intelligence framework (see Visser et al., 2006a; Waterhouse, 2006; Chen, Moran, & Gardner, 2009). Despite the influence of the theory, however, evidence for the existence of intelligences that operate independently without the influence of a general intelligence factor is sorely lacking. Gottfredson (2002) asserts that g involves the ability to "reason, learn, and solve problems" (p. 27), which helps to explain why it is affects performance across domains and across the lifespan. She also notes that no one has been able to develop a meaningful ability test that does not measure general intelligence. Without evidence for the existence of intelligences that are independent of each other and independent of a unifying ability, developing new teaching strategies emphasizing alterative educational values could do students a disservice if real-life opportunities continue to demand traditional intellectual abilities such as language, math, and reasoning skills (Barnett et al., 2006). Unfortunately, claims that multiple intelligence theory is "a proven approach to education for the twenty-first century" (Hoerr, 2003: 94) are generally made with little or no systematic evidence to support them.

Gardner (2011) criticized "the psychometric establishment …who believed (and continue to believe) that they have the right to define intelligence, to determine how it is measured, and to resist efforts to pluralize the concept" (pp. 127–128). In stark contrast to Gardner's perspective, Waterhouse (2006) suggested that the multiple intelligence model is easy to understand because it simply divides intelligence into separate components based on specific content, and therefore allows people to believe that they understand how human cognitive processes work even if the evidence is at odds with the theory. To date, there are many anecdotes and opinions, but little empirical evidence to conclude that human cognitive ability consists of many independent intelligences.

References

Barnett, S. M., Ceci, S. J., & Williams, W. M. (2006). Is the ability to make a bacon sandwich a mark of intelligence?, and other issues: Some reflections of Gardner's Theory of Multiple Intelligences. In: J. A. Schaler (Ed.), *Howard Gardner under fire: The rebel psychologist faces his critics* (pp. 95–114). Chicago: Open Court.

Chen, J., Moran, S., & Gardner, H. (2009). *Multiple intelligences around the world*. San Francisco: Jossey-Bass.

Furnham, A. (2009). The validity of a new, self-report measure of multiple intelligence. *Current Psychology, 28*, 225–239.

Galton, F. (1892). *Hereditary genius*. London: Macmillan.

Gardner, H. (1983). *Frames of mind*. New York: Basic Books.

Gardner. H. (1999). *Intelligence reframed: Multiple intelligences for the 21st century*. New York: Basic Books.

Gardner, H. (2006a). *Multiple intelligences: New horizons*. New York: Basic Books.

Gardner, H. (2006b). On failing to grasp the core of MI theory: A response to Visser et al. *Intelligence, 34*, 503–505.

Gardner, H. (2011). The theory of multiple intelligences. In: M. A. Gernsbacher, R. W. Pew, L. M. Hough, & J. R. Pomerantz (Eds.), *Psychology and the real world* (pp. 122–130). New York: Worth.

Gardner, H. & Moran, S. (2006). The science of multiple intelligences theory: A response to Lynn Waterhouse. *Educational Psychologist, 41*, 227–232.

Gardner, H. & Traub, J. (2010). A debate on "multiple intelligences." In: D. Gordon (Ed.)., *Cerebrum 2010: Emerging in brain science* (pp. 34–61). Washington, DC: Dana Press.

Gottfredson, L. S. (1997). Why *g* matters: The complexity of everyday life. *Intelligence, 24*, 79–132.

Gottfredson, L. S. (2002). Where and why *g* matters: Not a mystery. *Human Performance, 15*, 25–46.

Gregory, R. J. (2011). *Psychological testing: History, principles, and applications*. Boston, MA: Allyn & Bacon.

Guilford, J. P. (1967). *The nature of human intelligence*. New York: McGraw-Hill.

Hoerr, T. R. (2003). It's no fad: Fifteen years of implementing multiple intelligences. *Educational Horizons, 81*, 92–94.

Hogan, T. P. (2007). *Psychological testing: A practical introduction*. Hoboken, NJ: John Wiley & Sons.

Hunt, E. (2011). *Human intelligence*. New York: Cambridge University Press.

Jensen, A. R. (1986). *g*: Artifact or reality? *Journal of Vocational Behavior, 29*, 301–331.

Johnson, W., Bouchard, T. J., Krueger, R. F., McGue, M., & Gottesman, I. I. (2004). Just one *g*: consistent results from three test batteries. *Intelligence, 32*, 95–107.

Johnson, W., te Nijenhuis, J., Bouchard, T. J. (2007). Still just one *g*: Consistent results from five test batteries. *Intelligence, 36*, 81–95.

Kaplan, R. M. & Saccuzzo, D. P. (2013). *Psychological testing: Principles, applications, & issues*. Belmont, CA: Wadsworth.

Kincheloe, J. L. (1999). The foundations of a democratic educational psychology. In: J. L. Kincheloe, S. R Steinberg, & L. E. Villaverde (Eds.), *Rethinking intelligence: Confronting psychological assumptions about teaching and learning* (pp. 1–26). London: Routledge.

Lohman, D. F. (2001). Fluid intelligence, inductive reasoning, and working memory: Where the theory of multiple intelligences falls short. In: N. Colangelo & S. G. Assouline (Eds.), *Talent development IV: Proceedings from the 1998 Henry B. and Jocelyn Wallace National Research Symposium on Talent Development* (pp. 219–227). Scottsdale, AZ: Great Potential Press.

Lubinski, D. (2004). Introduction to the special section on cognitive abilities: 100 years after Spearman's (1904) "'General intelligence,' Objectively determined and measured." *Journal of Personality and Social Psychology, 86*, 96–111.

McRorie, M. & Cooper, C. (2004). Synaptic transmission correlates of general mental ability. *Intelligence, 32*, 263–275.

Roberts, R. D. & Lipnevich, A. A. (2012). From general intelligence to multiple intelligences: Meanings, models, and measures. In: K. R. Harris, S. Graham, T. Urdan, S. Graham, J. M. Royer, & M. Zeidner (Eds.), *APA educational psychology handbook, vol. 2: Individual differences and cultural and contextual factors* (pp. 33–57). Washington, DC: American Psychological Association.

Schmidt, F. L. & Hunter, J. (2004). General mental ability in the world of work: Occupational attainment and job performance. *Journal of Personality and Social Psychology, 86*, 162–173.

Spearman, C. (1904). "General intelligence": Objectively determined and measured. *American Journal of Psychology, 15*, 201–293.

Spearman, C. (1927). *The abilities of man*. Oxford: Macmillan.

Thurstone, L. L. (1938). Primary mental abilities. *Psychometric Monographs, 1*, ix.

Visser, B. A., Ashton, M. C., & Vernon, P. A. (2006a). Beyond *g*: Putting multiple intelligences theory to the test. *Intelligence, 34*, 487–502.

Visser, B. A., Ashton, M. C., & Vernon, P. A. (2006b). *g* and the measurement of multiple intelligences: A response to Gardner. *Intelligence, 34*, 507–510.

Visser, B. A., Ashton, M. C., & Vernon, P. A. (2008). What makes you think you're so smart? Measured abilities, personality, and sex differences in relation to self-estimates of multiple intelligences. *Journal of Individual Differences, 29*, 35–44.

Waterhouse, L. (2006). Multiple intelligences, the Mozart Effect, and emotional intelligence: A critical review. *Educational Psychologist, 41*, 207–225.

White, J. (2004). Howard Gardner: The myth of multiple intelligences. Available at: http://eprints.ioe.ac.uk/1263/1/WhiteJ2005HowardGardner1.pdf.

10 MYTH: SELF-ESTEEM IMPROVES ACADEMIC PERFORMANCE

A popular assumption among both educators and the general public is that self-esteem plays an important role in determining students' academic success. Self-esteem usually refers primarily to one's global self-evaluation rather than to beliefs about one's specific talents or abilities. It is particularly important to recognize that self-esteem pertains to perceptions of one's own characteristics rather than any objective evaluation of those characteristics (Baumeister, Campbell, Krueger, & Vohs, 2003; Baumeister, 2005). Therefore, one's self-evaluation may or may not be based on any specific accomplishments.

The idea that self-esteem might enhance academic performance goes back at least as far as the 1960s. Many researchers observed positive associations between students' self-reported levels of self-esteem and the grades those students earned in school. That is, students with higher self-esteem tended to perform better in school than students with lower self-esteem. Although it was certainly plausible that feeling good about oneself might enhance school performance, it was equally plausible that succeeding in school might enhance self-esteem, or that other factors might promote both high self-esteem and academic success. Despite the commonly known perils of confusing correlation with causation, many educators began to assume that increasing students' self-esteem would help students to be more successful in school.

Great Myths of Education and Learning, First Edition. Jeffrey D. Holmes.
© 2016 John Wiley & Sons, Inc. Published 2016 by John Wiley & Sons, Inc.

There are many intuitively appealing reasons why self-esteem should lead to improved academic performance. Students with high self-esteem might set higher academic goals for themselves and persist longer if they encounter challenges obtaining those goals (Bachman & O'Malley, 1977). Students with high self-esteem also might work harder to achieve success in order to maintain their positive self-view (Valentine, DuBois, & Cooper, 2004). In light of such appealing explanations and the evidence that self-esteem is correlated with school performance, educators began focusing on ways to increase students' self-esteem as a means to enhance academic performance (Schreier & Kraut, 1979; Byrne, 1986). By the late 1980s, the potential for self-esteem interventions to improve school performance seemed so compelling that the state of California established a task force to investigate the positive impact of high self-esteem and make public policy recommendations (California Task Force to Promote Self-Esteem and Personal and Social Responsibility, 1990). Despite identifying little evidence of a causal link between self-esteem and academic performance, the task force concluded from correlational studies and various testimonials that "good education requires good self-esteem" (p. 2). Consequently, the members of the task force recommended that all schools engage in an effort to raise student self-esteem, and that teacher training and credentialing requirements include self-esteem content. Such beliefs and interventions certainly have not disappeared as time has gone by (e.g., Zimmerman, Copeland, Shope, & Dielman, 1997; EduNova, 2012; Nabayunga, 2013; see also Forsyth, Lawrence, Burnette, & Baumeister, 2007; Stupnisky et al., 2007).

Many researchers have observed that self-esteem is positively correlated with academic performance for students across a wide variety of age groups. For example, in a small early study of American fifth graders, scores on a self-esteem inventory were positively associated with scores on an academic achievement test (Simon & Simon, 1975). In a much larger study more than 20 years later, Zimmerman and colleagues (1997) collected data from more than 1,000 students when the students were in sixth, seventh, eighth, and ninth grades. At each point in time, the students completed a self-esteem scale and also reported their grades. The researchers reported that self-esteem and grades were associated at each point of data collection, and that decreasing self-esteem over time was associated with decreasing grades, while increasing self-esteem was associated with increases in grades.

Although the majority of self-esteem research has been conducted in the United States, some researchers have studied students in other countries. For example, Seabi (2011) collected data from university engineering students in South Africa and found that self-esteem was positively associated with exam performance across several academic domains, including math, physics, and chemistry. In contrast, Leeson, Ciarrochi, and Heaven (2008) used standardized test scores and self-esteem survey scores from more than 600 Australian seventh graders to predict those students' academic performance in tenth grade. The researchers reported that the correlation between self-esteem in seventh grade and course grades three years later was nonsignificant. Moreover, the best predictors of course grades by far were the measures of actual academic ability. Interestingly, Leeson and colleagues' findings mimic those of Demo and Parker (1987), who found no association between self-esteem and grade point average in a sample of nearly 300 American college students. Unlike the study reported above by Zimmerman and colleagues (1997), in which self-esteem was correlated with student grades, Demo and Parker assessed academic performance by accessing college records rather than by relying on student self-report of their own grades.

In light of such inconsistent findings, integrative reviews of multiple studies are particularly valuable. Perhaps the two most important reviews were both published more than 30 years ago. The first of these was conducted by Wylie (1979), who cited many studies where self-esteem was positively correlated with students' grades and standardized test scores. She also suggested that the variations across studies in the degree to which self-esteem correlated with academic performance may be attributable to the wide variety of measures that researchers used to assess self-esteem and academic performance. Importantly, Wylie concluded more than three decades ago that "the correlations of achievement indices and over-all self-regard indices tend to be small in absolute terms, offering no support to the commonly accepted lore that achievement and self-regard are strongly associated" (p. 406).

The second important review was conducted by Hansford and Hattie (1982), who performed a meta-analysis statistically integrating the findings from studies of more than 39,000 participants. Like Wylie (1979), the researchers identified a large range of correlations across studies due to variations in self-esteem measures, outcome measures, and participant samples. They reported an overall correlation of .22 between academic performance and self-esteem measures, meaning that only 5% of the variation in student achievement was associated with variation in self-esteem. Hansford and Hattie also found that the average correlation for studies using nationally representative student samples was essentially zero – the positive overall association being accounted for entirely by smaller, less representative samples.

Although study results vary widely, there appears to be a small positive association between self-esteem and academic performance. However, this association often shrinks considerably when researchers control for other factors associated with achievement. For example, in a study of 530 twelve-year-olds, self-esteem was positively correlated with scores on a variety of achievement tests, but self-esteem accounted for very little (less than 3%) of the variation in student test scores after researchers accounted for students' IQ and socioeconomic status (Rubin, Dorle, & Sandidge, 1977). The researchers concluded that the practical significance of self-esteem as a predictor of academic performance was "negligible" (p. 506). Similarly, based on data from 800 college students, Stupnisky and colleagues (2007) reported a very weak correlation between self-esteem and first-year college grade point average, but this correlation was reduced to nonsignificance after the researchers controlled for students' age, sex, and high-school grades. In both of these studies, as well as several more reviewed by Wylie (1979), measures of ability and past academic performance were the best predictors of later academic performance and accounted for most, or all, of the variation in performance associated with self-esteem.

Personality variables may also supersede self-esteem in predicting academic performance. Crocker and Luhtanen (2003) collected data from more than 600 first-year college students and found, similar to other researchers, that self-esteem measured prior to the start of college was not associated with students' first-semester grade point average. Although self-esteem was weakly correlated with the number of academic problems that students reported during their first semester of college, the correlation was reduced to nonsignificance when the researchers controlled for personality variables such as neuroticism. It therefore appears that the association between self-esteem and academic performance may be better explained by other characteristics associated with both variables.

The most important question regarding the role of self-esteem in education – assuming the existence of at least a weak correlation – is whether self-esteem plays a causal role in academic performance. Drawing causal conclusions about the effects of self-esteem is challenging since it is not possible to conduct an experiment where participants are randomly assigned to have either high or low self-esteem. However, Baumeister and colleagues (2003) note that causal determinations can be informed by correlational findings. At a minimum, they state, causes must come before effects, so self-esteem at one point in time must first be shown to correlate with school performance at a later point in time. Accordingly, researchers have used longitudinal methods to study links between self-esteem and academic performance. A second approach has been for researchers to use a complex statistical technique known as structural equation modeling – often in conjunction with longitudinal data collection methods – to help determine the likely direction of influence between variables.

In one early longitudinal study, Bachman and O'Malley (1977) analyzed data from more than 1,600 tenth-grade boys who participated in a national study in the United States. Data were collected at five points in time beginning when the students were in tenth grade and continuing for eight years. A composite intellectual ability measure was administered in tenth grade, and students reported their course grades from the year before data collection began. At each point of data collection, students completed self-esteem surveys and reported information on their academic achievement. Each time data were collected, higher self-esteem was associated with greater educational attainment. The researchers then used structural equation modeling to examine possible causal links between the variables and determined that self-esteem in high school is correlated with later academic achievement because both variables are affected by other important factors such as actual academic ability, past academic performance, and family socioeconomic status. Bachman and O'Malley concluded that "self-esteem *adds* very little by way of a contribution to later attainment" (p. 377, italics in original). The researchers later reanalyzed the data from the same sample (Bachman & O'Malley, 1986). They concluded that actual academic ability is by far the most important determinant of academic performance and that self-esteem is not a causal factor, but rather that academic success leads to improved self-esteem.

In another longitudinal study, Ross and Broh (2000) analyzed data from 8,800 US students from whom data were collected in eighth, tenth, and twelfth grades. At each point in time, students completed academic achievement tests and the researchers recorded students' grades. The researchers found that earlier academic success predicted later self-esteem, but that increases in self-esteem did not predict later improvements in academic performance. Like other researchers, Ross and Broh found that the factor most highly correlated with academic performance was previous academic performance.

Researchers reached a similar conclusion based on an analysis of data from more than 23,000 high school students who were part of a national longitudinal study (Pottebaum, Keith, & Ehly (2001). Students in this study completed several standardized ability tests, a self-esteem measure, and a family background questionnaire during their sophomore year of high school and again two years later. Based on structural equation modeling, Pottebaum and colleagues found no evidence that self-esteem was a causal factor in academic performance and concluded that other variables are responsible for both self-esteem and school achievement. Using data from a representative US sample of nearly 1,900 boys who were likewise tested in tenth grade and again two years later, Rosenberg, Schooler, and Schoenbach (1989) found evidence that academic success as measured by class grades has a significant effect on later self-esteem, but that self-esteem has no significant impact on later academic performance.

In another study, researchers examined data from younger children assessed over a longer period of time (Maruyama, Rubin, & Kingsbury, 1981). Maruyama and colleagues analyzed data from a longitudinal research project involving children born in Minnesota over four consecutive years. The children's' socioeconomic status was assessed at birth, IQ was measured at age 7, standardized achievement tests were administered at ages 9, 12, and 15, and self-esteem was assessed at age 12. The researchers found no evidence of a causal link – in either direction – between self-esteem and academic success; rather, they concluded that the association between the two variables was due to the fact that intelligence and socioeconomic status caused both.

Some evidence even calls into question the very existence of a correlation between self-esteem measured at one point in time and academic performance measured at a later time. In her study of more than 900 high school students, Byrne (1986) observed only a very small correlation between self-esteem and academic achievement, and found no evidence to suggest a causal link. Valentine and colleagues (2004) performed a meta-analysis integrating the findings from 55 studies where researchers used a longitudinal design to examine the association between self-beliefs and later academic performance. In all the studies, the original researchers had controlled for initial academic achievement. Valentine and colleagues found that the overall link was extremely weak and concluded that "evidence is lacking to support theoretical or applied perspectives in which self-beliefs are characterized as a strong and pervasive influence on student achievement" (p. 127). Following their analysis of high school students, Stupnisky and colleagues (2007) likewise "found no evidence that students' level of self-esteem directly influences their academic achievement" (p. 316). Although most studies have been conducted in the United States, researchers studying more than 600 Norwegian elementary school students (Skaalvik & Hagtvet, 1990) and more than 5,000 German seventh graders (Trautwein, Lüdtke, Köller, & Baumert, 2006) have reached similar conclusions.

As noted early in this chapter, the emphasis on increasing students' self-esteem as a means to improve their academic performance was borne largely out of intuitive appeal and early correlational evidence. Many teachers and parents have assumed that how students feel about themselves plays a critical role in determining their academic success (Pottebaum et al., 2001). This assumption has triggered the development of countless interventions designed to directly increase student self-esteem. There is evidence that such interventions can in fact enhance self-esteem. Haney and Durlak (1998) meta-analyzed findings from 120 interventions and concluded that, on average, such interventions lead to a modest increase in participants' self-esteem. However, the researchers also found that interventions were far more effective in increasing self-esteem among participants with behavioral or mental health problems than participants without such problems. The average effect of such interventions among participants with no preexisting problems was very weak – calling into question the premise that self-esteem in normal populations can be meaningfully increased via educational interventions.

Despite the apparently modest effects of self-esteem interventions, it is important to test whether such interventions improve students' academic performance. Schreier and Kraut (1979) reviewed eight published and 18 unpublished studies on the effectiveness of self-concept improvement interventions for improving academic performance. The studies included students from preschool to high school, and several of the studies were based on large samples. Schreier and Kraut concluded that there was no reliable link between self-esteem interventions and academic achievement, and referred to the evidence for a causal link between self-views and academic performance as "overwhelmingly negative" (p. 145). They noted that many studies have methodological flaws such as lack of random assignment, but doubted that such limitations could account for the chronic lack of effect across studies. They argued that there have been too many trials to continue asserting that self-esteem interventions were bringing about significant changes in academic performance. It is noteworthy that this review was published over 30 years ago, but did little to dispel the belief that increasing student self-esteem would improve academic achievement.

Surprisingly, emphasizing students' self-esteem may sometimes be detrimental to their academic success. In a particularly thought-provoking study, researchers found that focusing on student self-esteem caused a decline in student performance (Forsyth et al., 2007). Forsyth and colleagues predicted that an intervention to increase self-esteem would boost academic performance in college students. They randomly assigned 90 students who earned a C, D, or F on the first exam in a large undergraduate psychology course to receive either six weekly emails containing review questions regarding course content, or six weekly emails containing both the review questions and messages indicating the importance of self-esteem. The self-esteem messages encouraged students to maintain a positive self-view. The researchers' prediction that the self-esteem messages would boost test scores was not supported, and in fact the opposite effect occurred. Students who had earned Ds and Fs on the first exam with an average of 57%, and who received the self-esteem intervention, earned an average of 38% on the final exam. The authors noted that this change was both statistically and practically significant – in that the average score dropped from nearly passing to far below passing. The average score of D and F students in the control condition did not change significantly from the first exam to the final, and C students' grades declined slightly across both conditions. Forsyth and colleagues recommended that self-esteem interventions used in schools be carefully evaluated, asserting that it may actually be detrimental to boost self-esteem without more directly helping students improve school performance. They concluded that "persuading students to think well of themselves despite having performed poorly on a first test seems, if anything, to make students do even worse" (p. 458).

A noteworthy body of evidence has emerged suggesting that academic achievement is more strongly associated with specific elements of self-esteem than with general self-esteem. Marsh and Craven (2006) argue that many inconsistent findings regarding the link between self-concept and academic performance can be explained by conceptualizing self-concept as a multidimensional factor rather than as a single global characteristic. General self-concept, they assert, can be better understood by considering specific components of self-worth – both academic and nonacademic. Accordingly, they maintain that academic self-concept will be a much stronger and more important factor than general self-esteem in predicting academic performance. Since aspects of self-concept that are relevant to a specific outcome will be better predictors, it is perhaps not surprising that global self-esteem is often associated minimally or not at all with academic performance.

A number of studies provide support for Marsh's and Craven's (2006) proposal. For example, Shavelson and Bolus (1982) had seventh and eighth grade students complete measures of both global self-esteem and academic self-esteem, as well as a standardized achievement test. Data were collected in February approximately two weeks after fall semester grades were distributed, and again in June just before the school year ended. The researchers also obtained students' class grades for both semesters. Shavelson and Bolus found that global self-esteem was only slightly associated with grades, academic self-concept was more strongly associated with grades, and subject-specific academic self-concept was even more strongly associated with grades in specific courses. For example, science grades correlated .12 with global self-esteem, .37 with academic self-concept, and .43 with self-concept specific to science ability. The same pattern emerged for math and English. The researchers concluded that self-esteem is actually a multifaceted and hierarchical characteristic in that subject-specific self-concept is a component of academic self-concept, which in turn is a component of global self-concept; prediction of performance improves with increasing specificity of the self-concept measures.

Many other studies similarly show that measures of self-esteem specific to academic ability are much stronger predictors of academic perfor-mance than are measures of global self-esteem (Wylie, 1979; Hansford & Hattie, 1982; Skaalvik & Hagtvet, 1990; Trautwein et al., 2006). Moreover, there is evidence that academic self-esteem accounts for the association between global self-esteem and academic performance. Pullman and Allik (2008) studied more than 4,500 Estonian students ranging from second graders through university applicants who com-pleted measures of general and academic self-esteem – the latter defined as beliefs about one's competence specific to academics. The correlations between general self-esteem and grade point average fell primarily in the .20–.28 range, and they tended to decline as students progressed through school so that the correlation for students in twelfth grade was only .09. In contrast, the association between academic self-esteem and grade point average was much higher with an average correlation of .53. Moreover, the link between general self-esteem and grades was no longer significant when the researchers accounted for academic self-esteem. Pullman and Allik concluded that academic self-esteem can contribute to overall self-esteem, but is only one component. It is interesting to note that, consist-ent with this conclusion, most researchers reporting the strongest correlations between general self-esteem and academic performance have used a measure of self-esteem that includes some items pertaining to self-concept regarding academic ability (e.g., Simon & Simon, 1975; Rubin et al., 1977; Seabi, 2011).

Other researchers have likewise emphasized the difference between general and specific self-esteem. Rosenberg, Schooler, Schoenbach, and Rosenberg (1995) described self-esteem as an attitude and asserted that like any attitude, self-esteem consists of both cognitive and affective components. They suggested that global self-esteem is primarily affective in nature and is therefore more relevant to psychological health, while specific types such as academic self-esteem are more cognitive in nature and are more relevant to behavior and behavioral outcomes. Accordingly, they suggested that researchers have often studied the "wrong type of self-esteem" when examining the link with academic achievement, and argued that studying predictors of a specific outcome requires studying specific types of self-esteem relevant to that outcome (p. 54).

Rosenberg and colleagues (1995) analyzed data from nearly 1,900 tenth grade boys who were part of a longitudinal study of students across the United States. Like Pullman and Allik (2008), they found that the link between academic self-esteem and grades is twice as strong as the link between general self-esteem and grades. Rosenberg and colleagues also found that controlling for academic self-esteem shrinks the correlation between global self-esteem and grades to an extremely small link, but the reverse is not true – controlling for global self-esteem barely affects the link between academic self-esteem and grades. The researchers then used structural equation modeling to estimate causal effects and found evidence that although global and academic self-esteem affect each other, the effect of academic self-esteem on global self-esteem is stronger than the reverse. Interestingly, Rosenberg and colleagues repeated their analysis after splitting the sample based on students' self-report of how much they valued academic success. The association between global and academic self-esteem was only replicated for students who highly valued academic success. The impact of academic self-esteem on global self-esteem for this group was nearly three times greater than the impact observed among students reporting low valuing of academic success. The researchers concluded that academic self-esteem affects global self-esteem only for students who value academic performance, and that neither global nor academic self-esteem cause students to value academic success. Instead, valuing academic success increases the role that academic success plays in one's global self-esteem.

The notion that self-concept affects behavior and that confidence in oneself leads to greater success is embedded in individualistic cultural beliefs (Schreier & Kraut, 1979; Forsyth et al., 2007). Therefore, it is perhaps not surprising that correlational studies have often been interpreted as evidence for a causal link, ultimately leading to a "fascination with self-esteem" among teachers, parents, and even researchers (Baumeister et al., 2003: 2). Educational objectives often emphasize teaching students that self-esteem is important for academic success (Stupnisky et al., 2007). Advocates of the so-called self-esteem movement often begin from the premise that a great many people suffer from low self-esteem, but in fact – at least in the United States – most people score above the midpoint on measures of self-esteem, which suggests that most people actually feel quite good about themselves (Baumeister et al., 2003). It also appears that overall self-esteem scores for people from elementary age through college have increased over the last several decades (Twenge & Campbell, 2001). Interestingly, this increase in population self-esteem over time coincided with a decrease in average SAT scores (Forsyth et al., 2007).

Researchers have concluded that self-esteem even among very young children tends to be very high. Bridgeman and Shipman (1978) studied 404 children who were between 3.5 and 4.5 years old at the beginning of a longitudinal study. Each year for four years, the children took a preschool version a self-esteem test that involved having adults ask questions using visual stimuli. They also completed various measures of academic achievement. Even in this sample, which was ethnically diverse and consisted mostly of low-income students, self-esteem scores among preschoolers were high. The vast majority of children expressed positive self-views before they entered school, and it was not until third grade that there was more variation across children in self-esteem. Since the variation in self-esteem arose following variation in school performance, Bridgman and Shipman concluded that differences in self-esteem emerge as an effect of school performance rather than a cause. Interestingly, Bridgman and Shipman also found that preschool self-esteem scores predicted third grade academic achievement. However, they speculated that given the nature of the preschool self-esteem task, the positive association may have actually been due to differences in students' ability to pay attention to and understand the tasks rather than actual self-esteem. This pattern would be consistent with other researchers' conclusions that the critical factor in educational success is actual ability rather than views about the self (Bachman & O'Malley, 1986).

If self-esteem results from academic success rather than causing it, educators wishing to improve students' achievement should perhaps focus on students' academic abilities rather than on their self-concepts (Bachman & O'Malley, 1986). Baumeister and colleagues (2003) point out that interventions designed to directly increase self-esteem without improving academic skills could backfire because students could experience the reward of high self-esteem without achieving actual success. This could lead students to expend less effort on school work because feeling good about themselves is no longer a potential reward for academic achievement.

Other researchers conclude that although interventions to improve students' global self-esteem are ineffective for improving academic achievement, increasing students' academic self-esteem might actually improve performance (Rosenberg et al., 1995). They point out, as others have (e.g., Shokraii, 1996), that educational interventions have typically focused on global self-esteem. Baumeister and colleagues (2005) concluded that promoting general self-esteem offers little benefit "beyond the seductive pleasure it brings to those engaged in the exercise" (p. 91). Even if educators emphasize academic self-esteem rather than global self-concept, the effects are likely to be short-lived in the absence of a con-current emphasis on academic competence (Marsh & Craven, 2006). Of course, none of this means that teachers and parents should be indifferent to how students feel about themselves – especially when students appear to be having mental health problems. However, the evidence that broad efforts to improve students' self-esteem will enhance their academic performance is extraordinarily weak.

References

Bachman, J. G. & O'Malley, P. M. (1977). Self-esteem in young men: A longitudinal analysis of the impact of educational and occupational attainment. *Journal of Personality and Social Psychology, 35,* 365–380.

Bachman, J. G. & O'Malley, P. M. (1986). Self-concepts, self-esteem, and educational experiences: The frog pond revisited (again). *Journal of Personality and Social Psychology, 50,* 35–46.

Baumeister, R. (2005). Rethinking self-esteem: Why nonprofits should stop pushing self-esteem and endorsing self-control. *Stanford Social Innovation Review, 3,* 34–41.

Baumeister, R. F., Campbell, J. D., Krueger, J. I., & Vohs, K. D. (2003). Does high self-esteem cause better performance, interpersonal success, happiness, or healthier lifestyles? *Psychological Science in the Public Interest, 4,* 1–44.

Baumeister, R. F., Campbell, J. D., Krueger, J. I., & Vohs, K. D. (2005). Exploding the self-esteem myth. *Scientific American, 292,* 84–91.

Bridgeman, B. & Shipman, V. C. (1978). Preschool measures of self-esteem and achievement motivation as predictors of third-grade achievement. *Journal of Educational Psychology, 70,* 17–28.

Byrne, B. M. (1986). Self-concept/academic achievement relations: An investigation of dimensionality, stability, and causality. *Canadian Journal of Behavioural Science, 18,* 173–186.

California Task Force to Promote Self-Esteem and Personal and Social Responsibility. (1990). *Toward a state of self-esteem.* Sacramento: California State Department of Education.

Crocker, J. & Luhtanen, R. K. (2003). Level of self-esteem and contingencies of self-worth: Unique effects on academic, social, and financial problems in college students. *Personality and Social Psychology Bulletin, 29,* 701–712.

Demo, D. H. & Parker, K. D. (1987). Academic achievement and self-esteem among black and white college students. *Journal of Social Psychology, 127,* 345–355.

EduNova (2012). Student confidence and self-esteem. Available at: www.edunova.com/articles/student-confidence.

Forsyth, D. R., Lawrence, N. K., Burnette, J. L., & Baumeister, R. F. (2007). Attempting to improve the academic performance of struggling college students by bolstering their self-esteem: An intervention that backfired. *Journal of Social and Clinical Psychology, 26,* 447–459.

Haney, P. & Durlak, J. A. (1998). Changing self-esteem in children and adolescents: A meta-analytic review. *Journal of Clinical Child Psychology, 27,* 423–433.

Hansford, B. C. & Hattie, J. A. (1982). The relationship between self and achievement/performance measures. *Review of Educational Research, 52,* 123–142.

Leeson, P., Ciarrochi, J., & Heaven, P. C. L. (2008). Cognitive ability, personality, and academic performance in adolescence. *Personality and Individual Differences, 45,* 630–635.

Marsh, H. W. & Craven, R. G. (2006). Reciprocal effects of self-concept and performance from a multidimensional perspective. *Perspectives on Psychological Science, 1,* 133–163.

Maruyama, G., Rubin, R. A., & Kingsbury, G. G. (1981). Self-esteem and educational achievement: Independent constructs with a common cause? *Journal of Personality and Social Psychology, 40,* 962–975.

Nabayunga, F. (2013). Uganda: Self-esteem improves students' grades. Available at: http://allafrica.com/stories/201305090847.html.

Pottebaum, S. M., Keith, T. Z., & Ehly, S. W. (1986). Is there a causal relation between self-concept and academic achievement? *Journal of Educational Research, 79,* 140–144.

Pullman, H. & Allik, J. (2008). Relations of academic and general self-esteem to school achievement. *Personality and Individual Differences, 45,* 559–564.

Rosenberg, M., Schooler, C., & Schoenbach, C. (1989). Self-esteem and adolescent problems: Modeling reciprocal effects. *American Sociological Review, 54,* 1004–1018.

Rosenberg, M., Schooler, C., Schoenbach, C., & Rosenberg, F. (1995). Global self-esteem and specific self-esteem: Different concepts, different outcomes. *American Sociological Review, 60,* 141–156.

Ross, C. E. & Broh, B. A. (2000). The roles of self-esteem and the sense of personal control in the academic achievement process. *Sociology of Education, 73,* 270–284.

Rubin, R. A., Dorle, J., & Sandidge, S. (1977). Self-esteem and school performance. *Psychology in the Schools, 14,* 503–507.

Schreier, M. A. & Kraut, R. E. (1979). Increasing educational achievement via self-concept change. *Review of Educational Research, 49,* 131–150.

Seabi, J. (2011). Relating learning strategies, self-esteem, intellectual functioning with academic achievement among first-year engineering students. *South African Journal of Psychology, 41,* 239–249.

Shavelson, R. J. & Bolus, R. (1982). Self-concept: The interplay of theory and methods. *Journal of Educational Psychology, 74*, 3–17.

Shokraii, N. H. (1996). *The self-esteem fraud: Why feel-good education does not lead to academic success*. Washington, DC: Center for Equal Opportunity.

Simon, W. E. & Simon, M. G. (1975). Self-esteem, intelligence and standardized academic achievement. *Psychology in the Schools, 12*, 97–100.

Skaalvik, E. M. & Hagtvet, K. A. (1990). Academic achievement and self-concept: An analysis of causal predominance in a developmental perspective. *Journal of Personality and Social Psychology, 58*, 292–307.

Stupnisky, R. H., Renaud, R. D., Perry, R. P., Ruthig, J. C., Haynes, T. L., & Clifton, R. A. (2007). Comparing self-esteem and perceived control as predictors of first-year college students' academic achievement. *Social Psychology and Education, 10*, 303–330.

Trautwein, U., Lüdtke, O., Köller, O., & Baumert, J. (2006). Self-esteem, academic self-concept, and achievement: How the learning environment moderates the dynamics of self-concept. *Journal of Personality and Social Psychology, 90*, 334–349.

Twenge, J. M. & Campbell, W. K. (2001). Age and birth cohort differences in self-esteem: A cross-temporal meta-analysis. *Personality and Social Psychology Review, 5*, 321–344.

Valentine, J. C., DuBois, D. L., & Cooper, H. (2004). The relation between self-beliefs and academic achievement: A meta-analytic review. *Educational Psychologist, 39*, 111–133.

Wylie, R. C. (1979). *The self-concept, vol. 2: Theory and research on selected topics*. Lincoln: University of Nebraska Press.

Zimmerman, M. A., Copeland, L. A., Shope, J. T., & Dielman, T. E. (1997). A longitudinal study of self-esteem: Implications for adolescent development. *Journal of Youth and Adolescence, 26*, 117–141.

11

MYTH: REPETITION IS A HIGHLY EFFECTIVE STUDY STRATEGY

Most students believe that repeatedly reviewing course material is an effective study method, and surveys indicate that rereading textbook chapters is students' most common study strategy (Amlund, Kardash, & Kulhavy, 1986; Karpicke, Butler, & Roediger, 2009). In one study, approximately two-thirds of students reported rereading text chapters in preparation for exams (Carrier, 2003). Repetition certainly can enhance memory. Surely everyone has experience with repeating a phone number or items from a shopping list in an effort to retain the information and perhaps transfer it to long-term memory. Not surprisingly, numerous studies demonstrate that memory is often enhanced when learners are exposed to information more than once (e.g., Rothkopf, 1968). However, most studies of this sort have been conducted in laboratory settings with immediate performance on a simple recall task as the criterion for successful learning. Research using learning content and assessments more directly relevant to education suggests that the benefits of repeated exposure to the same information – usually through rereading text materials – tend to be quite modest. Although students who report using more active study strategies that promote deeper processing and better retention tend to perform better on exams than students who simply reread text material, most students do not use these active strategies (Carrier, 2003).

Great Myths of Education and Learning, First Edition. Jeffrey D. Holmes.
© 2016 John Wiley & Sons, Inc. Published 2016 by John Wiley & Sons, Inc.

Researchers have demonstrated that repeated exposure to academic material enhances learning at least somewhat beyond what can be acquired through a single reading. This unsurprising finding has been demonstrated in a variety of laboratory studies. For example, Amlund and colleagues (1986) randomly assigned graduate students to read a text passage either once, twice, or three times. Participants who read the passage more than once did so in immediate succession. Next, the students took a free recall test where they reproduced all the text they could remember from the passage, and a cued test made up of completion items. Participants who read the passage more than once recalled a significantly greater number of words and correctly answered more of the test items than students who read the passage only a single time. This difference in learning was only partially retained when participants were retested a week later. Importantly, there was no difference in immediate test performance between students who read the material twice and those who read it three times. The authors therefore concluded that the benefits of repeated exposure to text information are greatest the first time the content is reread. Subsequent readings appear unlikely to offer much additional benefit.

Several characteristics of Amlund and colleagues' (1986) study may limit the generalizability of the findings to real-life academic settings. First, the roughly 700-word text passage that students read is much shorter than the text segments students typically read for their classes. Second, most students studying for actual classes probably do not reread the exact same text content immediately after reading it the first time. Finally, the differences between the single-read and multiple-read groups were significant when testing was immediate, but the benefits of rereading were small and were only partially retained on a delayed test. Given that there is generally some delay between when students do the bulk of their studying and when they take an exam, the benefits of rereading in preparation for a delayed test are more relevant to what happens in educational environments. Amlund and colleagues' findings suggest that students gain little in terms of delayed test performance from reading text multiple times.

Researchers have also compared the effects of rereading content immediately versus having a delay between readings. Dunlosky and Rawson (2005) had undergraduate students read six passages adapted from a Graduate Record Examination (GRE) practice test. Students were randomly assigned to read the passages a single time, to reread them immediately, or to reread them a week after the first reading. Students then answered multiple-choice questions assessing knowledge of specific factual information from each passage, as well as questions requiring them to make inferences based on the passage content. Dunlosky and Rawson reported that rereading – whether immediate or delayed – had no effect on students' test performance overall, nor did it improve performance specifically on either type of test question. Testing in this study was again conducted immediately after participants studied the text material. Researchers have extended such work by examining the effects of repetition on delayed test performance, which more closely mimics students' real-life study activities.

Rawson and Kintsch (2005) compared the effects of immediate and delayed rereading on both immediate and delayed tests. They conducted two experiments with a total of more than 400 undergraduate participants, again randomly assigned to read text material a single time, to reread immediately, or to reread a week after the first reading. Half of the students were tested on the material immediately after their final reading of the text, and half were tested two days after their final reading. The test included a free recall task where participants reproduced all the content they could remember from one section of the text, as well as short-answer questions testing comprehension of text material. Immediate rereading led to better performance on an immediate test, but did not improve performance on a delayed test. In contrast, spaced rereading improved performance on a delayed test, but not on an immediate test. The authors concluded that distributed repetition led to more durable learning, and that learning associated with immediate repetition was far more fragile.

In a particularly thought-provoking study, researchers investigated whether the benefits of rereading might depend on students' academic ability and the nature of the outcome measures used to assess learning. Barnett and Seefeldt (1989) used a median split of ACT scores to divide college students into groups of high and low academic ability. All students were randomly assigned to read, either once or twice, a passage on various legal principles. Students then took an essay test assessing knowledge of factual information taken directly from the passage, and also assessing their ability to apply what they had read to novel examples. The tests were scored by experimenters unaware of which students were in which experimental condition. When tested on direct factual information, high-ability students performed better than low-ability students, and those who read the passage twice performed better than those who read the passage once. More interestingly, when assessed on ability to apply what they had read, only high-ability students benefitted from reading the material a second time. Barnett and Seefeldt offered several possible explanations for this difference. They speculated that low-ability students may tend to emphasize concrete learning as they study or may put forth less effort when rereading because they have less insight into the shortcomings in their knowledge; alternatively, the study strategies used by high-ability students when rereading may be more sophisticated than those used by low-ability students. The researchers concluded that rereading can be an effective study strategy, but that students do not all benefit to the same degree and the benefits may not extend to all types of tests. Barnett and Seefeldt interpreted their findings in reference to students who complain that they read assigned material numerous times but still struggle on tests, emphasizing that when tests assess something beyond factual content, rereading is unlikely to offer much advantage – particularly for low ability students.

Several researchers have voiced concern that most studies of the effects of rereading have been conducted in laboratories rather than classrooms (e.g., Callender & McDaniel, 2009). Although laboratory research offers greater experimental control, the findings may have limited applicability to real-life educational practices. Callender and McDaniel attempted to bridge this gap by conducting four laboratory experiments using text content and test formats similar to those found in actual courses. In each experiment, undergraduate students were randomly assigned to either single or repeated reading groups. The text material was drawn from psychology textbooks and an article from a scholarly periodical appropriate for undergraduates, and the passages were longer (about 2,000 words) than those used in many laboratory studies. The effectiveness of rereading was assessed using multiple-choice and short-answer items focused on understanding of content rather than simple free recall of words.

Callender and McDaniel (2009) drew a number of important conclusions from their four experiments. Failing to replicate some earlier findings described above, the researchers found that rereading text did not improve learning regardless of whether students took a test of the material immediately or after a 24-hour delay. This was true regardless of participants' reading comprehension ability and prior familiarity with the material – students with strong reading comprehension skills did not benefit from rereading more than students with poorer comprehension skills, nor did students studying content about which they had some prior knowledge benefit more than students studying unfamiliar material. Callender and McDaniel concluded that, in general, test performance is the same whether the content is read once or twice, and asserted that improvements in learning associated with rereading do not translate to real-life educational practices.

Other researchers have drawn similar conclusions to those reached by Callender and McDaniel (2009). Dunlosky, Rawson, Marsh, Nathan, and Willingham (2013) conducted a comprehensive review of research on the effectiveness of numerous study strategies. They confirmed that rereading is one of the most common study techniques used by students across all levels of academic performance. They also reported that repetition does tend to have some positive effect on learning and that this effect occurs whether participants read text passages or listen to the passages on an audio recording. Consistent with research cited early in this chapter, they concluded that rereading tends to be more beneficial when there are time lags between repetitions than when participants reread content immediately, and that most of the benefits of rereading occur after just one repetition – with additional repetitions providing little additional benefit.

Notwithstanding some limited potential increase in learning as a result of rereading, Dunlosky and colleagues (2013) also identified several important caveats. They note, for example, that all the experimental research on the effects of rereading academic material has taken place in laboratory settings rather than classrooms. No published experiments have included actual course content in an actual course setting, nor have any experiments included real class exams as outcome measures. This is particularly important given that researchers have observed little or no benefit from rereading when experimental materials closely resemble text content and assessment measures found in educational settings (see Callender & McDaniel, 2009). Dunlosky and colleagues further note that in most studies, participants reread content immediately and were then tested immediately, which does not necessarily mimic the way students actually study and take exams – a concern echoed elsewhere (Rawson & Kintsch, 2005). When participants are tested after a delay, those who had reread the material often do no better than those who had read it only once. Finally, any potential gains from rereading likely depend in part on the nature of the outcome measure. Dunlosky and colleagues point out that in studies using free recall tests, where participants must simply reproduce as much text as possible from memory, repeated reading tends to produce positive effects. However, students generally do not encounter such tests in academic settings. The researchers explain that some studies have shown positive rereading effects on measures such as completion tests of factual information, but benefits on multiple-choice tests are generally weak or nonexistent. For tests requiring participants to apply what they have read, rereading has again produced mixed results, with some studies showing modest benefits, some studies showing no benefits, and some studies showing benefits only for students with high academic ability. Given the equivocal findings across hundreds of studies, and the fact that rereading effects, when observed, tend to be small, Dunlosky and colleagues concluded that rereading has "low utility" (p. 29) as a study technique.

Given that repeatedly rereading academic material appears to produce limited gains in terms of student learning, it is important to consider whether students' time would be better spent applying alternative study strategies. Alternative strategies would still require that students read information at least once, but might yield greater benefits than rereading because they require students to engage with the material in a more cognitively active manner. Students reading a text more than once may perform better on an exam than students who read only once and who do nothing else to prepare for the exam. Moreover, rereading content may be similarly effective to other relatively passive study techniques such as highlighting or summarizing (Rawson and Kintsch, 2005). However, in direct comparison with rereading, some techniques have proven to be far superior in terms of students' test performance. The most noteworthy of these techniques is practice testing. Although there are other strategies that are also more effective than rereading, practice testing is unique in that students can apply the technique with very little training.

The testing effect, also known as test-enhanced learning, is addressed in Chapter 12, below, on multiple-choice testing, but is also relevant to the topic of studying by repetition. Research on the testing effect originated decades ago, but has expanded tremendously in recent years. The testing effect refers to the fact that taking a test tends to improve performance on subsequent tests of similar content, and tends to produce greater benefits than would occur from simply restudying the content (Roediger & Karpicke, 2006a). In a particularly vivid illustration of test-enhanced learning, Roediger and Karpicke (2006b) conducted two experiments involving academic text material. In the first experiment, undergraduate students read two brief text passages and then either read the text again or took a free recall test where they recalled as much of the text as possible from memory. All participants then took a recall test five minutes, two days, or one week later. When tested after only five minutes, students who reread performed better on a recall test than students who had taken a practice recall test. However, when tested after either two days or one week – a scenario more closely resembling what happens in real life – students who had taken a practice test performed better than students who had reread the text. That is, students who had taken a practice test rather than rereading retained more of the text material over time.

In their second experiment, Roediger and Karpicke (2006b) used an even more sophisticated research design. They assigned undergraduate students to one of three conditions in which some students read passages four times, some read three times and then took a free recall practice test, and some read only once and took three practice recall tests. Students then took a final recall test either five minutes or one week later. Replicating the pattern from the first experiment, students who read multiple times performed better on the immediate recall test than students in either of the practice test conditions. When tested after a week's delay, however, students who had taken three practice tests recalled more information than students tested only once, and students tested once recalled more than students who simply reread the passages. Once again, taking a practice test led to better retention than simply rereading, and taking multiple practice tests led to better retention than taking a single practice test. What makes the findings even more striking is that Roediger and Karpicke used five-minute reading sessions and students were instructed to read the passage as many times as they could in that time frame. Students kept a tally of the number of times they had read the passage. Over the four sessions, students in the rereading condition read the passage an average of 14.2 times, whereas those in the repeated testing condition read it an average of only 3.4 times. Nonetheless, students in the testing condition retained a great deal more information a week later despite having received no feedback on their practice test performance.

In another recent study of test-enhanced learning, Weinstein, McDermott, and Roediger (2010) investigated whether students would benefit more by producing their own practice test questions than from taking an existing practice test. The researchers conducted three experiments in which students read three academic passages and then either reread them, produced their own practice test questions and answers based on the text, or took a practice test provided by the researchers. Students then took a final test on the content either immediately or after a two-day delay. The final test included both free recall and short-answer sections. Weinstein and colleagues reported that rereading led to poorer performance than either generating or responding to practice test items, and that this pattern occurred on both the immediate and delayed tests. The researchers also noted that students who responded to existing practice test items did as well on the outcome tests as students who generated their own practice items. Since generating one's own items is more time-consuming than using existing items, the researchers suggest that students can use this strategy when practice tests are unavailable, but will benefit just as much from the more efficient technique of using existing practice tests when possible.

A variety of other studies substantiate the advantages of practice testing over repeatedly studying content, and demonstrate that these advantages are neither short-lived nor limited to material explicitly appearing on the practice tests. For example, Larsen, Butler, and Roediger (2009) found that the benefits of practice testing relative to simple restudying were still present on a test given after a six-month delay. There is also evidence that practice testing leads to deeper and more meaningful cognitive processing of material, as evidenced by the fact that practice testing improves learning of related but untested content (McDaniel, Thomas, Agarwal, McDermott, & Roediger, 2013). The testing effect even translates to learning classroom lecture content. Students who took a short-answer test after viewing a lecture tended to retain more information than students who restudied a summary of the lecture (Butler and Roediger, 2007).

A thorough review of the research on the benefits of practice testing is beyond the scope of this chapter, but interested readers are encouraged to examine comprehensive reviews available elsewhere (Roediger & Karpicke, 2006a; Roediger, Agarwal, Kang, & Marsh, 2010; Dunlosky et al., 2013). Dunlosky and colleagues noted that research demonstrating the benefits of practice testing goes back more than a century, but given the sheer volume of recent research they focused mainly on the more than 100 studies conducted just in the ten years preceding their review. They drew several conclusions from the existing literature. First, practice testing using a variety of test formats – including free recall, short-answer, completion, and multiple-choice – can enhance performance on later tests. Free-recall and short-answer tests generally produce greater retention benefits than other formats – probably because they require students to engage in the more effortful retrieval process of producing answers rather than recognizing them. Nonetheless, practice testing is generally more beneficial than rereading regardless of the practice test format. Second, practice testing likewise produces benefits on a variety of outcome test formats, including those most commonly used in education (short-answer, completion, and multiple-choice). Third, practice testing can improve learning even when the final test is of a different format than the practice test, when the material on the final test is related but not identical to the material on the practice test, and when the tests involved go beyond content knowledge to include comprehension and application of learned material. Finally, the benefits of practice testing are evident in studies across a wide range of participant ages, educational levels, and ability levels, and the effects appear to be quite durable – having been demonstrated after as long as several years following initial study. Dunlosky and colleagues' overall assessment is that as a study strategy, practice testing has "high utility" (p. 35).

It is important to note that practice testing is not the only study strategy that generally produces greater learning benefits than rereading. Roediger and Pyc (2012) identify two other active study strategies that tend to provide advantages over restudying content. When using the technique known as elaborative interrogation, students actively produce their own explanations for the claims they have read about. A related technique known as self-explanation is a metacognitive strategy whereby students monitor and actively explain their learning as they read. The limitation of these strategies is that they require more time than either rereading material or taking a practice test, which might limit their practicality – particularly with less motivated students.

Students often have limited awareness of the relative effectiveness of various study techniques, and most students report that no one has ever taught them how to study (Kornell & Bjork, 2007). Karpicke and colleagues (2009) surveyed undergraduate students from a highly competitive university about the strategies they use to prepare for exams. Repeatedly rereading text material was by far the most commonly reported strategy, and more than half of the students reported it as their primary strategy. Only a small minority of students reported using strategies that involve active memory retrieval, and only 1% reported that such a strategy was their primary study technique. Interestingly, using practice testing as a deliberate study strategy is positively associated with grade point average (Hartwig & Dunlosky, 2012). Fewer than one in five of the students in Karpicke and colleagues' study reported that they would use practice testing rather than some other method such as rereading, and most of these students indicated that they would use practice tests to identify what they still needed to study rather than to enhance their learning. Karpicke and colleagues concur with other researchers (e.g., Fritz, Morris, Bjork, Gelman, & Wickens, 2000; Wiley, Griffin, & Thiede, 2005) that repeated exposure to text content tends to make students feel more familiar with the material without necessarily increasing their knowledge or comprehension of the content. Accordingly, Roediger and Karpicke (2006b) found that students who read text content repeatedly without practice testing were more confident than students who took practice tests about how much information they would remember a week later – confidence that subsequent tests of the material revealed to be unfounded.

Roediger and Pyc (2012) assert that students should be taught about the effectiveness of active study techniques that are likely to produce much greater benefits than rereading course material. Practice testing is likely to be particularly advantageous because it does not require a great deal of special instruction and is generally no more time consuming than rereading. Of course, the effectiveness of any study technique depends on student motivation. Rereading, practice testing, and all other study strategies are irrelevant for students who do not study the first time, but motivated students will likely learn more effectively by applying alternatives to rereading.

References

Amlund, J. T., Kardash, C. A. M., & Kulhavy, R. W. (1986). Repetitive reading and recall of expository text. *Reading Research Quarterly, 21*, 49–58.

Barnett, J. E. & Seefeldt, R. W. (1989). Read something once, why read it again? Repetitive reading and recall. *Journal of Reading Behavior, 21*, 351–360.

Butler, A. C. & Roediger, H. L. (2007). Testing improves long-term retention in a simulated classroom setting. *European Journal of Cognitive Psychology, 19*, 514–527.

Callender, A. A. & McDaniel, M. A. (2009). The limited benefits of rereading educational texts. *Contemporary Educational Psychology, 34*, 30–41.

Carrier, L. M. (2003). College students' choices of study strategies. *Perceptual and Motor Skills, 96*, 54–56.

Dunlosky, J. & Rawson, K. A. (2005). Why does rereading improve metacomprehension accuracy? Evaluating the levels-of-disruption hypothesis for the rereading effect. *Discourse Processes, 40*, 37–55.

Dunlosky, J., Rawson, K. A., Marsh, E. J., Nathan, M. J., & Willingham, D. T. (2013). Improving students' learning with effective learning techniques: Promising directions from cognitive and educational psychology. *Psychological Science in the Public Interest, 14*, 4–58.

Fritz, C. O., Morris, P. E., Bjork, R. A., Gelman, R., & Wickens, T. D. (2000). When further learning fails: Stability and change following repeated presentation of text. *British Journal of Psychology, 91*, 493–511.

Hartwig, M. K. & Dunlosky, J. (2012). Study strategies of college students: Are self-testing and scheduling related to achievement? *Psychonomic Bulletin & Review, 19*, 126–134.

Karpicke, J. D., Butler, A. C., & Roediger, H. L. (2009). Metacognitive strategies in student learning: Do students practice retrieval when they study on their own. *Memory, 17*, 471–479.

Kornell, N. & Bjork, R. A. (2007). The promise and perils of self-regulated study. *Psychonomic Bulletin & Review, 14*, 219–224.

Larsen, D. P., Butler, A. C., & Roediger, H. L. (2009). Repeated testing improves long-term retention relative to repeated study: A randomised controlled trial. *Medical Education, 43*, 1174–1181.

McDaniel, M. A., Thomas, R. C., Agarwal, P. K., McDermott, K. B., & Roediger, H. L. (2013). Quizzing in middle-school science: Successful transfer performance on classroom exams. *Applied Cognitive Psychology, 27*, 360–372.

Rawson, K. A. & Kintsch, W. (2005). Rereading effects depend on time of test. *Journal of Educational Psychology, 97*, 70–80.

Roediger, H. L. & Karpicke, J. D. (2006a). The power of testing memory: Basic research and implications for educational practice. *Perspectives on Psychological Science, 1*, 181–210.

Roediger, H. L. & Karpicke, J. D. (2006b). Test-enhanced learning: Taking memory tests improves long-term retention. *Psychological Science, 17*, 249–255.

Roediger, H. L. & Pyc, M. A. (2012). Inexpensive techniques to improve education: Applying cognitive psychology to enhance educational practice. *Journal of Applied Research in Memory and Cognition, 1*, 242–248.

Roediger, H. L., Agarwal, P. K., Kang, S. H. K, & Marsh, E. J. (2010). Benefits of testing memory: Best practices and boundary conditions. In: G. M. Davies & D. B. Wright (Eds.), *New frontiers in applied memory* (pp. 13–49). Brighton: Psychology Press.

Rothkopf, E. Z. (1968). Textual constraint as function of repeated inspection. *Journal of Educational Psychology, 59*, 20–25.

Weinstein, Y., McDermott, K. B., & Roediger, H. L. (2010). A comparison of study strategies for passages: Rereading, answering questions, and generating questions. *Journal of Experimental Psychology: Applied, 16*, 308–316.

Wiley, J., Griffin, T. D., & Thiede, K. W. (2005). Putting the comprehension in metacomprehension. *Journal of General Psychology, 132*, 408–428.

12 MYTH: MULTIPLE-CHOICE EXAMS ARE INFERIOR TO OTHER EXAM FORMATS

Multiple-choice tests are one of the most maligned educational tools in existence. Instructors often criticize multiple-choice tests, based primarily on the assumption that such tests can only assess superficial knowledge and therefore other forms of examination are better measures of deeper and more meaningful student learning (see Frederiksen, 1984). Students sometimes complain that multiple-choice tests are tricky (Appleby, 2008), even going as far as to claim a multiple-choice learning disability (Demystifying learning disabilities, n.d.). Moreover, it is easy to identify critics who claim that multiple-choice tests are "nearly always worthless" (Yermish, 2010: para. 1). The key to evaluating such claims is to determine whether multiple-choice tests assess fundamentally different forms of knowledge than tests in other formats. Hundreds of studies concerning multiple-choice tests have been conducted over nearly a century. These studies vary widely in terms of both research methodology and the specific subject matter being tested. The objective of this chapter is not to demonstrate that the multiple-choice format is superior to other formats, but rather to briefly review some representative findings to demonstrate that multiple-choice tests have their place and are not the educational boogeymen they are often made out to be.

Many researchers have compared multiple-choice with alternate test formats. These alternate formats vary, but always involve some sort of

Great Myths of Education and Learning, First Edition. Jeffrey D. Holmes.
© 2016 John Wiley & Sons, Inc. Published 2016 by John Wiley & Sons, Inc.

open-ended or constructed response so that the test-taker must provide an answer rather than choosing an answer from a set of provided options. To evaluate whether tests in various formats are assessing the same type of knowledge or skill, it is useful to begin by reviewing tests where data are available from large samples of students taking the same test. Classroom research generally does not provide such an opportunity, but large data sets are available for research using Advanced Placement exams, which hundreds of thousands of high school students take each year to earn college credit. One group of researchers (Lukhele, Thissen, & Wainer, 1994) compared multiple-choice to essay items on a number of Advanced Placement exams. These researchers pointed out that, relative to multiple-choice exams, essay exams carry great costs in terms of the time required for students to take them and instructors to score them. Moreover, essay exams introduce concerns about inter-rater reliability – whether different scorers evaluate essay responses in the same way – that are of little concern on more objective multiple-choice tests. Justifying this relative inefficiency, and the potential for subjectivity in scoring, demands a search for evidence that essay items provide information that multiple-choice items do not.

Lukhele and colleagues (1994) analyzed data from Advanced Placement Chemistry and United States History exams, and determined that the multiple-choice items were better measures of student proficiency than the essay items. Moreover, they concluded that at least for these two exams, "There is no evidence to indicate that these two kinds of questions are measuring fundamentally different things" (p. 245). The researchers also examined five years of data from seven different Advanced Placement exams and found that multiple-choice and essay sections correlated more highly than essays did with other essays. In other words, multiple-choice items are superior to essay items in predicting a student's performance on other essay items. Lukhele and colleagues note that Advanced Placement essays are constructed by highly-trained test developers and scored by highly-trained raters, which reduces measurement error. On less rigorously designed and scored tests, the researchers concluded, multiple-choice items would present an even greater advantage over essays.

Other researchers have likewise examined the equivalence of the multiple-choice and free-response sections of Advanced Placement exams. Bennett, Rock, and Wang (1991) tested the claim that free-response items assess higher-order thinking skills, while multiple-choice items assess only recognition of factual knowledge. Bennett and colleagues examined data from the Advanced Placement Computer Science test, which, they note, is designed specifically so that the multiple-choice and open-ended items assess the same content, but differ in terms of the required depth of analysis. The researchers examined data from 2,000 students drawn randomly from all students who took the computer science exam in one year. Using factor analysis, a statistical procedure for detecting underlying factors that link various tasks together, the researchers concluded that a single-factor best fit the exam data. That is, both item formats appeared to measure the same underlying psychological characteristic. Bennett and colleagues noted that although individual multiple-choice items might have some limitations in terms of measuring some cognitive processes, groups of items together likely assess many processes usually assumed to be measured only by open-ended items. They concluded that there is little evidence that multiple-choice and open-ended items are measuring different things. In a subsequent study of both computer science and chemistry Advanced Placement exams (Thissen, Wainer, & Wang, 1994), researchers reached essentially the same conclusion, asserting that although there may be some very small statistical effects associated with differences in test format, these effects are likely to have little practical significance.

In another interesting study, Bridgeman and Lewis (1994) compared the effectiveness of the multiple-choice and essay sections of several Advanced Placement exams for predicting subsequent college course grades. The researchers analyzed data from more than 7,000 students from 32 public and private colleges. For biology and American history exams, scores on the multiple-choice sections correlated more highly than essay scores with first-year college grade point average (GPA). Further, composite scores using both multiple-choice and essay items did not predict first-year GPA any better than multiple-choice items alone. In the case of English and European History exams, multiple-choice and essay sections correlated equally well with first-year GPA. There was no subject test where the essay portion was more highly correlated than the multiple-choice portion with college GPA. Bridgeman and Lewis acknowledge that Advanced Placement exams are not designed to predict future college performance, but the observed pattern of correlations does not support the notion that the essay and multiple-choice portions of the exams are measuring different things, nor that the essays are better measures of deeper knowledge or understanding.

Although most researchers comparing test formats study achievement tests designed to assess acquired knowledge, Ward (1982) examined format equivalence on a test of verbal aptitude. Based on previous research, Ward suspected that tests requiring examinees to produce an answer might demand different skills than tests requiring examinees to select an answer. He gave verbal aptitude tests containing multiple-choice items and three open-ended formats of varying complexity to 315 college students. After correcting for measurement error – the imprecision inherent in measuring any characteristic – the median correlation between test formats was .80 on a scale where 1.00 would indicate a perfect association between formats. A factor analysis revealed a single primary factor underlying all item types. Ward concluded that with respect to verbal aptitude, open-ended items provide little information not assessed by multiple-choice items, and both types of items assess similar abilities.

Rodriguez (2003) used meta-analysis, a technique for combining the results from multiple studies, to examine the equivalence of test formats across a variety of domains and educational levels. He combined the results from 67 studies and found that the average correlation between multiple-choice and open-ended tests, after correcting for measurement error, was .87. There was some variation in the correlations across studies based on whether the items with different response formats contained similar wording, but all correlations between test formats designed to measure the same content knowledge or cognitive process were very high, suggesting that tests in different formats are assessing similar characteristics. Rodriguez further noted that the correlation between different test formats was very similar regardless of whether the study had been conducted with primary, secondary, or post-secondary students.

Perhaps most relevant to teachers deciding what test format to use in their classes are studies conducted in actual classroom settings. In one study conducted more than four decades ago, Bracht and Hopkins (1970) gave students in five college psychology courses an exam containing 24 multiple-choice items assessing content from assigned reading, and two essay items designed to measure higher-order thinking such as application and analysis. A unique strength of this study is that the essays were scored by course instructors who were trained to apply a carefully constructed rubric. The correlations between the multiple-choice and essay sections, after correcting for measurement error, ranged from .81 to .95. Bracht and Hopkins concluded that many common concerns about multiple-choice tests are not grounded in empirical evidence, and that empirical data are not consistent with the claim that multiple-choice and essay exams assess different things.

In one very impressive study in a classroom setting, Hancock (1994) designed items to evaluate both knowledge and higher-order thinking skills. Hancock cited many common criticisms of multiple-choice tests, most notably that they can measure only knowledge and that open-ended items are necessary for measuring important thinking skills. He suggested that many critics fail to define what they mean by higher-order thinking and assume that essay exams measure complex thinking when often they do not. Hancock used Bloom's (1984) taxonomy of learning objectives as a framework for constructing tests for two undergraduate courses. Bloom's well-known framework hierarchically categorizes levels of learning ranging from memory of content knowledge to evaluation of information based on evidence. Each exam in Hancock's study contained both multiple-choice and open-ended items assessing course content along four of Bloom's dimensions: knowledge, comprehension, application, and analysis. Like other researchers, Hancock found that the two types of items were highly correlated, and that a single factor appeared to underlie both types of tasks – suggesting that the two test formats are comparable in terms of what they assess. He acknowledged that multiple-choice and open-ended items may at times demand somewhat different skills, but the skills are highly correlated. Hancock asserted that a multiple-choice test must be carefully designed if it is to measure higher thinking skills, but this is equally true of open-ended exams. He noted common assumptions that open-ended items measure complex thinking and multiple-choice items cannot measure complex thinking, and concluded that both assumptions are incorrect.

There is at least one specific academic skill – writing ability – that may not be adequately assessed by multiple-choice tests. Ackerman and Smith (1988) cited evidence that for tests of writing, multiple-choice and essay formats may measure different abilities. These researchers studied over 200 tenth grade students who took a multiple-choice test of basic skills such as spelling and punctuation, as well as more complex writing skills such as verbal expression and appropriate paragraph structure. Two weeks after taking the multiple-choice test, the students completed a free-response essay exam, which was scored by six English teachers who were not employed at the school from which the students were recruited. The researchers concluded from the students' test scores that when assessing writing, multiple-choice and essay exams provide different types of information. This is perhaps unsurprising for two reasons. First, the multiple-choice and essay exams used in this study were specifically designed to assess different types of knowledge. Second, an essay test in writing assesses a specific skill rather than knowledge in some particular content domain. Since declarative and procedural memory represent distinct systems pertaining to factual information and skills, respectively, it makes sense that an adequate test of writing skills would require the procedural task of actual writing. Ackerman and Smith recommend that instructors assessing writing skills use both multiple-choice and essay formats, since multiple-choice items are effective for assessing declarative aspects of writing skills and essay items are effective for assessing procedural writing skills.

Aside from the question of whether tests in differing formats assess similar constructs, a secondary criticism of multiple-choice tests is that many students are consistently disadvantaged by such tests. It is common to hear students assert that they are simply bad test-takers or do not do well on multiple-choice tests. Three researchers (Bleske-Rechek, Zeug, & Webb, 2007) recently investigated this issue. The researchers studied students in three different college psychology courses. The exams in these courses all contained both multiple-choice and short, open-ended items assessing the same content. All items were designed to assess application of concepts in addition to general retention and comprehension. The researchers compared discrepancies in performance between multiple-choice and open-ended sections across students and exams, and made two important observations. First, students' performance was not usually discrepant across the two exam formats. In other words, students tended to perform at approximately the same level on both types of exam item. Second, even students whose multiple-choice and open-ended performance was discrepant on one exam tended not to repeat the pattern on other exams. In fact, students whose scores on one test suggested format discrepancies in favor of one type of item were just as likely to demonstrate the opposite pattern on other tests. Bleske-Rechek and colleagues concluded that "students were not consistently favored by one form of assessment over another" (p. 98).

The bulk of the existing research does not support claims that multiple-choice and other exam formats assess meaningfully different constructs, or that many students are disadvantaged by having to demonstrate their knowledge using a multiple-choice format. Although students perceive essay tests to be more effective for assessing knowledge (Zeidner, 1987), Bleske-Rechek and colleagues (2007) concluded that little is objectively gained by using such tests. Wainer and Thissen (1993) went as far as to challenge readers to provide any evidence they could to counter the conclusion, based on numerous large data sets, that the multiple-choice format is superior to the open-ended format when effective item writers design tests to assess specific knowledge. These authors emphasized, however, that rather than claiming that multiple-choice tests are always superior, they were simply insisting that conclusions should be based on data rather than rhetoric. In their words: "Departing from a test format that can span the content domain of a subject without making undue time demands on examinees and that yields objective, reliable scores ought not to be done without evidence that the replacement test format does a better job" (p. 116).

Students' beliefs about test formats certainly seem to affect their approach to studying. Although many students complain that multiple-choice tests are unfair, Zeidner (1987) found that most students tend to view multiple-choice tests more positively than essay tests – believing the former to be easier, clearer, fairer, and less anxiety-provoking than the latter. In one study (Kulhavy, Dyer, & Silver, 1975), researchers found that students prepare differently for multiple-choice exams than they do for open-ended exams, but the results of the study did not show that students' study strategies for multiple-choice tests are necessarily less effective. In a subsequent study, Rickards and Friedman (1978) found that students expecting to take an essay exam took better quality notes than students expecting a multiple-choice test, but that these differing approaches did not lead to differences in subsequent test performance.

In recent years there has been a great expansion of research on how test-taking can actually enhance student learning – a phenomenon known as the testing effect. Most research on the testing effect has been based on multiple-choice tests. This research illustrates that the potential utility of multiple-choice tests goes well beyond their efficiency. For example, Roediger and Marsh (2005) had undergraduate students read nonfiction reading comprehension passages and then take a multiple-choice test on the content. A short time later, the students took a recall test on the same material. Although taking the initial multiple-choice test led students to provide some incorrect information on the recall test, students also answered more recall items correctly as a result of having taken the multiple-choice test – despite the fact that they received no feedback on their multiple-choice performance.

In a review of research on the testing effect (Marsh, Roediger, Bjork, & Bjork, 2007), researchers cited many studies demonstrating that testing improves performance on subsequent tests. Marsh and colleagues acknowledged that multiple-choice tests expose students to incorrect information in the form of incorrect response options, but they argued that the benefits of multiple-choice testing with respect to enhancing memory and improving later test performance outweigh the effects of misinformation. Butler and Roediger (2008) further demonstrated that providing feedback to students after they respond to multiple-choice items strengthens the testing effect and also reduces the amount of misinformation retained by students. Importantly, students' likelihood of retaining misinformation from having been exposed to incorrect alternative answers was reduced whether the feedback they received came immediately or after a delay. Instructors can therefore maximize the learning benefits of multiple-choice testing whether or not it is practical to provide feedback immediately.

In addition to enhancing performance on subsequent multiple-choice tests, recent evidence suggests that taking multiple-choice tests can enhance later performance on tests in another format. A group of researchers (Little, Bjork, Bjork, & Angello, 2012) had undergraduate participants read nonfiction passages and then complete either a multiple-choice or completion test on the material. After a short delay, all students took another completion test. The researchers found that taking the multiple-choice test led to better subsequent performance than taking the completion test. Moreover, taking the multiple-choice test slightly enhanced student performance on subsequent items related (but not identical) to those on the original test, whereas taking a completion test actually led to poorer performance on subsequent related items. Little and colleagues concluded that multiple-choice tests can enhance learning of content that is specifically tested, as well as related content associated with plausible incorrect alternative response options – conclusions echoed in other current literature (e.g., Glass & Sinha, 2013). Although the learning benefits of taking tests may not be limited to the multiple-choice format, the demonstrated positive effects of responding to multiple-choice items further demonstrate that the multiple-choice format has value.

Given that realities in contemporary education are likely to continue to make multiple-choice testing necessary, it is fortunate that a rich literature exists to assist instructors and other professionals who must construct such exams. Cantor (1987) noted that multiple-choice is the most popular testing format because it can be used to assess knowledge of many different subject areas as well as higher-order thinking. Cantor and others (Aiken, 1982; Stupans, 2006) provide useful guidelines for writing good multiple-choice items. In addition, Haladyna, Downing, and Rodriguez (2002) conducted a comprehensive review of research and textbook guidelines for writing multiple-choice items. Their work is an excellent resource for instructors wishing to maximize the reliability, validity, and perceived fairness of their multiple-choice tests. Appleby (2008) even developed a teaching exercise, in which students read a brief passage about different memory systems and then consider multiple-choice questions designed to assess different levels of thinking about the passage content, to help students recognize the "myth" that multiple-choice tests can assess only simple recognition and rote memory (p. 119).

In light of practical educational realities it appears that multiple-choice tests are here to stay. As class sizes at many schools continue to increase, there is a corresponding necessity to develop assessment instruments that are both valid and efficient. Fortunately, research to date suggests that many common concerns about multiple-choice testing are exaggerated or unfounded. Multiple-choice items allow instructors to assess student knowledge of broad content domains in a short period of time. Although open-ended test formats appear to permit instructors to assess higher cognitive processes and greater depth of content knowledge, evidence is sparse that typical free-response tests achieve such objectives – or that open-ended and multiple-choice tests consistently assess different things. Tests are tools and, as is always the case, choosing the right tool depends on an accurate assessment of the specific objectives one wishes to achieve.

References

Ackerman, T. A. & Smith, P. L. (1988). A comparison of the information provided by essay, multiple-choice, and free-response writing tests. *Applied Psychological Measurement, 12*, 117–128.

Aiken L. R. (1982). Writing multiple-choice items to measure higher-order educational objectives. *Educational and Psychological Measurement, 42*, 803–806.

Appleby, D. C. (2008). A cognitive taxonomy of multiple-choice questions. In: L. T. Benjamin Jr. (Ed.), *Favorite activities for the teaching of psychology* (pp. 119–123). Washington, DC: American Psychological Association.

Bennett, R. E., Rock, D. A., & Wang, M. (1991). Equivalence of free-response and multiple-choice items. *Journal of Educational Measurement, 28*, 77–92.

Bleske-Rechek, A., Zeug, N., & Webb., R. M. (2007). Discrepant performance on multiple-choice and short-answer assessments and the relation of performance to general scholastic aptitude. *Assessment & Education in Higher Education, 32*, 89–105.

Bloom, B. (Ed.). (1984). *Taxonomy of educational objectives, book 1: Cognitive domain.* 2nd edn. New York: Longman.

Bracht, G. H. & Hopkins, K. D. (1970). The communality of essay and objective tests of academic achievement. *Educational and Psychological Measurement, 30*, 359–364.

Bridgeman, B. & Lewis, C. (1994). The relationship of essay and multiple-choice scores with grades in college courses. *Journal of Educational Measurement, 31*, 37–50.

Butler, A. C. & Roediger, H. L. (2008). Feedback enhances the positive and reduces the negative effects of multiple-choice testing. *Memory & Cognition, 36*, 604–616.

Cantor, J. A. (1987). Developing multiple-choice test items. *Training and Development Journal, 41*, 85–88.

Demystifying learning disabilities (n.d.). Available at: http://www.emory.edu/ACAD_EXCHANGE/2000/octnov/learningdis.html.

Frederiksen, N. (1984). The real test bias: Influences of testing on teaching and learning. *American Psychologist, 39*, 193–202.

Glass, A. L. & Sinha, N. (2013). Multiple-choice questioning is an efficient instructional methodology that may be widely implemented in academic courses to improve exam performance. *Current Directions in Psychological Science, 22*, 471–477.

Haladyna, T. M., Downing, S. M., & Rodriguez, M. C. (2002). A review of multiple-choice item-writing guidelines for classroom assessment. *Applied Measurement in Education, 15*, 309–334.

Hancock, G. R. (1994). Cognitive complexity and the comparability of multiple-choice and constructed-response test formats. *Journal of Experimental Education, 62*, 143–157.

Kulhavy, R. W., Dyer, J. W., & Silver, L. (1975). The effects of notetaking and test expectancy on the learning of text material. *Journal of Educational Research, 68*, 363–365.

Little, J. L., Bjork, L. B., Bjork, R. A., & Angello, G. (2012). Multiple-choice tests exonerated, at least of some charges: Fostering test-induced learning and avoiding test-induced forgetting. *Psychological Science, 23*, 1337–1344.

Lukhele, R., Thissen, D., & Wainer, H. (1994). On the relative value of multiple-choice, constructed-response and examinee-selected items on two achievement tests. *Journal of Educational Measurement, 31*, 234–250.

Marsh, E. J., Roediger, H. L., Bjork, R. A., & Bjork, E. L. (2007). The memorial consequences of multiple-choice testing. *Psychonomic Bulletin & Review, 14*, 194–199.

Rickards, J. P. & Friedman, F. (1978). The encoding versus the external storage hypothesis in note taking. *Contemporary Educational Psychology, 3*, 136–143.

Rodriguez, M. C. (2003). Construct equivalence of multiple-choice and constructed-response items: A random effects synthesis of correlations. *Journal of Educational Measurement, 40*, 163–184.

Roediger, H. L. & Marsh, E. J. (2005). The positive and negative consequences of multiple-choice testing. *Journal of Experimental Psychology: Learning, Memory, and Cognition, 31*, 1155–1159.

Stupans, I. (2006). Multiple-choice questions: Can they examine application of knowledge? *Pharmacy Education, 6*, 59–63.

Thissen, D., Wainer, H., & Wang, X. (1994). Are tests comprising both multiple-choice and free-response items necessarily less unidimensional than multiple-choice tests? An analysis of two tests. *Journal of Educational Measurement, 31*, 113–123.

Wainer, H. & Thissen, D. (1993). Combining multiple-choice and constructed-response test scores: Toward a Marxist theory of test construction. *Applied Measurement in Education, 6*, 103–118.

Ward, W. C. (1982). A comparison of free-response and multiple-choice forms of verbal aptitude tests. *Applied Psychological Measurement, 6*, 1–11.

Yermish, A. (2010). Bubble, bubble, toil and trouble … (multiple choice exams). Available at: https://davincilearning.wordpress.com/2010/12/23/bubble-bubble-toil-and-trouble-multiple-choice-exams.

Zeidner, M. (1987). Essay versus multiple-choice type classroom exams: The student's perspective. *Journal of Educational Research, 80*, 352–358.

13 MYTH: STUDENTS SHOULD NOT CHANGE ANSWERS ON MULTIPLE-CHOICE EXAMS

One of the most persistent myths in education is that once a student decides on a response to a multiple-choice exam item, he or she is best advised to retain that response rather than changing to a different one. This belief has come to be known as the "first instinct fallacy," and most students have heard that changing answers on multiple-choice tests is ill advised. Indeed, it takes little time to locate sources offering strategies for taking multiple-choice exams that include the guidance that students' first response is usually correct (e.g., Top ten SAT test tips, n.d.; SAT test taking tips and techniques, n.d.).

Foote and Belinky (1972) referred to this advice as folk wisdom held by both students and instructors, and they found that 99% of the college students in their sample had heard such advice. Skinner (1983) likewise found that virtually all the college students in his sample had heard that answer-changing was inadvisable. In a small survey, Benjamin, Cavell, and Shallenberger (1984) reported that a majority of college instructors similarly believe that changing answers tends to lower scores, and most students report that instructors have advised them not to change answers (Ramsey, Ramsey, & Barnes, 1987; Geiger, 1997). Most students clearly trust the advice. Many researchers have found that the majority of students believe that initial responses are more likely to be correct, and that changing answers is therefore likely to lower test scores (Ballance, 1977; Benjamin et al., 1984; Geiger, 1991a). What is most interesting about this particular myth is the amount and consistency of the evidence against it. It is not merely that the majority of published studies show that students tend to benefit from changing answers, but that there are virtually no studies indicating otherwise.

The first study of answer-changing beliefs and effects was conducted more than 80 years ago. Matthews (1929) examined survey data from college students in an educational psychology course, and actual exam data from a larger sample of students. All but four of 28 students surveyed believed that their own answer changes on exams more often yielded incorrect answers than correct ones. Matthews studied exam responses from students in eight different college classes and found that of the answers that were changed, 53% were changed from wrong to right, while only 21% were changed from right to wrong. Matthews also reported that low-scoring students tended to make more changes than high-scoring students; low-scoring students were also less likely than high-scoring students to change answers from wrong to right. However, students at all levels tended to make more wrong-to-right changes than right-to-wrong changes. That is, high-scoring students benefitted more from changing answers than did low-scoring students, but students at all levels tended to benefit.

The pattern of results that Matthews (1929) reported nearly a century ago has been replicated numerous times across numerous subject areas with minimal variation. The most straightforward of these studies involve students taking class exams and researchers comparing the number of answers that were changed from right to wrong with the number changed from wrong to right. Researchers also tend to report the frequency of changes from one wrong response to another wrong response, but these are of less importance because they do not alter the total score on the exam. In many studies, researchers also report the proportion of students whose scores increase versus decrease as a result of changing answers. Studies of this type have been conducted with samples of chemistry students (Copeland, 1972), nursing students (Cassidy, 1987; Nieswiadomy, Arnold, & Garza, 2001), medical students (Davis, 1975; Harvill & Davis, 1997), undergraduate economics students (Reiling & Taylor, 1972), accounting students (Geiger, 1991b), graduate-level measurement students (Mueller & Shwedel, 1975; Schwarz, McMorris, & DeMers, 1991), and research and statistics students (Heidenberg & Layne, 2000), to name a few. In all these studies, responses were far more likely to have been changed from wrong to right than from right to wrong by ratios ranging from a minimum of approximately 2 to 1 to a maximum of more than 5 to 1. That is, for every answer that students changed from right to wrong, they changed an average of between two and five from wrong to right. Moreover, the majority of students – typically 65–75% – in each study increased their total exam scores by changing answers from their initial responses; only a small minority – typically 5–7% of students – had a net loss in exam score as a result of their answer changing.

The studies cited in the preceding paragraph all involved classroom examinations in American higher education. However, researchers have also studied answer-changing effects in other samples and with other types of exam. Smith and Moore (1976) wondered whether students with less experience taking multiple-choice tests would benefit from changing answers. They studied data from 240 examinees who had dropped out of high-school – a weak proxy for having less experience with tests – and who had later taken a standardized national high-school equivalency exam containing 370 items covering five broad academic domains. When students changed their answers on this exam, they were more than twice as likely to change from wrong to right than from right to wrong. In another study with students even less experienced with multiple-choice exams, Casteel (1991) gave 53 eighth grade students a standardized critical thinking test during one class, and an opportunity to revise their answers during the following class. Nearly two-thirds of the changes made were from wrong to right, with fewer than one in five changed from right to wrong. Geiger (1991b) noted that few answer-changing studies had been conducted using items requiring numerical calculation. He therefore examined multiple-choice responses from business administration students in an accounting class and found that there was no difference between numerical and non-numerical items – changes to both types of item were more likely to be beneficial than harmful by a ratio of three to one.

The tendency for students to generate net gains by changing answers is also apparent in international samples. Al-Hamly and Coombe (2005) examined data from nearly 300 students at a college in the Middle East who took a standardized English proficiency test. Wrong-to-right changes again outnumbered right-to-wrong changes by more than two to one. In another study, Di Milia (2007) compared students with Western and non-Western educational backgrounds. He analyzed data from more than 2,700 students at an Australian university – comparing Australian students with international students primarily from India, China, and

Bangladesh. The students had completed either a human resource management exam or a law exam. For both types of exam, wrong-to-right changes outnumbered right-to-wrong changes and far more students improved than lowered their scores by changing answers. Moreover, the authors observed no meaningful differences in terms of benefitting from changing answers based on whether students were from Western or non-Western educational backgrounds.

The tendency to benefit from changing answers has also been observed in samples outside formal academic settings. Stoffer, Davis, and Brown (1977) compared college students with military personnel in terms of answer-changing effects. They compared undergraduates enrolled in introductory psychology who took classroom exams with men enlisted in the United States Air Force who took Air Force qualifying exams assessing knowledge of aircraft maintenance as well as general technical skills. The results for these divergent participant samples and varying exam types were quite similar. In both cases, roughly 67% of changed answers were wrong-to-right and only about 20% of changes were right-to-wrong. Consistent with this pattern, 67% of the college students and 72% of the military personnel increased their scores by changing answers.

Replicating Matthews's (1929) findings, Stoffer and colleagues (1977) observed that high-scoring students tended to benefit more than low-scoring students by changing answers. However, the researchers recognized a potential confound in that whether someone achieves a high score is associated with whether he or she successfully changes incorrect answers. In other words, whether students are categorized as high-scoring or low-scoring for purposes of predicting their likelihood of successfully changing answers is affected by the frequency with which they have successfully changed answers. Stoffer and colleagues accounted for this confound by comparing high-scorers with low-scorers based on their test performance prior to changing answers. Although high-scoring students gained more on average than low-scoring students, students at all levels tended to gain. This finding was replicated once again in a more recent study (Heidenberg & Layne, 2000), in which researchers again controlled for potential confounding by comparing high and low scorers based on initial test performance rather than on performance that was affected by answer changing.

Several studies have similarly shown that stronger students make more wrong-to-right changes than weaker students. In his study of chemistry students cited earlier, Copeland (1972) reported that among "A" students – based on exam score – 90% of changes were from wrong to right; this proportion decreased steadily as a function of letter grade. Among failing students, only 24% of changes were from wrong to right. However, it is important to note that at no grade level did right-to-wrong changes outnumber wrong-to-right changes. Even failing students tended to break even as a result of changing answers and students at all non-failing levels tended to gain. In Smith and Moore's (1976) study of students taking a high-school equivalency exam, changes made by passing students were more likely to be beneficial than harmful by a ratio of three to one, but even among failing students the ratio was two to one. Mueller and Shwedel (1975) likewise found that high-scoring students gained more points by changing answers, but that students at all levels tended to benefit. They also observed that while low-scoring students were slightly more likely than high-scoring students to decrease their scores by changing answers, the majority of even low-scoring students increased their scores.

In an important review of answer-changing research completed nearly 30 years ago (Benjamin et al., 1984), the authors noted that up until that time researchers had treated all answer changes as the same. The reviewers therefore recommended that researchers start to account for varying reasons why students change specific answers. Several subsequent teams of researchers addressed this question by asking students to choose from several explanations for each change they made on exams. Shatz and Best (1987) made such an inquiry to students in introductory psychology and found that nearly three-quarters of changes were from wrong to right when the student's reason for changing was something other than guessing – such as finding a clue in a subsequent question. In cases where guessing was the student's explanation, only one in three changes were from wrong to right which was comparable to the proportion of right-to-wrong changes when guessing. That is, students changing an answer based on guessing were as likely to change from right to wrong as from wrong to right. Harvill and Davis (1997) similarly found that changes based on guessing tend to average out and thus create little net gain. In contrast, when students changed answers based on re-evaluating or better understanding the question, wrong-to-right changes outnumbered right-to-wrong changes by nearly four to one. Changing answers based solely on guessing may even be detrimental. Heidenberg and Layne (2000) found that among changes based on guessing, right-to-wrong changes outnumbered wrong-to-right changes by three to one. Shatz's and Best's conclusion is well supported by their findings and those of other researchers: changing answers is worthwhile only when the student has a good reason for doing so; otherwise it is not worth the student's time and energy to dwell on a question because the subsequent guess is unlikely, on average, to be beneficial.

Some researchers have directly compared student perceptions about changing answers with students' actual performance on exams. Geiger (1996) surveyed almost 300 advanced accounting students from two universities. He found that while 73% of the students increased their overall exam scores in the class by changing answers, only 12% of the students believed that changing answers had helped them and 69% believed it had lowered their scores. Only one student in five accurately perceived the effects that answer changing had on his or her exam score, and the vast majority underestimated the benefits of changing answers. The results of other studies on student perceptions (Ballance, 1977; Smith, White, & Coop, 1979; Geiger, 1990; 1991a) are highly consistent with those observed by Geiger. In all cases, the majority of students believed that changing answers had lowered their exam scores when in fact the majority of students improved by changing answers.

Student beliefs about answer changing appear relatively intractable even when instructors offer strong contrary evidence. Foote and Belinky (1972) found that providing feedback to students about the positive effects of answer changing based on data from their own class exams had no effect on students' answer-changing patterns on subsequent exams. In two studies (McMorris & Weidman, 1986; McMorris, DeMyers, & Schwarz, 1987), the instructor of graduate-level educational and psychological measurement courses specifically taught students about the literature demonstrating the benefits of changing answers. The information was included in class discussion and students were tested on it during the first class exam. The instruction did not reduce the benefit of answer-changing by causing students to change answers haphazardly, nor did it change the proportion of students who gained and lost by changing answers. However, this may have been because students who had received this explicit instruction were no more likely to change answers on subsequent exams than students with no such instruction. The training appeared to have no effect on students' reluctance to change answers.

Kruger, Wirtz, and Miller (2005) conducted four studies to explore the reasons why students believe the first instinct fallacy despite contrary data. In the first study, the researchers examined test data from more than 1,500 introductory psychology students, 51 of whom were randomly selected to also provide predictions for the whole class on the likely outcomes of answer changing. Replicating past research, 75% of surveyed students believed that an initial response is more likely to be correct than an alternative – even if the alterative begins to seem correct. Also consistent with other studies, students grossly underestimated the frequency of wrong-to-right changes and the proportion of students who improve their scores by changing answers. In their second study, Kruger and colleagues found that students report more regret from getting an answer wrong after changing it than they experience from getting an answer wrong after failing to change it. Students were also much more likely to report that they would feel foolish and be upset with themselves for getting a question wrong after changing a correct answer than they would after failing to change an incorrect answer.

In a third study, Kruger and colleagues (2005) gave 27 college students a multiple-choice test containing items from either the SAT or the Graduate Record Examination. For items where students were uncertain about the correct answer, they were instructed to narrow the options to two choices and then make a final decision. Students also reported which option reflected their first instinct. Then the researchers provided the correct answers. When the students were contacted between four and six weeks later, their memories of the consequences of changing answers were inconsistent with the actual consequences. Although participants were more likely to get a question wrong if they maintained their initial response on items for which they were uncertain, participants later remembered that changing their initial responses led to worse consequences than it actually did and that maintaining an initial response was more beneficial than it was.

In a final study, Kruger and colleagues (2005) had 68 college students watch one of two video versions of a mock game show involving a contestant responding to multiple-choice trivia questions. In one version of the video, the contestant always stuck with an initial answer and in the other version, the contestant always changed answers. In both versions the contestant got half of the questions correct. Research participants imagined that the contestant was a teammate and that they would themselves gain or lose money along with the contestant. Participants watching their "teammate" get questions wrong after switching answers reported greater frustration than participants whose teammate got the same number of questions wrong by not switching. Moreover, participants remembered the contestant doing better by retaining initial answers although this was not the case. Kruger and colleagues concluded from their four studies that when changing an answer results in getting a question wrong, participants experience more frustration, regret, and self-recrimination than when they get a question wrong by retaining an initial response. Such emotional consequences promote the first instinct fallacy by making answers changed from right to wrong more memorable than answers left unchanged or those changed from wrong to right. This pattern is consistent with the well-known availability heuristic: a mental shortcut in which people base their judgments on ideas that most readily come to mind. Since answers changed from right to wrong are more memorable, they come to mind more easily in later situations and disproportionately affect students' beliefs and decisions.

Despite the fact that most students believe changing answers is likely to lower one's test score, most students change some answers on most exams. In fact, in many studies, nearly all students changed answers (Geiger, 1990; 1991a; 1996; Schwarz et al., 1991), although most students change only a very small number of items on any particular test. Skinner (1983) inferred from this pattern that in fact the folk wisdom prohibiting answer-changing is correct and surmised that the reason why changes are more likely to be wrong-to-right is that students set a high threshold for changing – only doing so when they are quite certain about correctness of the change. He stated that students would be wise to change an answer only if they were at least 75% certain that the change was correct. However, Ramsey and colleagues (1987) found that changes were more likely than not to be beneficial even when students expressed low confidence that the change was correct. It is important to note that the methodology employed in most answer-changing studies likely underestimates the actual number of changed answers because students often lean toward their first instinct and then make a change before recording an answer (Schwarz et al., 1991). This would sometimes be the case when a student leaves a question blank and comes back to it later. Such changes would go undetected. It is also important to note that on any exam, a small minority of students lower their scores by changing answers, and it is not possible to predict who these students will be (Mueller & Wasser, 1977).

In light of the fact that low-scoring students are less likely than other students to benefit from changing answers, Best (1979) suggested that admonitions not to change might be appropriate for poorer students. He concluded that "it may now be appropriate to supply students with a more sophisticated answer changing strategy" (p. 230). The practical limitation to such a refined strategy is that it would require instructors to inform students prior to exams that if they are poor students, they should not change answers. It is difficult to imagine a humane instructor making such an announcement. Even if an instructor made such an announcement, the strategy would also depend on students having a great deal of insight about their own knowledge – an unlikely scenario among poor students (see Chapter 1 on students' judgment of their own knowledge). Based on his research suggesting that students are more likely to gain by changing difficult items than easy items, Pascale (1974) suggested that students can improve their test performance by reconsidering their answers – especially on tests that they perceive as challenging. The potential limitation of this advice is that poor students are likely to perceive most tests as challenging so this approach, in contrast with Best's advice, would encourage them to change more answers rather than fewer.

Although factors such as student ability play a role in the degree to which students gain by changing answers on multiple-choice exams, virtually all studies to date suggest that students at all levels change more answers from wrong to right than from right to wrong. Accordingly, Geiger (1997) asserts that warning students not to change answers adds unnecessary psychological difficulty to the task of completing an exam. Like many of the researchers cited in this chapter, he advises that instructors inform their students of the potential benefits of changing answers. Traditional advice against changing answers is clearly at odds with the objective evidence.

References

Al-Hamly, M. & Coombe, C. (2005). To change or not to change: investigating the value of MCQ answer changing for Gulf Arab students. *Language Testing, 22*, 509–531.

Ballance, C. T. (1977). Students' expectations and their answer-changing behavior. *Psychological Reports, 41*, 163–166.

Benjamin, L. T., Cavell, T. A., & Shallenberger, W. R. (1984). Staying with initial answers on objective tests: Is it a myth? *Teaching of Psychology, 11*, 133–141.

Best, J. B. (1979). Item difficulty and answer changing. *Teaching of Psychology, 6*, 228–230.

Cassidy, V. R. (1987). Response changing and student achievement on objective tests. *Journal of Nursing Education, 26*, 60–62.

Casteel, C. A. (1991). Answer changing on multiple-choice test items among eight-grade readers. *Journal of Experimental Education, 59*, 300–309.

Copeland, D. A. (1972). Should chemistry students change answers on multiple-choice tests? *Journal of Chemical Education, 49*, 258.

Davis, R. E. (1975). Changing examination answers: An educational myth? *Journal of Medical Education, 50*, 685–687.

Di Milia, L. (2007). Benefitting from multiple-choice exams: The positive impact of answer switching. *Educational Psychology, 27*, 607–615.

Foote, R. & Belinky, C. (1972). It pays to switch? Consequences of changing answers on multiple-choice examinations. *Psychological Reports, 31*, 667–673.

Geiger, M. A. (1990). Correlates of net gain from changing multiple-choice answers: Replication and extension. *Psychological Reports, 67*, 719–722.

Geiger, M. A. (1991a). Changing multiple-choice answers: Do students accurately perceive their performance? *Journal of Experimental Education, 59*, 250–257.

Geiger, M. A. (1991b). Changing multiple-choice answers: A validation and extension. *College Student Journal, 25*, 181–186.

Geiger, M. A. (1996). On the benefit of changing multiple-choice answers: Student perception and performance. *Education, 117*, 108–116.

Geiger, M. A. (1997). Educators' warnings about changing examination answers: Effects on student perceptions and performance. *College Student Journal, 3*, 429–432.

Harvill, L. M. & Davis, G. (1997). Test-taking behaviors and their impact on performance. *Academic Medicine, 72*, S97–S99.

Heidenberg, A. J. & Layne, B. H. (2000). Answer changing: A conditional argument. *College Student Journal, 34*, 440–450.

Kruger, J., Wirtz, D., & Miller, D. T. (2005). Counterfactual thinking and first instinct fallacy. *Journal of Personality and Social Psychology, 88*, 725–735.

Matthews, C. O. (1929). Erroneous first impressions on objective tests. *Journal of Educational Psychology, 20*, 280–286.

McMorris, R. F. & Weidman, A. H. (1986). Answer changing after instruction on answer changing. *Measurement and Evaluation in Counseling and Development, 18*, 93–101.

McMorris, R. F., DeMers, L. P., & Schwarz, S. P. (1987). Attitudes, behaviors, and reasons for changing responses following answer-changing instruction. *Journal of Educational Measurement, 24*, 131–143.

Mueller, D. J. & Shwedel, A. (1975). Some correlates of net gain resultant from answer changing on objective achievement test items. *Journal of Educational Measurement, 12*, 251–254.

Mueller, D. J. & Wasser, V. (1977). Implications of changing answers on objective test items. *Journal of Educational Measurement, 14*, 9–13.

Nieswiadomy, R. M., Arnold, W. K., & Garza, C. (2001). Changing answers on multiple-choice examinations taken by baccalaureate nursing students. *Journal of Nursing Education, 40*, 142–144.

Pascale, P. J. (1974). Changing initial answers on multiple-choice achievement tests. *Measurement and Evaluation in Guidance, 6*, 236–238.

Ramsey, P. H., Ramsey, P. P., & Barnes, M. J. (1987). Effects of student confidence and item difficulty on test score gains due to answer changing. *Teaching of Psychology, 14*, 206–210.

Reiling, E. & Taylor, R. (1972). A new approach to the problem of changing initial responses to multiple choice questions. *Journal of Educational Measurement, 9*, 67–70.

SAT test taking tips and techniques (n.d.). Available at: http://www.educationcorner.com/sat-test-taking-tips.html.

Schwarz, S. P., McMorris, R. F., & DeMers, L. P. (1991). Reasons for changing answers: An evaluation using personal interviews. *Journal of Educational Measurement, 28*, 163–171.

Shatz, M. A. & Best, J. B. (1987). Students' reasons for changing answers on objective tests. *Teaching of Psychology, 14*, 241–242.

Skinner, N. F. (1983). Switching answers on multiple-choice questions: Shrewdness or shibboleth? *Teaching of Psychology, 10*, 220–222.

Smith, A. & Moore, J. C. (1976). The effects of changing answers on scores of non-test-sophisticated examinees. *Measurement and Evaluation in Guidance, 8*, 252–254.

Smith, M., White, K. P., & Coop, R. H. (1979). The effect of item type on the consequences of changing answers on multiple-choice tests. *Journal of Educational Measurement, 16*, 203–208.

Stoffer, G. R., Davis, K. E., & Brown, J. B. (1977). The consequences of changing initial answers on objective tests: A stable effect and a stable misconception. *Journal of Educational Research, 70*, 272–277.

Top ten SAT test tips (n.d.). Available at: http://testprep.about.com/od/tipsfortesting/a/SAT_TestTips.htm.

14 MYTH: COACHING PRODUCES LARGE GAINS IN COLLEGE ADMISSION TEST SCORES

Most people who have applied for admission to American baccalaureate colleges and universities understand something about the role that standardized testing plays in the admissions process. The vast majority of students seeking to enroll in four-year colleges in the United States complete either the SAT or the ACT (Briggs, 2009). Indeed, the SAT alone is taken by more than 2 million students every year (College Board, n.d.). The majority of colleges and universities require applicants to submit standardized admission test scores – although the number of institutions discontinuing this requirement is growing (Peligri, 2014). The publishers of tests such as the SAT recommend that colleges use scores as part of a comprehensive picture of applicants' qualifications (College Board, n.d.). However, for students seeking admission to college – especially to colleges whose admission standards are particularly selective – the appeal of strategies to enhance one's credentials by boosting standardized test scores is undeniable. A popular strategy for increasing one's admission test scores is to participate in commercial coaching programs that promise

Great Myths of Education and Learning, First Edition. Jeffrey D. Holmes.
© 2016 John Wiley & Sons, Inc. Published 2016 by John Wiley & Sons, Inc.

large test score increases to aspiring college students with the motivation and financial resources to take advantage of them.

Coaching for college admissions testing is certainly big business. MacMillan (2010) cited evidence that the test preparation business is worth more than $1 billion per year. One of the biggest test coaching companies, Kaplan, was purchased by the Washington Post newspaper company in 1984. As of 2007, the Kaplan Educational Division, of which its test preparation program is a major component, brought in more revenue for the Washington Post Corporation than its journalism division (Jaffe, 2007). The profit-driven nature of test preparation programs is what raises concerns for many observers. The primary concern is that if SAT coaching is effective, it could lead to increased inequality in access to higher education. One reason for using standardized tests in college admissions is to level the playing field for students from poorer schools who have fewer resources (Montgomery & Lilly, 2012). Because coaching programs are often quite expensive – costing a minimum of several hundred dollars for the simplest programs and far exceeding $1,000 for premium programs – students with greater financial resources tend to have disproportionate access to them, which presumably could lead to fewer disadvantaged students being admitted to college. It is also important to keep in mind that SAT scores are commonly used by colleges and universities not only to inform decisions about who gets admitted, but also to help decide who receives scholarship funding (Montgomery & Lilly, 2012).

The vast majority of the research on coaching for college admissions tests focuses on the SAT – probably because the SAT is the test most widely used by American colleges and universities to inform admissions decisions. The SAT was first published in 1926 as the Scholastic Aptitude Test. Since its original publication, the test has changed names numerous times to reflect evolving perspectives on the nature of the exam and is now simply called the SAT. The shift away from referring to the test as a measure of aptitude carries important implications. An aptitude test is a test that is designed to measure potential in some particular domain. Over the years there has been ongoing debate concerning whether the SAT truly assesses future potential, or is better described as an achievement test assessing acquired knowledge. According to the website of the College Board, which publishes the SAT, the test assesses "academic readiness for college" (College Board, n.d., "About the Tests," para. 1). The test contains math and verbal sections, each scored on a scale from 200 to 800. In 2005, a writing section was added that is scored on the same scale. The research cited in this chapter addresses coaching effects on the math and verbal tests only, as research on coaching for the writing test is not yet available.

There are many different approaches to coaching for test preparation. This variety is in part what sometimes makes it difficult to draw broad conclusions about the effectiveness of coaching, as little consistency exists across the methods tested by various researchers. Commercial coaching companies are a major source of the coaching strategies that researchers have examined, and they are likewise a source of many extravagant claims concerning the potential for coaching to produce dramatic score increases. For example, the Princeton Review (2015) guarantees a 200-point increase in combined SAT scores for students who enroll in one of its coaching programs. Coaching sometimes involves teaching test content, but this approach is often impractical because admissions tests contain such a vast domain of potential content. Preparing for the SAT is unlike preparing for the academic achievement tests that most students are familiar with from their years in school. It is designed to be a broad measure of skills and knowledge so that the test content is not tied to any specific type of coursework. Therefore, test coaching programs often emphasize skills such as test wiseness (Becker, 1990), by providing students with guidance on test-taking strategies in addition to specific content knowledge. Such coaching might involve strategies such as teaching students how to approach particular types of test items in order to give them an edge when they are not able to answer based on content knowledge.

Test coaching of one kind or another has existed for many decades, and reviews of coaching effectiveness have a long history as well. One of the earliest studies examining the effectiveness of coaching for the SAT was commissioned by the College Board itself in 1951 (Dyer, 1953). In this study, boys who were seniors at two high schools served as experimental and control groups. The schools were chosen because they were similar across a variety of relevant characteristics such as student ability and the teaching approaches typically used at the schools. Students at both schools took the SAT at the start of their senior year and again the following March. In the interim, students at one of the schools participated in a variety of coaching exercises administered by math and English teachers, and specifically designed to increases student SAT scores. Students at the comparison school completed no such exercises. After the researchers controlled for years of enrollment at the school, foreign language coursework, mathematics coursework, and initial SAT scores, the students in the coached group scored an average of 4.6 points higher on the verbal section of the SAT and 12.9 points higher on the math section. Dyer concluded that although the difference in math scores was statistically significant, coaching had no practically significant effect on either math or verbal scores – especially given the number of hours of preparation required to produce the observed increases.

Dyer's (1953) work serves as a prologue to a noteworthy list of subsequent studies suggesting that coaching produces positive – but quite modest – increases in students' SAT scores. By the end of the 1970s, a sufficient number of studies were available for researchers to begin pooling results using a method called meta-analysis. Individual studies often have important flaws such as small samples or other methodological weaknesses. Researchers use meta-analysis to merge the data from a large number of existing studies in order to minimize the effect of such weaknesses in individual studies and draw more definitive conclusions.

Slack and Porter (1980) conducted one of the first reviews of research on SAT coaching. The researchers examined the findings from a variety of studies and concluded that coaching does in fact lead to notable increases in SAT scores, and that these increases are large enough to have practical significance in terms of students' chances of admission to college. Slack and Porter were highly critical of the widespread use of the SAT in college admissions, and were likewise critical of the Educational Testing Service (ETS) – the parent company of the College Board – for supposedly ignoring studies suggesting that SAT scores could be improved by formal training. They took issue with claims that the SAT measured student aptitude (as opposed to achievement), and applauded the faculty of one college who decided as early as 1970 to eliminate the requirement that candidates for admission submit SAT scores.

Response to Slack's and Porter's critique of the SAT was swift. In the same issue of the same journal, Jackson (1980), representing the ETS, took issue with what he claimed were false arguments made by Slack and Porter. Although Slack and Porter criticized the claim that the SAT is an aptitude test measuring students' capacity for learning and is therefore not subject to coaching effects, Jackson denied that such a claim had ever been made. He argued that Slack and Porter had ignored literature – including ETS publications – portraying the SAT as a test of learned abilities. Jackson noted that coaching usually refers to efforts to increase scores through short-term training, and that the existing research suggested that such training tends to produce very small gains. Jackson arrived at different conclusions from those reached by Slack and Porter in part because he defined coaching differently. The literature base that emerged over subsequent years followed a similar pattern, with different authors reviewing different studies using different criteria to reach different conclusions.

In another review, Messick and Jungeblut (1981) examined SAT coaching studies published up until 1980. They found that coaching effects are positively associated with the number of student contact hours in coaching programs. That is, coaching programs spanning more hours tended to produce greater gains. Although such an effect might not be surprising, Messick's and Jungeblut's analysis suggested that the time required to produce gains much greater than 20 or 30 points would likely not be feasible. For example, they estimated that a 10-point increase in SAT verbal scores would require 12 hours of coaching; a 20-point increase would require 57 hours of coaching; and a 30-point increase would require 260 hours. Their estimates for coaching for the math portion were slightly more modest, but still great enough that large score increases would require unrealistic amounts of coaching. They also noted that in the available studies, coaching time is heavily confounded with coaching method. In other words, coaching programs that are longer in duration tend to involve different strategies than those of shorter duration. Coaches in longer-term programs have more time to focus on increasing students' content knowledge, in contrast to short-term programs in which coaches are likely to place greater emphasis on test-taking skills that can be more quickly communicated. Therefore, it is difficult to separate the effects of coaching time versus coaching method.

The confounding of variables is just one of numerous methodological flaws that characterize many coaching studies. For example, the only way to demonstrate that a coaching program has a causal effect on test performance is to randomly assign students to either a coaching program or to a control condition whose members receive no coaching. This insures that the groups are similar at the beginning of the study so that any subsequent improvement in test scores among those receiving coaching can be attributed to the coaching itself. However, many coaching studies are nonrandomized so there is no equivalent control group with which to make comparisons. Conclusions based on such studies are far more limited because the characteristics of participants can affect the observed results (Messick & Jungeblut, 1981). When participants are not randomly assigned to coached and uncoached groups, it is possible that preexisting group differences account for some or all of the observed effects. DerSimonian and Laird (1983) conducted a meta-analysis of SAT coaching studies and found that higher quality studies produce much lower average coaching effects. In fact, they found that "The uncontrolled studies show mean gains of four to five times the corresponding mean gains of the matched and randomized studies" (p. 10). They also found that uncontrolled studies produced widely varying results, whereas randomized studies produced very consistent results. In fact, the coaching effects observed in high-quality studies were no greater than the effects that would be expected based on sampling error only. DerSimonian and Laird noted that Slack's and Porter's (1980) review revealed much larger average coaching gains because there was no control for the quality of the studies; moreover, the coaching effect observed in methodologically sound studies "seems too small to be practically significant" (p. 1), and "it appears that the benefits of coaching are indeed negligible" (p. 13). The authors of another meta-analysis of 14 SAT coaching studies that all used a pre-test–post-test design and a control group likewise concluded that the effects of coaching are small (Kulik, Bangert-Downs, & Kulik, 1984), and a review published several years later of all prior coaching studies revealed an average coaching effect of nine points on the verbal section and 16 points on the math section (Becker, 1990).

In 1994, the publisher of the SAT instituted a number of changes to the exam. Partly in response to concerns about the potential for coaching effects, antonym items were removed from the verbal section and replaced with additional reading comprehension items (Montgomery & Lilly, 2012). New content was added to the math portion as well. Shortly after the changes were implemented, the College Board commissioned a new survey of a nationally representative sample of students who took the SAT during the 1995–96 academic year (Powers & Rock, 1999). The researchers collected data from more than 4,000 students who registered for the SAT. Of these students, 12% reported using coaching programs outside any SAT training offered at their schools. Coaching was associated with an average increase of eight points on the verbal section and 18 points on the math section. The researchers reported that although the scores of a small proportion of students did increase more dramatically, far more students' scores either stayed the same or decreased after coaching. It is important to note that students who enroll in coaching programs are self-selected and tend to be highly-motivated (Messick & Jungeblut (1981). Therefore, any observed difference between coached and uncoached students based on survey data must be interpreted with caution, because students who pursue coaching are likely to differ in many ways from students who do not pursue coaching.

The authors of the most recent meta-analysis of SAT coaching research concluded that coaching may actually lead to larger gains than reported in previous reviews. Montgomery and Lilly (2012) estimated the effect of coaching to be 23.5 points for the verbal test and 32.7 points for the math test. Increases of this magnitude, the authors point out, could affect college admission decisions in the real world. However, after identifying over 300 possible studies for review, the researchers included only ten in their analysis. They also acknowledged that, like most studies of SAT coaching effects, the studies in their review all contained important methodological limitations such as small and non-representative samples, and high attrition rates. The researchers further noted that publication bias in favor of positive results might have affected which findings had been published in the past, potentially inflating the average score increases associated with coaching.

Most reviewers have concluded that the average effects of coaching are small and are unlikely to be of much practical significance (Becker, 1990; Powers & Rock, 1999). However, what constitutes meaningful increases in SAT scores remains an open question. Briggs (2009) surveyed admissions directors at four-year institutions in the United States to better determine how admissions tests are used in higher education. Nearly all the responding institutions reported that they use either the SAT or the ACT (with the majority using the SAT). Twenty-one percent of those using the SAT maintained a specified minimum score for admission. This subset of institutions consisted primarily of highly selective schools. In 2013, the combined math and verbal SAT score above which 75% of admitted students scored was 1,380 for Stanford, 1,410 for Harvard, and 1,430 for MIT (College Profiles, n.d.). Responses from admissions officers to Briggs' survey suggest that, at least at such selective schools where applicants' SAT scores tend to fall within a greatly restricted range toward the high end of scores, a small increase of even 10 or 20 points could "significantly improve students' likelihood of admission" (p. 19).

Although dozens of individual studies have been published on the effects of SAT coaching, nearly all of them are marred by methodological flaws that greatly limit the certainty of their conclusions. Small and biased samples are the norm. Coached groups sometimes have lower scores at pre-test than their uncoached comparison groups (Smyth, 1990), so observed increases as a function of coaching might partially reflect simple regression toward the mean. Powers and Rock (1999) noted in their observational study that coached students differed significantly from uncoached students along a host of relevant variables. Compared with uncoached students, coached students had higher high school grades and aspired to more esteemed careers; were more likely to have taken practice tests; had taken more math, foreign language, and science courses; preferred more selective colleges; perceived SAT scores to be more important; had parents with more education and higher income; and were more likely to be Asian American than from any other ethnic group. Coached students also were far more likely than uncoached students to have utilized additional voluntary test-preparation strategies as they prepared to take the SAT. As noted earlier in this chapter, students whose data appear in existing studies were self-selected to attend coaching because they were highly motivated to do well on the SAT (Messick & Jungeblut, 1981). Therefore, any observed gains may not apply to less motivated students or those mandated to attend coaching. Coaching itself is often poorly defined in the literature supposedly documenting its effectiveness (Becker, 1990). Moreover, many researchers have used inappropriate outcome measures such as shortened or obsolete forms of the SAT or even proxies for the SAT made up by researchers (Messick & Jungeblut, 1981).

Most researchers – regardless of their interpretations of the existing data – agree that more methodologically rigorous research is needed (Powers & Rock, 1999; Montgomery & Lilly, 2012). Many of the limitations of past studies could be overcome if researchers took steps to avoid ambiguities resulting from a lack of random assignment and the use of inappropriate comparison groups – ambiguities that arise when researchers compare test data from students who self-select into coaching programs with students who do not pursue coaching. Largely for practical reasons, however, few researchers have done this. It is therefore challenging to separate the effects of coaching from the effects of numerous confounding variables, including score improvements that come simply from taking a test more than once.

Even if coaching produces small to moderate increases in SAT performance, the magnitude of improvement promised by test coaching companies is dubious and far exceeds the increases reported in published research (Briggs, 2009). In some cases, coaching companies administer pre-tests that are much more difficult that the SAT (Smyth, 1990). When students later take the real SAT, it is likely that their scores will be higher regardless of any coaching effect. Other researchers have argued that the effects reported by coaching companies based on changes observed between pre-testing and post-testing of coached students are "simply not effects at all" because they fail to control for so many threats to their validity such as failure to randomize students to treatment and control groups (Powers & Rock, 1999: 112). Becker (1990) argued that published studies are likely to be the best quality studies available and that because the effects observed in well-conducted studies are small, "we must expect only modest gains from *any* coaching intervention" (p. 405). Powers and Rock (1999) noted that they could pick out isolated cases in their data in which a student appeared to have exhibited a large score increase after coaching. However, the researchers pointed out that such positive anecdotes are not representative, but are simply more memorable than the negative anecdotes also easily detected in the data.

There is agreement among most reviewers of SAT coaching research that coaching produces small but significant average increases in scores. It is noteworthy that the standard error of measurement – a statistic quantifying how discrepant from test-takers' actual ability their scores on a particular test tend to be – for the SAT is approximately 30 points for each of the subtests (College Board, 2012). This margin of error is consistent with or exceeds the observed coaching effects observed in most studies. That is, the average difference in coached students' scores from pre-test to post-test seldom exceeds the difference that would be expected based on measurement error. Although estimated coaching effects vary widely from study to study, the effects shrink as the quality and rigor of the studies increase (DerSimonian & Laird, 1983). It may in fact be true that coaching can benefit highly talented and highly motivated students who wish to increase their scores slightly to enhance their chances of admission to highly selective academic institutions. Nevertheless, claims that coaching routinely produces dramatic gains in test scores, or that coaching is part of an academic program that is "the scholastic equivalent of steroids" (Freedman, 2006: para. 3), are overstated.

References

Becker, B. J. (1990). Coaching for the scholastic aptitude test: Further synthesis and appraisal. *Review of Educational Research, 60,* 373–417.

Briggs, D. C. (2009). *Preparation for college admission exams.* Arlington, VA: National Association of College Admission Counseling.

College Profiles (n.d.). Available at: http://collegeapps.about.com/od/collegeprofiles, last accessed March 12, 2015.

College Board (n.d.). About the tests. Available at: https://sat.collegeboard.org/about-tests.

College Board (2012). Test characteristics of the SAT: Reliability, difficulty levels, completion rates. Available at: http://professionals.collegeboard.com/testing/sat-reasoning/scores/sat-data-tables.

DerSimonian, R. & Laird, N. M. (1983). Evaluating the effect of coaching on SAT scores: A meta-analysis. *Harvard Educational Review, 53,* 1–15.

Dyer, H. S. (1953). Does coaching help? *College Board Review, 19,* 331–335.

Freedman, S. G. (2006). In college entrance frenzy, a lesson out of left field. Available at: http://www.nytimes.com/2006/04/26/education/26education.html?_r=0.

Jackson, R. (1980). The Scholastic Aptitude Test: A response to Slack and Porter's "critical appraisal." *Harvard Educational Review, 50,* 382–391.

Jaffe, H. (2007). Practice tests, not news, bring in the big bucks for the post. Available at: http://www.washingtonian.com/blogs/capitalcomment/post-watch/practice-tests-not-news-bring-in-the-big-bucks-for-the-post.php.

Kulik, J. A., Bangert-Downs, R. L., & Kulik, C. C. (1984). Effectiveness of coaching for aptitude tests. *Psychological Bulletin, 95*, 179–188.

MacMillan, D. (2010). Grockit takes on Kaplan, Princeton Review in $1 billion test-prep market. Available at: http://www.bloomberg.com/news/2010-06-22/grockit-takes-on-kaplan-princeton-review-in-1-billion-test-prep-market.html.

Messick, S. & Jungeblut, A. (1981). Time and method in coaching for the SAT. *Psychological Bulletin, 89*, 191–216.

Montgomery, P. & Lilly, J. (2012). Systematic reviews of the effects of preparatory courses on university entrance examinations in high school-age students. *International Journal of Social Welfare, 21*, 3–12.

Peligri, J. (2014). No, the SAT is not required. More colleges join test-optional train. *USA Today*. Available at: http://college.usatoday.com/2014/07/07/no-the-sat-is-not-required-more-colleges-join-test-optional-train.

Powers, D. E. & Rock, D. A. (1999). Effects of coaching on SAT I: Reasoning test scores. *Journal of Educational Measurement, 36*, 93–118.

Princeton Review (2015). Guarantee details (SAT/ACT). Available at: http://www.princetonreview.com/guarantee-sat-act.aspx.

Slack, W. V. & Porter, D. (1980). The Scholastic Aptitude Test: A critical appraisal. *Harvard Educational Review, 50*, 154–175.

Smyth, F. L. (1990). SAT coaching: What *really* happens to scores and how we are led to expect more. *Journal of College Admission, 129*, 7–17.

15 MYTH: STANDARDIZED TESTS DO NOT PREDICT ACADEMIC PERFORMANCE

Standardized tests used as part of academic admissions decisions have many critics. Many students hold the tests they are required to take in order to apply to various academic institutions in disdain and are convinced that they measure nothing useful. Moreover, scholarly critiques include accusations that tests such as the SAT primarily measure students' family wealth rather than true academic ability, and contribute to gender and ethnic inequities in access to higher education (Guinier, 2015). Concerns about the potential disadvantages of using standardized tests to inform admissions decisions are long-standing, and hundreds of colleges no longer require applicants to submit test scores (Peligri, 2014). Despite occasional ideological vitriol, admissions tests do predict academic performance. This simply means that scores on standardized tests correlate positively with later academic success. Rather than dismissing the broad evidence for this correlation, discussions about the appropriateness of using standardized tests might more appropriately revolve around the strength of the association and whether the potential disadvantages of using tests to inform admissions decisions outweigh the advantages.

To evaluate the predictive validity of a test – the degree to which a test predicts performance on some other variable – researchers examine the correlation between test scores and measures of subsequent performance such as college grade point average (GPA). If the test scores correlate significantly with later performance, researchers conclude that the test has some criterion-related validity. That is, the test can be used to predict subsequent performance on some criterion, which is usually academic grades. In practice, however, the interpretation of such correlations often becomes more complicated. Correlations indicate associations between variables for groups of people. Many people know of someone who did relatively poorly on college admission tests but did very well in college, and someone else who did well on the exams but did poorly in college. Such anecdotes do not negate the correlation – they simply reflect the reality that the correlation will always be far less than perfect. Doubting the association because of noteworthy exceptions is no different than assuming that smoking poses no health hazard because some smokers do not become ill. Few people would make such an argument.

Over the past 80 years or so, researchers have conducted hundreds of studies examining the validity of standardized admissions tests for predicting subsequent academic performance in undergraduate and graduate programs. It is impossible to cover them all in a single chapter, but it is useful to examine findings based on large data sets and meta-analyses. Researchers use meta-analysis to integrate the findings from many existing studies in order to overcome some of the limitations of the individual studies and draw more reliable conclusions. The findings from meta-analyses and large-scale studies on the association between stand-ardized tests and subsequent academic performance are remarkably consistent: nearly all large studies reveal correlations that are significant, positive, and modest in magnitude. This pattern holds for tests used to predict undergraduate academic performance, as well as those used to inform decisions on graduate school admissions.

By far the most commonly used criterion in studies examining the validity of academic admissions tests is GPA in higher education programs. Researchers typically focus on the correlation between stand-ardized test scores and the grades students achieve during their first year of college or graduate school. Correlations of this nature are reported as decimals on a scale from 0 to 1 – with a zero correlation indicating no association between the variables and a coefficient of 1.0 indicating a perfect association. As one example, Ramist, Lewis, and McCamley-Jenkins (1994) conducted a meta-analysis using data from more than 46,000 students who completed the SAT and attended one of 45 colleges in the 1980s. The researchers reported an overall correlation of .36 between SAT scores and first-year GPA. All large-scale SAT validity studies reveal correlations of similar magnitude.

The SAT has undergone many revisions over the years. One major revision took effect in 1994. There were changes to the verbal portion of the exam, including elimination of antonym items, and the addition of items requiring students to evaluate different points of view. The time allotted to complete the test also was extended by 15 minutes so that students could complete more items. Each time a test is revised, new questions arise concerning the utility of the test and new validity studies must be conducted. Bridgeman, McCamley-Jenkins, and Ervin (2000) compared the predictive validity of the revised SAT to that of the previous version of the test. The researchers compared data from two large samples: one whose members had taken the SAT in 1994 prior to the revisions, and the other consisting of students who had taken the SAT in 1995 after the revisions had been implemented. There were more than 45,000 students in each sample. Bridgeman and colleagues found that the predictive validity of the SAT had remained essentially unchanged. The correlation between SAT scores and first-year college GPA was .35 for the new version of the SAT, compared with .34 for the prior version. Despite some noteworthy changes to the test, its association with college GPA was quite stable.

Another major revision of the SAT went into effect in 2005. A writing section was added, which was something that had never before been part of the test. The College Board, which publishes the SAT, commissioned a study (Kobrin, Patterson, Shaw, Mattern, & Barbuti, 2008) to evaluate the validity of the revised and expanded test. Kobrin and colleagues analyzed data from a sample of more than 151,000 students from more than 100 colleges and universities. The researchers reported a correlation of .35 between a composite test score that included all three sections of the SAT – critical reading, math, and writing – and first-year college GPA. Even with the addition of a major new task, the correlation between the test and college performance was equivalent to the correlations from studies evaluating earlier versions of the test. Interestingly, the newly-added writing subtest by itself predicted first-year college performance nearly as well as the test as a whole: correlating .33 with first-year GPA.

It is apparent that across large samples of students, SAT scores predict first-year college performance. Camara and Echternacht (2000) explained why first-year GPA is the criteria most commonly used in SAT validity studies. They noted that courses at the freshman level are more similar to each other in difficulty than upper-level courses, so first-year courses provide a more reliable validity criterion. Furthermore, the largest available data sets focus on first-year GPA, and first-year GPA is highly correlated with later cumulative GPA. Camara and Echternacht also cite potential problems with using cumulative GPA in validity studies of college admission tests. For instance, since upper-level courses tend to vary more in terms of difficulty, the correlation between pre-college tests and academic performance becomes suppressed because students do not pursue equally difficult courses. However, Wilson (1983) reviewed all known studies conducted between 1930 and 1980 in which the SAT was used to predict cumulative college GPA. He concluded that standardized admissions tests are just as valid for predicting cumulative GPA as they are for predicting first-year GPA. Burton and Ramist (2001) reviewed studies that were not part of Wilson's review because they were conducted after 1980. Analyzing data from more than 30,000 students, the researchers reported a correlation of .36 between SAT scores and cumulative GPA at graduation – the same level of association observed in studies of first-year grades.

It is important to note that most of the large-scale studies of SAT validity were commissioned by the College Board, which also publishes the test. This is somewhat understandable since the College Board has access to large data sets and also has a vested interest in demonstrating the validity of the SAT. However, the results from studies conducted by the College Board and by independent researchers are quite consistent. As one example, Geiser and Studley (2002) analyzed data from nearly 78,000 students entering the University of California between 1996 and 1999. For these students the correlation between SAT scores and first-year GPA was .36 – equivalent to correlations observed in other studies. It is possible to locate studies of smaller and more select student samples where the predictive validity of the SAT appears more equivocal. However, meta-analyses and studies with very large and diverse samples produce far more reliable and generalizable results (Sackett, Borneman, & Connelly, 2008). For reasons addressed in more detail later in this chapter, SAT validity coefficients are particularly vulnerable to suppression when researchers use restricted samples.

The conclusions summarized above concerning the predictive validity of standardized tests are not limited to tests used in undergraduate admissions. Kuncel, Hezlett, and Ones (2001) conducted a large meta-analysis of studies of the Graduate Record Examination (GRE). They analyzed data from more than 82,000 graduate students from nearly 1,800 separate research samples. The correlation between GRE scores and graduate school GPA was very similar to SAT validity coefficients. Correlations between GRE scores and graduate GPA ranged from .32 to .36 for different subsections – verbal, quantitative, and analytical – of the GRE. Moreover, GRE scores correlated more highly than undergraduate GPA with both graduate GPA and scores on comprehensive examinations in graduate school. A smaller meta-analysis (Kuncel, Wee, Serafin, & Hezlett, 2010) revealed somewhat smaller GRE validity coefficients, but demonstrated that GRE scores predict both first-year and cumulative GPA for both master's and doctoral students.

Julian (2005) analyzed data from more than 4,000 medical students and found that scores on the Medical College Admission Test (MCAT) correlated .44 with cumulative medical school GPA. In a large meta-analysis of more than 65,000 students who took the Graduate Management Admission Test (GMAT), test scores correlated .32 with first-year GPA and .31 with cumulative GPA in graduate business school (Kuncel, Crede, & Thomas, 2007). Finally, in a large meta-analysis of more than 90,000 law students, scores on the Law School Admission Test (LSAT) correlated .38 with first-year law school grades (Linn & Hastings, 1984). On all three of these tests – the MCAT, GMAT, and LSAT – the validity of test scores for predicting graduate GPA surpassed the predictive validity of undergraduate GPA. In a recent synthesis of meta-analyses of graduate admissions exams, Kuncel and Hezlett (2007) conclude: "For all tests across all relevant success measures, standardized test scores are positively related to subsequent measures of student success" (pp. 1080–1081).

Although the positive association between standardized test scores and later academic performance is remarkably consistent across studies of both undergraduate and graduate performance, it is also consistently modest in magnitude. Critics of standardized academic admissions tests often cite the rather modest correlations as reason to question the validity and utility of such tests. However, researchers have provided many explanations for why the correlations are not higher than usually observed. Foremost among these is the issue of range restriction.

Researchers evaluating test validity must use correlation coefficients that show the association between two continuous variables – such as test scores and GPA. To accurately reveal a correlation, a data set must contain a full range of scores on both variables. If the range is restricted, the correlation becomes suppressed. For instance, if one could measure both the jumping ability and basketball skill of every person in the United States, the data set would contain a wide range of each of the abilities. There would be some people whose jumping ability was extremely limited and others whose jumping ability would approach world-record levels – with everyone else falling somewhere in between. The same would be true for basketball skill. Given the range of data and the fact that jumping ability provides an advantage in basketball, the correlation between the two variables would likely be quite high. However, the correlation between the same two variables in a data set consisting only of professional basketball players would be much weaker – not because jumping ability is less important among elite basketball players, but because the range of the data set would be greatly restricted. With so little variability on both measures, the correlation coefficient would be artificially suppressed.

Range restriction is a common concern among researchers who study the predictive validity of standardized tests (e.g., Burton & Ramist, 2001; Sackett et al., 2008). When test scores are correlated with academic performance, the data sets generally do not contain a full range of scores. For example, among the more than 1 million students who take the SAT each year, many will never attend college. Although this occurs for many reasons, the students who ultimately do not attend college are disproportionately those with low SAT scores. Since these students cannot be included in validity studies, the range in available data sets is restricted. The range becomes further restricted because students are admitted to higher education based in part on their test scores. Therefore, the range of scores for students at any particular school – especially elite schools – will be further limited. If the students at a particular school were drawn randomly from the population of SAT takers, the correlation between test scores and academic performance would be higher.

A second factor that suppresses the correlations between test scores and academic outcomes has to do with the reliability of measures used to evaluate test validity – typically subsequent course grades. Reliability is simply another name for the consistency with which something is measured. A particular course grade can have different meanings in different contexts. Since any particular grade depends not only on student learning and performance, but also institution and instructor standards, the reliability of course grades tends to be low. When the outcome measure has low reliability, the correlation with other variables such as test scores is further reduced. There are several reasons why this may occur. First, college courses vary widely in terms of difficulty. Sackett and colleagues (2008) explain that two students with the same level of ability may earn different grades because of the courses they choose. Accordingly, the GPAs that show up in data sets are unreliable in that they do not control for course difficulty. Whereas admission test scores are standardized in the sense that everyone is assessed on the same scale, college and graduate school grades are far more contingent on the difficulty of chosen courses and programs, and the grading idiosyncrasies of individual instructors. Further, students with low SAT scores tend to choose different courses and majors than students with high SAT scores (Bridgeman et al., 2000). This inconsistency serves to reduce observed validity coefficients.

Fortunately, researchers can statistically correct for problems such as range restriction and inconsistency in grading to obtain estimates of what the validity coefficients would be without such limitations. When researchers apply this strategy, the predictive validity of admissions tests looks much more impressive. For example, Ramist and colleagues arrived at a correlation of .57 between SAT scores and first-year GPA after correcting for range restriction and the unreliability of college grades. Similarly, when Bridgeman et al. (2000) corrected for range restriction and course difficulty, the SAT validity coefficient increased to .56. Correcting for range restriction only, Kobrin et al. (2008) arrived at an estimated SAT validity coefficient of .53, and Julian (2005) estimated the corrected validity of the MCAT to be .59.

In one particularly comprehensive study of range restriction and course choice with respect to SAT validity, Berry and Sackett (2009) analyzed course-level data from more than 5 million grades earned by more than 168,000 students from 41 colleges. When correcting for range restriction at the national level – as if accepted students were drawn randomly from all students who took the SAT – the estimated validity coefficient was .51. After controlling for course choice, the researchers concluded that typical validity studies underestimate the predictive validity of the SAT by 30–40%.

Although standardized academic admission tests do predict subsequent academic performance, there are many issues pertaining to the use of such tests that are not readily resolved based on such validity data. For instance, correlations between test scores and later performance tend to be modest – although they increase notably when researchers control for imperfect data. Without correcting for data limitations, the validity coefficients for admissions tests hover around .35. This means that about 12% of the variation in students' academic performance is associated with their admissions test performance. Obviously, test scores are just one of many variables that predict academic performance. Nonetheless, many researchers argue that even correlations at this level can enhance prediction of success in meaningful ways (Sackett et al., 2008; Kuncel & Hezlett, 2010).

Another common criticism is that standardized test scores are a proxy measure of socioeconomic status (SES) (Guinier, 2015). Two recent studies involving very large data sets call this claim into question. In the first of these studies (Sackett, Kuncel, Arneson, Cooper, & Waters, 2009), researchers analyzed data from more than 155,000 students. They reported that the correlation between SAT scores and first-year GPA was .47 after correcting for range restriction. Controlling for student SES reduced this correlation only slightly to .44. In a follow-up meta-analysis of various college admissions tests, the researchers found that the validity coefficient was reduced from .37 to .36 after controlling for SES. The second study (Sackett et al., 2012) included two large data sets totaling more than 250,000 students. Again the correlation between SAT scores and college grades was barely affected by controlling for SES. In both studies, the authors concluded that controlling for SES does not reduce the predictive validity of the SAT in any meaningful way and therefore the SAT is not simply a measure of SES.

Finally, concerns often arise that standardized tests are biased against minorities. For example, Freedle (2003) argues that the SAT is both statistically and culturally biased. As evidence of this, he notes the well-known discrepancies in average test scores across various racial and ethnic groups, and states specifically that some items are differentially valid for Whites and African Americans. Although he acknowledges that such item-level differences are small, he argues for an alternative score calculation method, "to increase dramatically the number of minority individuals who might qualify for admission into our nation's select colleges and universities" (p. 28). Importantly, Freedle provides no evidence of bias in criterion-related validity – differences in the degree to which the SAT predicts academic performance across groups – which is the most important concern among test developers and those using tests to predict academic performance. Research on this question shows that instead of underpredicting academic performance for minorities, standardized tests in fact tend to overpredict performance for minorities (Kuncel & Hezlett, 2007; Sackett et al., 2008). Camara and Sathy (2004) cite numerous flaws in Freedle's alternate scoring proposal, demonstrating that his method would result in a test that is far less valid for predicting college performance. Despite mean differences in scores, there is little evidence that college admission tests are differentially valid across ethnic groups (Fleming & Garcia, 1998).

It is likely that many critics of standardized academic admissions tests tend to think of individuals – perhaps themselves or people they know – whose abilities they feel are not adequately revealed on standardized tests. They may not consider that using tests for screening large numbers of people is based on a different perspective. The question is whether knowing how students performed on a standardized test provides any information about their likely academic success. Psychological assessments have always been more prone to measurement error than other varieties of measurement such as those used in the physical sciences. Furthermore, tests do not measure all personal characteristics that predict success in higher education (Burton & Ramist, 2001; Kuncel & Hezlett, 2007). Nonetheless, prediction of success is enhanced when test scores are considered. No predictor of success is ever going to approach perfect accuracy. Regardless of the criteria used to admit students, there will always be some candidates who could have been successful but who are not selected. Admissions tests have the advantage of being the only measure that is standardized across all applicants. Other admissions criteria such as past academic grades, personal statements, and letters of recommendation are vulnerable to many subjective biases. Standardized test scores predict academic success beyond what is predicted by prior grades alone, and researchers have consistently found that the best predictor is a combination of prior academic performance and standardized test scores (Ramist et al., 1994; Camara & Echternacht, 2000; Linn & Hastings, 2004; Julian, 2005; Kobrin et al., 2008; Berry & Sackett, 2009). Test scores certainly do not provide all the information that admissions officers need to know about candidates. Moreover, the use of test scores has pros and cons meriting ongoing debate given the specific institutional contexts in which they are used. However, it is inaccurate to assert that standardized admission tests are uncorrelated with academic performance.

References

Berry, C. M. & Sackett, P. R. (2009). Individual differences in course choice result in underestimation of the validity of college admissions systems. *Psychological Science, 20*, 822–830.

Bridgeman, B., McCamley-Jenkins, L., & Ervin, N. (2000). Predictions of freshman grade-point average from the revised and recentered SAT I: Reasoning Test. *College Board Research Report No. 2000-1*. New York: College Entrance Examination Board.

Burton, N. W. & Ramist, L. (2001). Predicting success in college: SAT studies of classes graduating since 1980. *College Board Research Report No. 2001-2*. New York: College Entrance Examination Board.

Camara, W. J. & Echternacht, G. (2000). The SAT I and high school grades: Utility in predicting success in college. *College Board Research Note (RN-10)*. New York: College Entrance Examination Board.

Camara, W. & Sathy, V. (2004). College Board response to Harvard Educational Review article by Freedle. Available at: http://research.collegeboard.org/publications/content/2012/05/college-board-response-harvard-educational-review-article-freedle.

Fleming, J. & Garcia, N. (1998). Are standardized tests fait to African Americans? *Journal of Higher Education, 69*, 471–495.

Freedle, R. O. (2003). Correcting the SAT's ethic and social-class bias: A method for re-estimating SAT scores. *Harvard Educational Review, 73*, 1–43.

Geiser, S. & Studley, R. (2002). UC and the SAT: Predictive validity and differential impact of the SAT I and SAT II at the University of California. *Educational Assessment, 8*, 1–26.

Guinier, L. (2015). Ivy leagues meritocracy lie: How Harvard and Yale cook the books for the 1 percent. Available at: http://www.salon.com/2015/01/11/ivy_leagues_meritocracy_lie_how_harvard_and_yale_cook_the_books_for_the_1_percent/?wptouch_preview_theme=enabled.

Julian, E. R. (2005). Validity of the Medical College Admission Test for predicting medical school performance. *Academic Medicine, 80*, 910–917.

Kobrin, J. L., Patterson, B. F., Shaw, E. J., Mattern, K. D., & Barbuti, S. M. (2008). Validity of the SAT for predicting first-year college grade point average. *College Board Research Report No. 2008-5*. New York: The College Board.

Kuncel, N. R. & Hezlett, S. A. (2007). Standardized tests predict graduate students' success. *Science, 315*, 1080–1081.

Kuncel, N. R., & Hezlett, S. A. (2010). Fact and fiction in cognitive ability testing for admissions and hiring decisions. *Current Directions in Psychological Science, 19*, 339–345.

Kuncel, N. R., Crede, M., & Thomas, L. L. (2007). A meta-analysis of the predictive validity of the Graduate Management Admission Test (GMAT) and undergraduate grade point average (UGPA) for graduate student academic performance. *Academy of Management Learning & Education, 6*, 51–68.

Kuncel, N. R., Hezlett, S. A., & Ones, D. S. (2001). A comprehensive meta-analysis of the predictive validity of the Graduate Record Examinations: Implications for graduate student selection and performance. *Psychological Bulletin, 127*, 182–181.

Kuncel, N. R., Wee, S., Serafin, L., & Hezlett, S. A. (2010). The validity of the Graduate Record Examination for master's and doctoral programs: A meta-analytic investigation. *Educational and Psychological Measurement, 70*, 340–352.

Linn, R. L. & Hastings, C. N. (1984). A meta analysis of the validity of predictors of performance in law school. *Journal of Educational Measurement, 21*, 245–259.

Peligri, J. (2014). No, the SAT is not required. More colleges join test-optional train. *USA Today*. Available at: http://college.usatoday.com/2014/07/07/no-the-sat-is-not-required-more-colleges-join-test-optional-train.

Ramist, L., Lewis, C., & McCamley-Jenkins, L. (1994). Student group differences in predicting college grades: Sex, language, and ethnic groups. *College Board Research Report No. 93-1*. New York: College Entrance Examination Board.

Sackett, P. R., Borneman, M. J., & Connelly, B. S. (2008). High-stakes testing in higher education and employment: Appraising the evidence for validity and fairness. *American Psychologist, 63*, 215–227.

Sackett, P. R., Kuncel, N. R., Arneson, J. J., Cooper, S. R., & Waters, S. D. (2009). Does socioeconomic status explain the relationship between admissions tests and post-secondary academic performance? *Psychological Bulletin, 135*, 1–22.

Sackett, P. R., Kuncel, N. R., Beatty, A. S., Rigdon, J. L., Shen, W., & Kiger, T. B. (2012). The role of socioeconomic status in SAT-grade relationships and in college admissions decisions. *Psychological Science, 23*, 1000–1007.

Wilson, K. M. (1983). A review of research on the prediction of academic performance after the freshman year. *College Board Research Report No. 83-2*. New York: College Entrance Examination Board.

16

MYTH: STANDARDIZED ABILITY TESTS ARE BIASED AGAINST SOME MINORITY GROUPS

The issue of potential cultural bias on standardized tests is one of the most emotionally-laden topics in psychology. Advocates of standardized tests see the tests as efficient and objective tools for assessing all sorts of abilities; in contrast, critics cite average group differences in test scores as evidence that the tests are tools of prejudice and discrimination. The latter of these views has contributed most recently to a trend at many colleges and universities of eliminating the requirement that applicants submit scores from admissions tests (Anderson, 2015). With so many people convinced that standardized tests are biased against members of some minority groups, the legitimate pursuit of fairness in university admissions makes tests an easy target. However, opponents of test-optional policies assert that tests such as the SAT assess important characteristics and worry that some proposed policies for eliminating test requirements would do more harm than good (Hambrick & Chabris, 2014). It is unlikely that testing advocates endorse testing in a deliberate effort to discriminate against members of any group. To the contrary, test

Great Myths of Education and Learning, First Edition. Jeffrey D. Holmes.
© 2016 John Wiley & Sons, Inc. Published 2016 by John Wiley & Sons, Inc.

developers have devised a host of strategies for detecting test bias and methods for reducing it. Nonetheless, bias in testing remains a topic of contentious debate.

The literature addressing test bias is vast and complex – having originated soon after the emergence of standardized testing itself approximately a century ago. In fact, entire books have been written on this single topic (e.g., Jensen, 1980). Moreover, testing and test development practices themselves are very complex, and most people – even psychologists – have limited expertise with regard to these practices. Like many scientific issues, test bias is often discussed and debated in sound bites. The topic also carries with it a great deal of social and emotional baggage that triggers additional confusion and misinformation.

Concerns about cultural bias in standardized testing arise out of the very long history of average group differences in test scores. For nearly as long as standardized cognitive testing has existed, psychometricians – people who develop and use tests – have observed systematic differences in the average scores obtained by various ethnic groups. To the understandable chagrin of many scholars, the presence of such differences in average scores is among the most consistent findings in psychological research. It is important to note here two very important caveats. First, the average observed differences in test scores are difficult to refute, but the meaning and origin of those differences are the subject of constant debate. Authors of books such as *The Bell Curve* (Herrnstein & Murray, 1994) have triggered firestorms of controversy and contributed to the politicization of testing by suggesting that group differences in test scores are partially due to genetic influences. However, definitive evidence explaining the differences remains elusive. Second, regardless of the presence or absence of test bias, data on average group differences do not apply to specific individuals. At all levels of performance on all ability tests, there are members of every demographic group.

Research and controversy concerning group differences in ability test performance go back more than a century. Francis Galton (1892) observed differences in average performance among demographic groups long before the development of modern standardized tests. The largest proportion of the enormous body of subsequent research addresses differences between African Americans and White Americans, but many studies include data for other groups as well. The overall trend in this literature is that standardized test scores are generally highest among people of Asian descent, with Whites usually scoring nearly as highly. Average scores for African Americans tend to be about one standard deviation below those of Whites, with the averages for Latinos and Native

Americans falling roughly halfway between Whites and African Americans. It should be noted that this summary is an oversimplification of data on millions of examinees taking standardized tests over the past century. Although individual studies sometimes vary in the magnitude of the differences, the pattern is quite consistent and is present in most large-scale tests including IQ tests (Jensen, 1980), the SAT (College Board, 2013), the ACT (ACT, 2012), the Graduate Record Examination (GRE) (Educational Testing Service, 2012; 2013), the Law School Admissions Test (LSAT) (Dalessandro, Anthony, & Reese, 2012), the Medical College Admission Test (MCAT) (Association of American Medical Colleges, 2012), and the Graduate Management Admissions Test (GMAT) (Bridgeman & McHale, 1996). The differences are also present on tests administered to younger students such as the National Assessment of Educational Progress (NAEP) – a national proficiency exam administered to large samples of US students at four-year intervals beginning in fourth grade (US Department of Education, National Center for Education Statistics, 2012). Camara and Schmidt (1999) provide a helpful overview of group differences on a variety of standardized tests. Researchers have periodically suggested that the test score gaps – particularly between White and African Americans – may be shrinking (Jones, 1984). However, recent research suggests that group differences on most major tests remain stable (Roth, Bevier, Bobko, Switzer, & Tyler, 2001).

Many scholars and members of the public have cited such long-standing group differences in average test performance as evidence of chronic test bias against members of minority groups (see Reynolds & Lowe, 2009). The problem with this conclusion is that it presupposes the absence of real group differences – a conclusion that is appealing, but not empirically defensible. It is scientifically inappropriate to assume either the presence or absence of group differences without sufficient supporting data. This point is noted by the *Standards for Educational and Psychological Testing*, the benchmark guide for appropriate test use published jointly by three national organizations (AERA, APA, & NCME, 2014). The authors of the *Standards* assert that although group differences in test scores demand scrutiny, "group differences in outcomes do not in themselves indicate that a testing application is biased or unfair" (p. 54).

Test bias occurs when a test measures fundamentally different things for members of different groups. Bias is closely linked with the principle of test validity – the degree to which a test accurately measures what its developers intended to measure. For example, a valid intelligence test is one that assesses intelligence without being unduly affected by other factors. When scores on a test are affected by factors other than the variable of interest, they are said to be contaminated with measurement error. Measurement error is not something that can be eliminated – it exists in all types of measurement. Even measures of physical characteristics such as height and weight often have a small degree of error and are therefore not perfectly reliable. For example, many people have had the experience of stepping on a digital bathroom scale and observing the result, then stepping off and immediately stepping back on – only to see a slightly different number. It is unlikely that a person's weight changed in those few seconds to a degree great enough to be detected by a bathroom scale. When researchers use psychological instruments, the amount of measurement error is much greater because the target of measurement does not have physical characteristics that can be measured directly.

Two broad varieties of error can affect measurement. The first is known as random error, which can alter scores in either direction and therefore does not generally affect research conclusions in any consistent way. If your bathroom scale is affected by random error and you step on it 100 times, you will see some variation in the results because each individual measurement is a function of both your true weight and measurement error. Fortunately, since the error is random, it leads to some results that exceed your true weight and some that are below it. Therefore, such effects tend to balance out so the average of your multiple measurements likely would be very close to your true weight. In contrast, test bias would represent systematic error. Imagine that unbeknownst to you, someone behind you placed his or her foot on the scale each time you stepped on it. In this case, each reading would be biased and the measurement error would not average out over time.

Scores on standardized tests can likewise be affected by both random and systematic error. Each year, as hundreds of thousands of students sit down to take the SAT, countless factors cause random measurement error. For example, some students arrive at the testing site having had sufficient sleep and an adequate breakfast; some do not. Some students are in a good mood; some are not. Such factors tend to average out across students and therefore do not lead to group differences in average performance. Test bias would occur if some important factor affected different groups in systematically different ways. For example, if female students were given 30 minutes for each math subtest and male students were given 20 minutes, the test would no longer be measuring exactly the same thing for females and males so the results would be biased. Such vivid illustrations of bias obviously do not occur in real life because standardization procedures are designed to guarantee that everyone taking a test does so under the same conditions. Therefore, any potential bias in standardized testing would have to result from much more subtle and complex factors.

One of the most long-standing concerns among critics of standardized ability tests is that such tests might contain specific content that is more difficult for members of minority groups than for members of the majority – even when examinees' underlying ability is equivalent (Reynolds & Lowe, 2009). This situation could occur for a variety of reasons, including systematic group differences in educational opportunity and the use of language that is less familiar to members of minority groups. Historically, test developers have attempted to deal with this issue by having panels of expert judges evaluate each individual item on a test to determine if its content is culturally biased (see Flaugher, 1978). These panels usually consist of members of various minority groups who would presumably be best qualified to identify biased items.

Unfortunately, research does not support the view that anyone – expert or otherwise – can reliably identify biased test items based solely on content. Sandoval and Miille (1980) had 100 African American, Mexican American, and White college students from a range of socioeconomic backgrounds rate items from one of the most frequently used intelligence tests for children. Fifteen of the items had been shown in advance to be significantly more difficult for African Americans than for White Americans, and 15 items had been shown to be more difficult for Mexican Americans than for White Americans. An additional 15 items were included that were equivalent in difficulty across the groups. Participants in the study rated each item based on whether he or she thought it would be more difficult for minority children, more difficult for majority children, or equally difficult across groups. The results demonstrated that judges could not identify which items were more difficult for various groups, and that minority judges were no better than White judges in determining which items were more difficult for minority children.

Whereas Sandoval and Miille (1980) studied the judgments of lay item evaluators, Jensen (1976) evaluated the quality of expert judgment in detecting biased items. He identified the eight items from an intelligence test that showed the greatest discrimination between White and African American examinees, and the eight items that showed the least discrimination. He then asked ten psychologists – five African American and five White – to differentiate the items that discriminated between groups from the items that did not. The psychologists performed no better than chance at judging which items discriminated. Interestingly, Miele (1979) found that the intelligence test item most frequently cited – based on the item's content – as evidence of cultural bias against African Americans was actually relatively *easier* for African Americans than for Whites.

Given the inability of even expert judges to identify potential bias by subjectively evaluating item content, researchers have turned to statistical strategies for identifying biased items. For example, Flaugher and Schrader (1978) analyzed SAT data from approximately 1,000 White and 1,000 African American students. They rescored the tests after eliminating 27 items that African American examinees answered correctly less often than White examinees. Eliminating these items had almost no impact on the magnitude of average group differences because the eliminated items tended to be relatively easy items. Therefore, eliminating the items made the overall test more difficult for everyone and the mean differences persisted.

A more recent and more complex method of identifying biased items involves examining differential item functioning. Applying this type of analysis, researchers identify groups of test-takers who all have the same score on the overall test and therefore appear to have equivalent levels of ability. Researchers then examine the test data to identify items that members of different groups get correct at different rates. Such items are potentially biased because they show group differences when overall group differences have been controlled by only studying examinees at one level of ability. Research on differential item functioning can be summarized in terms of two broad conclusions. First, even when evaluators know which items have been identified as statistically biased, they are unable to explain why the differences occurred (Reynolds & Lowe, 2009). Given the lack of any consistent pattern among the items, the information is not useful for avoiding bias in future tests. Second, items that are answered correctly at different rates across groups with the same overall level of ability are rare, and tend to account for very little of the group differences in average scores; removing them therefore does little to reduce average group differences (Reynolds, 1998). Moreover, some item discrepancies may represent what researchers refer to as Type 1 errors: identifying a difference that does not actually exist. When researchers examine group differences on a large set of variables – such as each individual item on a test – they are likely to observe some differences based only on chance.

Another type of potential test bias has to do with whether a test is measuring the same underlying ability or construct for members of different groups. This issue is not independent of questions concerning content bias as discussed above, but it is evaluated statistically without reliance on expert judgment. Researchers use statistical techniques such as factor analysis and internal consistency analysis to determine whether tests are assessing similar constructs across groups. Factor analysis is a method for determining patterns of abilities underlying test items. Although factor analysis can be complex, it is based on correlations between items and the notion that highly correlated items are assessing similar abilities. Likewise an internal consistency analysis can help to determine whether items on a test are measuring the same characteristic. High consistency among a group of items – meaning that people who get one item correct tend to get others correct – suggests that the items are measuring similar abilities. Test bias would be suspected if the pattern of abilities underlying performance on a particular test, or the degree of internal consistency among test items, was dramatically different for members of different groups. Such a pattern might lead one to conclude that for some reason, the test as a whole does not measure the same characteristic across groups.

Most researchers investigating the internal consistency or factor structure of tests across different groups have examined intelligence tests. Miele (1979) analyzed test results from 274 African American and White children who had taken the Wechsler Intelligence Scale for children (WISC) in preschool, first grade, third grade, and fifth grade. Miele reported that for comparisons at all grade levels, the primary factor structure of the test was not significantly different for White and African American children. Other researchers have reported similar results for children from these and additional ethic groups (Reschly, 1978; Oakland & Feigenbaum, 1979; Gutkin & Reynolds, 1980; 1981). Internal consistency within each WISC subtest also tends to be similar across African Americans, Mexican Americans, and White Americans (Oakland & Feigenbaum, 1979; Sandoval, 1979). These similar patterns of factor structure and test reliability conflict with the notion that the tests are measuring different things for different groups.

Finally, tests can be biased in terms of their validity for predicting performance on other tasks. Predictive bias is usually evaluated using a statistical analysis called regression, which allows researchers to evaluate the utility of tests for predicting various outcomes such as college grade point average. A test could be considered biased if the predictions it yields are different for members of different groups. In other words, a test has predictive bias when members of two groups have the same average test score, but different average performance on some criterion. For example, "if African American performance on the criterion variables (school achievement, college GPA, etc.) were systematically higher than the same subjects' test scores would predict," test bias would be indicated (Neisser et al. 1996: 93). In such a case, the academic performance of African

Americans would be underpredicted because their actual performance would likely be higher than what their tests scores would predict.

In contrast to this hypothetical example, researchers have generally reported that standardized tests tend to predict equally well for members of different groups. However, evidence of predictive bias does arise for some tests, but not in the direction usually assumed by test critics. The assumption that tests underpredict for members of minority groups is inconsistent with existing data. For example, Mattern and Patterson (2013) examined data from over 475,000 students who took the SAT and went on to college. The researchers reported a very small degree of difference between African American and White students in terms of the level of college performance that would be predicted by SAT scores, but the test actually overpredicted for African Americans. That is, for African Americans the test predicted slightly better college performance than the students actually achieved, and for Whites the test predicted slightly lower performance than they actually achieved. This pattern is consistent with the results of other large-scale studies and reviews on the SAT, which have also revealed overprediction for other minority groups with the exception of people of Asian descent (Young, 2001; Kobrin, Sathy, & Shaw, 2007; Mattern, Patterson, Shaw, Kobrin, & Barbuti, 2008). Researchers have similarly concluded that tests such as the MCAT (Koenig, Sireci, & Wiley, 1998; Davis et al., 2013) and IQ tests (Reschly & Sabers, 1979; Jensen, 1980; Neisser et al., 1996) do not systematically underpredict minority group performance on relevant outcomes.

It is important to recognize that test bias is not the same as test fairness. Bias is primarily investigated using statistical procedures to determine whether tests are measuring the same characteristic across groups. In contrast, fairness is about appropriate use of tests and involves values and subjective judgments. A test that is shown to be unbiased might still be judged to be unfair, if using the test causes differential outcomes. For example, average group differences in test performance might lead to the disproportionate admission of members of various groups to selective colleges. Therefore, using the test might mean that some students' opportunities are limited based on their test performance, which might inspire some critics to argue that test scores should not be part of the selection process. A challenge arises, however, because test scores are often valid predictors of performance on some important outcome. In the absence of an appropriate substitute, ignoring test scores can lead to the admission of students who will be more likely to struggle and less likely to succeed – a scenario that is problematic for both students and institutions (Sander &

Taylor, 2012). The important point, however, is that judgments about test fairness are subjective and are not evidence of test bias.

The broad consensus among psychometricians is that standardized tests are not systematically biased against members of minority groups. This conclusion is based on the evidence that even experts cannot identify ostensibly biased items based on content, that tests do not appear to have differential statistical characteristics across groups, and that tests do not systematically underpredict performance of minority group members on relevant outcomes such as academic performance. Research on test bias is always becoming more sophisticated. Much of the research investigating potential bias in test content was published decades ago and has dwindled – perhaps because any benefits from eliminating obviously biased content have already been realized. Likewise, there is little contemporary research comparing the underlying statistical characteristics of tests across groups, probably because researchers have generally failed to find evidence that standardized ability tests measure different things for different groups. Contemporary researchers tend to focus on predictive bias and statistically-identified item bias as described earlier in this chapter. However, these approaches resemble earlier methods in their failure thus far to reveal consistent or widespread evidence of test bias.

Average group differences in standardized test scores are stubbornly consistent across time and across different tests. However, adequate explanation for the differences remains elusive. If tests are biased, other explanations for group differences in test performance are unnecessary. Scholars could conclude that all groups are the same and that tests create differences rather than reveal them. If tests are not biased, scholars – and other interested parties – would be forced to conclude that real group differences exist and must be addressed. Even if average differences in test performance reflect real differences between groups, it would in no way demonstrate the existence of intrinsic or immutable differences in aptitude. The differences might more legitimately be attributed to unequal access to wealth, education, and other resources, or even systematic prejudice and discrimination, which are reflected in test performance. Such a conclusion is consistent with a recent study in which researchers detected a link between socioeconomic status and characteristics of children's brains. Using brain-imaging technology to study seventh and eighth graders, Mackey and colleagues (2015) observed that the brains of low-income children had thinner cortexes than the brains of high-income children. Moreover, these brain differences accounted for almost half of the difference between the groups in scores on a standardized achievement test. Given that ethnicity is confounded with socioeconomic status, it is possible that unbiased tests are revealing real and pervasive societal biases.

Wiesen (2013) reviewed more than 100 rationales that researchers have offered to explain group differences in test performance. What is perhaps most important to recognize, however, is that if the differences are due to differential educational and economic opportunity, attributing them to test bias is akin to addressing group discrepancies in diabetes prevalence by dismissing diabetes tests. As Reynolds (2000) points out: "we find it anathema that racial or ethnic differences in aptitude or ability might be real ... so, we search for reasons why these differences are not true" (p. 148); blaming tests is perhaps easier than examining other potential causes.

Again, test bias is an extraordinarily complex and controversial topic. The literature extends back over many decades, scores of different tests, hundreds of studies, thousands of analyses, and millions of participants – not to mention countless opinions and interpretations. To better appreciate this complexity, interested readers are encouraged to consult more comprehensive reviews such as those by Brown, Reynolds, and Whitaker (1999), and Reynolds and Lowe (2009).

References

ACT (2012). *ACT Profile Report – National*. Available at: http://www.act.org/newsroom/data/2012/pdf/profile/National2012.pdf.

American Educational Research Association, American Psychological Association, & National Council on Measurement in Education. (2014). *Standards for educational and psychological testing*. Washington, DC: American Educational Research Association.

Anderson, N. (2015). George Washington University applicants no longer need to take admissions tests. Available at: http://www.washingtonpost.com/news/grade-point/wp/2015/07/27/george-washington-university-applicants-no-longer-need-to-take-admissions-tests.

Association of American Medical Colleges (2012). *MCAT Scores and GPAs for applicants and matriculants to U.S. medical schools by race and ethnicity, 2012.* Available at: https://www.aamc.org/download/321498/data/2012factstable19.pdf.

Bridgeman, B. & McHale, F. (1996). *Gender and ethnic group differences on the GMAT analytical writing assessment*. Educational Testing Service Research Report No. 96-2. Available at: http://www.ets.org/Media/Research/pdf/RR-96-02.pdf.

Brown, R. T., Reynolds, C. R., & Whitaker, J. S. (1999). Bias in mental testing since *Bias in mental testing*. *School Psychology Quarterly, 14*, 208–238.

Camara, W. J. & Schmidt, A. E. (1999). Group differences in standardized testing and social stratification. *College Board Research Report No. 99-5*. New York: College Entrance Examination Board.

College Board (2013). *Total Group Profile Report.* Available at: http://media.collegeboard.com/digitalServices/pdf/research/2013/TotalGroup-2013.pdf.

Dalessandro, S. P., Anthony, L. C., & Reese, L. M. (2012). *LSAT performance with regional, gender, and racial/ethnic breakdowns: 2005–2006 through 2011–2012 testing years.* Law School Admissions Council LSAT Technical Report No. 12-03. Available at: http://www.lsac.org/docs/default-source/research-(lsac-resources)/tr-12-03.pdf.

Davis, D., Dorsey, J. K., Franks, R. D., Sackett, P. R., Searcy, C. A., & Zhao, X. (2013). Do racial and ethnic group differences in performance on the MCAT exam reflect test bias? *Academic Medicine, 88,* 593–602.

Educational Testing Service (2012). *GRE General Test Score information by ethnicity/racial groups, 2009–2010.* Available at: http://www.ets.org/s/gre/pdf/gre_general_test_score_information_by_ethnicity_2009_2010.pdf.

Educational Testing Service (2013). *A snapshot of the individuals who took the GRE revised General Test.* Available at: http://www.ets.org/s/gre/pdf/snapshot.pdf.

Flaugher, R. L. (1978). The many definitions of test bias. *American Psychologist, 33,* 671–679.

Flaugher, R. L. & Schrader, W. B. (1978). Eliminating differentially difficult items as an approach to test bias. *ETS Research Report No. RB-78-04.* Princeton, NJ: Educational Testing Service.

Galton, F. (1892). *Hereditary genius.* London: Macmillan.

Gutkin, T. B. & Reynolds, C. R. (1980). Factorial similarity of the WISC-R for Anglos and Chicanos referred by psychological services. *Journal of School Psychology, 18,* 34–39.

Gutkin, T. B. & Reynolds, C. R. (1981). Factorial similarity of the WISC-R for White and Black children from the standardization sample. *Journal of Educational Psychology, 73,* 227–231.

Hambrick, D. Z. & Chabris, C. (2014). Yes, IQ really matters: Critics of the SAT and other standardized testing are disregarding the data. Available at: http://www.slate.com/articles/health_and_science/science/2014/04/what_do_sat_and_iq_tests_measure_general_intelligence_predicts_school_and.html.

Herrnstein, R. J. & Murray, C. (1994). *The bell curve.* New York: Free Press.

Jensen, A. R. (1976). Test bias and construct validity. *Phi Delta Kappa, 58,* 340–346.

Jensen, A. R. (1980). *Bias in mental testing.* New York: Free Press.

Jones, L. V. (1984). White–black achievement differences. *American Psychologist, 39,* 1207–1213.

Kobrin, J. L., Sathy, V., & Shaw, W. J. (2007). A historical view of subgroup performance differences on the SAT Reasoning Test. *College Board Research Report No. 2006-5.* New York: College Entrance Examination Board.

Koenig, J. A., Sireci, S. G., & Wiley, A. (1998). Evaluating the predictive validity of MCAT scores across diverse applicant groups. *Academic Medicine, 73,* 1095–1106.

Mackey, A. P., Finn, A. S., Leonard, J. A., Jacoby-Senghor, D. S., West, M. R., Gabrieli, C. F. O., & Gabrieli, J. D. E. (2015). Neuroanatomical correlates of the income–achievement gap. *Psychological Science, 26*, 925–933.

Mattern, K. D. & Patterson, B. F. (2013). Test of slope and intercept bias in college admissions: A response to Aguinis, Culpepper, and Pierce (2010). *Journal of Applied Psychology, 98*, 134–147.

Mattern, K. D., Patterson, B. F., Shaw, E. J., Kobrin, J. L., & Barbuti, S. M. (2008). Differential validity and prediction of the SAT. *College Board Research Report No. 2008-4.* New York: College Entrance Examination Board.

Miele, F. (1979). Cultural bias in the WISC. *Intelligence, 3*, 149–163.

Neisser, U., Boodoo, G., Bouchard, T. J., Boykin, A. W., Brody, N., Ceci, S. J., Halpern, D. F., Loehlin, J. C., Perloff, R., Sternberg, R. J., & Urbina., S. (1996). Intelligence: Knowns and unknowns. *American Psychologist, 51*, 77–101.

Oakland, T. & Feigenbaum, D. (1979). Multiple sources of test bias on the WISC-R and Bender–Gestalt test. *Journal of Consulting and Clinical Psychology, 47*, 968–974.

Reschly, D. J. (1978). WISC-R factor structures among Anglos, Blacks, Chicanos, and Native-American Papagos. *Journal of Consulting and Clinical Psychology, 46*, 417–422.

Reschly, D. J. & Sabers, D. L. (1979). Analysis of test bias in four groups with the regression definition. *Journal of Educational Measurement, 16*, 1–9.

Reynolds, (1998). Cultural bias in testing of intelligence and personality. In: A. Bellack, M. Hersen, & C. Belar (Eds.), *Comprehensive clinical psychology: Cross-cultural psychology* (pp. 53–92). New York: Elsevier Science.

Reynolds, C. R. (2000). Why is psychometric research on bias in mental testing so often ignored? *Psychology, Public Policy, and Law, 6*, 144–150.

Reynolds, C.R. & Lowe, P.A. (2009). The problem of bias in psychological assessment. In: T. B. Gutkin & C. R. Reynolds (Eds.), *The Handbook of School Psychology*. 4th edn. (pp. 332–374). Hoboken, NJ: John Wiley & Sons.

Roth, P. L., Bevier, C. A., Bobko, P., Switzer, F. S., & Tyler, P. (2001). Ethnic group differences in cognitive ability in employment and educational settings: A meta-analysis. *Personnel Psychology, 54*, 297–330.

Sander, R. H. & Taylor, S. (2012. *Mismatch: How affirmative action hurts students it's intended to help and why universities won't admit it.* New York: Basic Books.

Sandoval, J. (1979). The WISC-R and internal evidence of test bias with minority groups. *Journal of Consulting and Clinical Psychology, 47*, 919–927.

Sandoval, J. & Miille, M. P. W. (1980). Accuracy of judgments of WISC-R item difficulty for minority groups. *Journal of Consulting and Clinical Psychology, 48*, 249–253.

US Department of Education, National Center for Education Statistics. (2012). *Digest of education statistics, 2011.* NCES 2012-001. Available at: https://nces.ed.gov/programs/digest/d11/ch_2.asp.

Wiesen, J. P. (2013). Possible reasons for the black–white differences seen with many cognitive ability tests. Available at: http://appliedpersonnelresearch.com/papers/adimpact.pdf.

Young, J. W. (2001). Differential validity, differential prediction, and college admission testing: A comprehensive review and analysis. *College Board Research Report No. 2001-6.* New York: College Entrance Examination Board.

INDEX

Great Myths of Education and Learning, First Edition. Jeffrey D. Holmes.
© 2016 John Wiley & Sons, Inc. Published 2016 by John Wiley & Sons, Inc.